NATIVE WISDOM

Native Wisdom

Perceptions of the Natural Way

Ed McGaa, Eagle Man

Illustrated by Rudy Chasing Hawk, Hunkpapa Sioux

Four Directions Publishing, Minneapolis

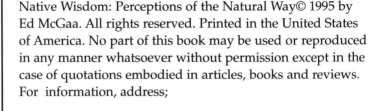

Four Directions Publishing

P.O. Box 24671, Minneapolis, MN 55424
Phone: 952-922-9322, Fax: 952-922-7163
E-mail: eagleman4@aol.com
Website: http://members.aol.com/eagleman4

First Edition

Cover and text illustrations by Rudolph Chasing Hawk.
Portraits and illustrations by Mary McGaa.
Art Direction by Kimberlea' A. Weeks.
Photo by Thomas Kingrey.
Project Coordinator—Mike Poquette.
Cover Beadwork—Prevalent design found on medicine bags of Lakota Sioux. Signifies a tipis' reflection in the water. Life today and a life beyond. "The Great Spirit assures us that we have a home here and one in the beyond. You will enter that tipi reflecting in the water when you pass on." Musings of Chief Eagle Feather while sitting beside a tipi reflecting in the Cheyenne River —1969.

Cataloging-in-Publication Data

McGaa, Ed
    Native Wisdom : perceptions of the Natural Way /
    Ed McGaa; illustrated by Rudy Chasing Hawk. —
    Minneapolis, MN : Four Directions Pub., c1995.
    p. cm.
    Includes bibliographical references and index.
    ISBN 0-9645173-1-0
    1. Oglala Indians — Religion. 2. Oglala Indians —
Philosophy. 3. Human ecology — Religious aspects.
    I. Chasing Hawk, Rudy, ill. II. Title.
    E99.O3M34 1995   299'.785
                                      QB195-20269
        00 01 02 03   RRD(H) 10 9 8 7 6 5

Contents

Foreword

Catlin's Creed:

I love a people who have always made me welcome to the best they had.
I love a people who are honest without laws, who have no jails and no poorhouses.
I love a people who keep the commandments without ever having read them or heard them preached from the pulpit.
I love a people who never swear, who never take the name of God in vain.
I love a people who love their neighbors as they love themselves.
I love a people who worship God without a bible, for I believe that God loves them also.
I love a people whose religion is all the same, and who are free from religious animosities.
I love a people who have never raised a hand against me, or stolen my property, where there was no law to punish for either.
I love a people who have never fought a battle with white men, except on their own ground.
I love and don't fear mankind where God has made and left them, for there they are children.
I love a people who live and keep what is their own without locks and keys.
I love all people who do the best they can.
And oh, how I love a people who don't live for the love of money!

George Catlin(1796-1872)[1]

George Catlin, Artist, who lived for eight years among Native American tribes, said in 1841: "All history of the subject goes to prove that, when first visited by civilized people, the American Indians have been found friendly and hospitable—from the days of Christopher Columbus to the Lewis and Clark Expedition... and so also have a great many other travelers, including myself. Nowhere, to my knowledge, have they stolen a six-pence worth of my property, though in their countries there are no laws to punish for theft. I have visited forty-eight different tribes, and I feel authorized to say that the North American Indian in his native state is honest, faithful, brave... and an honorable and religious being."[2]

* * * *

I am often asked the related questions, "How can I become more environmental? How can I help save the Earth? What can people do to help the environment?"

If we modern era inhabitants could go back only a few centuries to those indigenous people who made the environment work for them, we could observe a working environmental system which humans lived within for thousands of years.

The basic answer lies within Spirituality. The North American indigenous people were truly spiritual and encompassed environmentalism within their spiritual beliefs. It is simple. We must go back to a belief system that provides an understanding that we are a part of the whole universe, especially this planet. We are related to all things. But to understand Mitakuye Oyasin (We are all related), we will have to understand the concepts of indigenous thought.

* * * *

Humanities II

The class was titled—Humanities II. A selected list of questions from students had been compiled by the teacher over a period of years. These intriguing questions were given to all speakers who had agreed to speak on spirituality and religion before the class. The entire list is found in the Appendix.

Humanities II was taught in an upper income, midwestern, metropolitan suburban school. I suspect that this class of young minds, their curiosity, wonderment, optimism, skepticism, and their set convictions, are fairly reflective of present day youth in the realm of philosophy, religion and spirituality. Because I am from a culture that suffered severe religious oppression, I was most appreciative of the progress which I discerned by such a list from young, questing, forming minds. My gratitude was also buoyed by the fact that other speakers aside from the dominant society belief system were actually requested to come into the classrooms to share their views.

These profound questions would never have been submitted when I was a student in high school. Speakers outside of the dominant mainstream were not invited into our schools. In those days, students held the same iron clad convictions as their parents. Indigenous Spirituality was forbidden by the federal government which administrated Native American educational institutions. In these schools, North American native people were processed not to re-examine beneficial indigenous culture and history but instead, were programmed to ridicule and degrade their own indigenous culture.

In my grandparent's time, missionary educators established schools on federal tribal lands and had open access to the government boarding schools in order to promote religious indoctrination. They were even given federal lands to build their schools upon, which was a direct violation of the constitutional protection of church and state separation. Academic education was secondary to their primary goal which was complete eradication of native religion, spirituality and culture. Within both school systems, missionary and federal, the educational curriculum was designed to foster submissive assimilation into the mainstream society.

Maybe such a past has influenced me to appreciate these times now that our tribe is allowed a new sense of religious freedom. Maybe that is why I could be moved to such a degree that I have undertaken this task to respond to these questions which have been brought before me. They struck deep, deep down in some mysterious way into my psyche, or were they actually reaching into my DNA?

I tend toward an upbeat attitude in respect to the abundance of knowledge which is coming to two leggeds (humans) as this millennium is here upon us. The first half of the twentieth century primarily depended on books to extend communication, questioning, reasoning, exploration and story-telling. Radio, movies and then television began to capture increasing audiences through this powerful force called technology. By mid-century, daily news, world events, the front lines of war or the midst of catastrophe were radio broadcasted. Within a few decades, world events were videoed into the living room. Indeed, the twentieth century is a new world of communication where innovative technology has played a strong role towards an exponential understanding based on reams of information available on a daily and changing basis.

The students who wrote these questions signal a harmonic change that is beginning to stir. The colossal information system which is now available is also becoming more accurate. An information access system reaches across the land where millions of like-minded students are not afraid to think, to question religion, science, politics, government and entrenched systems. In classrooms, and more so in colleges, I sense a healthy rejection of that portion of old religious molds which forbade or restricted questioning religious thought. As they evolve into adulthood, more questions will be asked. A new reference and a respect for the observed truths of Nature is definitely spawning. I think that these questions are quite powerful and could lead us toward a planet saving harmony. Whatever, they have given me a renewed hope and a new energy to continue questing forward.

* * * *

Acknowledgements

To the many friends, supporters, and critics who have contributed to my path: My thanks to each of you.

Special appreciation to my major influencers, Bill Eagle Feather, Frank Fools Crow and Ben Black Elk.

To Senior Editor Sharon Diotte

To Copy Editors Colleen Wasner and Pam Brittain.

To Rudy Chasing Hawk, Sonny Hare, Bill Swift Hawk, John Nordlum and lifetime friend, Stan Curtis.

To my sister LaVerne, for her many stories and lasting friendship. To sister Chick and brother DeWayne for their loyalty.

To the Earth, for all that it teaches.

To the teacher, Judy Layzell, who compiled these questions from young minds.

* * * *

Note: The subjects; Lakota, Dakota, and Sioux will be used interchangeably throughout this text. At this time, my tribe is still officially addressed as the Oglala Sioux as is the adjoining tribe, the Rosebud Sioux. That is how the tribal councils have been referring to themselves for quite awhile. The terms Native American, American Indian and Indian will also be used. Most older Native Americans have been called Indian all their lives and have become quite used to that term, therefore interchange is preferred by the author who is much more concerned about spiritual content than linguistic semantics whose overplay has too often proven more of a distraction than being of harmonic value.

NATIVE WISDOM

Who is God?

I love a people whose religion is all the same, and who are free from religious animosities.

* * * *

How does your religion define the Supreme Being?
Share your thoughts on God: Did He create us?
How does your religion explain the unknown, such as creation?
Is this religion based on the existence of an immortal being?
How did the 'higher power' become the 'higher power'?
How does your God manifest itself to humans? Is He always watching?
Does your God have a gender?
Is your religion defined by what one thinks and does?
What is the underlying theme of your religion?
Where do you believe your Supreme Being exists?

* * * *

Who is God? Before I can begin to answer such a question, I must explain that any answer, or attempt to answer, is based on my own background, my personal experiences and that which has influenced me upon my personal journey down the Red Trail of Life or as some may call it, my journey within the Natural Way. Indigenous teachers were major influencers at the beginning of my travels and on into middle age. Serious works from truth seeking authors continue to leave their imprint within my spirit.

I do not speak for my tribe, nor the indigenous tribes. No one can. If some one says that they do, cast a wary eye of suspicion. Another indigenous person will not offer the same answers as mine or of another's. No one speaks for the dominant society so why should members of the dominant society expect that one of us should speak for all indigenous people? Some native peoples may exhibit a commonality, especially if they are of the same tribe. Others will not.

It has been my observance that too many non-Indians elevate every utterance a Native American makes as if it is what all Native Americans will agree with. I have a simple statement in that regard. I have never known two Indians to conduct a sweat lodge in the same way. Even Chief Fools Crow and Chief Eagle Feather used differing procedure in conducting their ceremonies. Both used the same symbolic colors of Black Elk's vision, red, yellow, black and white, but neither had them in the same arrangement as stated in the book, *Black Elk Speaks*. Red was east, yellow was south, black was west and white was north in Black Elk's vision. Aside from that difference, however, the two Sioux holy men's wisdom, advice, suggestions, conduct, sacrifice and attitude conveyed a considerable amount of commonality reflected in Black Elk's words. Commonality is an important ingredient when the Indigenous Way, the Natural Way, is being considered.

I was further influenced by Black Elk's son, Ben and also the daughter of John Neihardt, Hilda Neihardt. In regard to these two influencers, I have observed a high degree of similarity with Fools Crow's and Eagle Feather's philosophies, regardless of the arrangement of colors for each direction.

Detractors and criticizers love to center in on a color or a mere ceremonial procedure to draw attention away from the magnitude of a knowledgeable person. Detractors often know very little in reference to what they are pretending to know. Therefore, they will attempt to divert attention toward what anyone could recognize as a minor difference. The detractors get their recognition by this method and hence they bloom in the spotlight like a moth before a flame for a few moments. Always ask a detractor or a criticizer, "What is your background, what is your experience, where is your "knowledge" coming from?" If you are going to allow a detractor to become a "knowledge" source for your trail of life, you are a fool if you do not probe deeply into their background and track record.

An insignificant paper hanger, who rose only to the rank of corporal in the military, once captured a whole nation by utilizing distraction, criticism, hate and lies. In a few short years, his detracting vitriol led his nation down a horrible trail that cost millions of lives and terrible suffering. His country was eventually split in two and separated. Adolph Hitler was not a gifted person, certainly not gifted with positive traits. He swayed a whole nation to do unimaginable acts simply because of his ability to criticize, detract, condemn and manipulate. That is how dangerous and damaging an ignorant detractor can become.

Many of my suppositions are strongly influenced by my native teachers and a particular pair of books, *Black Elk Speaks* and *The Sacred Pipe*. I consider these writings as the words of a great holy man from my tribe. For me, these books are a representation of the spiritual thought of my tribe, back when they were truly traditional and lived freely within created nature upon the Great Plains. (Black Elk's vision will be explored in depth in a subsequent chapter.)

A Christian would not be able to write about Christian belief without mentioning Jesus; a Moslem would surely speak of Muhammad when he or she would write about their Moslem faith. I would have to offer Black Elk's vision as an integral part of my belief system. Other writings have affected me as well. They are found in Suggested Readings at the end of this book.

The works of Jack Weatherford have taught me some important facts regarding what can happen when a people are Earth centered. His book, *Indian Givers*, established that indigenous people were the true cultivators of democracy and also exhibited an exemplary environmental track record. His work is a history book and would not be classified as a philosophical or a religious text. At the local library I discovered the Pilgrim's logs which admitted that a generous people kept them alive. I hope this emphasizes that my spiritual influences are not based on pure religious form, nor are they based only on native originated works; far from it. My experiences, adventures and observations of Mother Earth are my main influencers, especially since my teacher influencers have gone on. This text will emphasize that what one learns, observes and experiences; these happenings implant spiritual beliefs.

My trail has not lacked experience or teachers and it has consumed a major portion of this century. I was influenced by tribal thought, values, culture, art, teachers, history, stories, research, many books and other related information. I have also been fortunate, and appreciate that I live in an age of technology where vast amounts of information are available if one will exercise the initiative to look.

At this point I must confess that I do not offer any answers, really. Rather, my attempt at answers are but mere suppositions. A supposition is an attempt to offer a response with a reserve clause that the supposition could be wrong, or only partially accurate, especially when the subject being discussed lies within the realm of religion and spirituality. Can you imagine reading an author who states he could be wrong? This is indeed a historic publication. "Everything I say is very correct and I am a leading world authority," is what most authors seem to intend or imply, such are the established rules and habits that so-called learned circles have fallen into.

Nature based culture accepts mystery within spiritual thought. A person who follows or respects the Natural Way could very well answer, "This is my view, my opinion, my belief but the subject is so vast that it is beyond my total purview if I am to be honest or truthful." The entire area or subject of the beyond, the Supreme Being, its creation, is one of profound mystery. I do not believe that any two leggeds know for sure what they are commenting about, regarding these subjects. I will not become angry with you if you civilly or respectfully disagree with my viewpoints, my suppositions. At best, I can only tell you how or why I arrive at my suppositional conclusions; what facts or evidence lead me toward my views. "I could be wrong! You might be right. I don't know!" Wouldn't the world be a better place if people could just shed their false egos and learn to honestly make these three statements? Another important admission should also become a part of everyone's communication: "Maybe both of us have no idea of what we are talking about but let us explore with open minds and an open heart."

Mother Earth Spirituality was intended to introduce a tribe's culture in order to establish a deeper understanding of tribal spiritual depth. I wanted to bring forth native historical accounts and contributions from an American Indian point of view while also exposing delusive stereotyping. *Rainbow Tribe* was an attempt to verify the many paths which embrace and experience Natural Way philosophy. *Native Wisdom* is a response to religious and philosophical questions from probing minds in these environmental times of great crisis. For those who wonder, question or are on the edge of an extensive meadow of thought about this Natural Way concept of spirituality, hopefully this will help them walk into that meadow to observe, touch, feel and become more familiar with what influenced and guided ancient ancestors in spiritual commonality to all descendants of two leggeds.

I have attempted to "answer" the issue within each question. Often, what an indigenous influenced person might perceive as an issue may contrast sharply with how the reader will comprehend; especially a reader who is strongly influenced by dominant society values. Often, a question will receive historical or social dialogue related to specific indigenous material, information or influence. My intentions are to lend support to my perceptions which are influenced by this dialogue. Occasionally, I differ with some cultural aspects of what may be considered generally recognized indigenous custom or code. We are all human and differ more than we think. This variance aspect might prove to be a healthy symbol and allow adaptation when it might be beneficial for the earth or evolving society. Nature abounds with variance within species.

Bear in mind that these questions were projected to me through the context and dialogue of the dominant society. Young, inquisitive minds from dominant society households asked these questions, yet their openness and broad perspective indicates to me that they are forthright, straightforward and unpretentious queries. Such a change has so suddenly come over our youth! The new technology to which they have access has made all of this happen regardless of how the dominant society's religious establishments have attempted to keep everyone in a particular mold and/or a closed mind set.

My suppositions, opinions or attempts to answer often rely on thought, history, values and examples within dominant religious beliefs that I was initially exposed to. "Just as one cannot understand the structure of a language (for example, English) if one only knows that language—one must be able to compare it with another language (for example—Chinese) from another linguistic family—so also one cannot really understand a particular religious system unless it can be compared with other religious systems."[1]

I am not attempting to make people angry, I am trying to communicate. This method can become an avenue for positive and creative introspection. Introspection is difficult for many people whether they are indigenous or non-indigenous in thought.

Who is God? This is an impossible question for most indigenous people from the North American portion of this hemisphere who have resisted the religious exactness attitude of Euro-centric, dominant society. For me, it is possible that the Great Mystery (Wakan Tanka to the Sioux) could be represented, in part, by the Six Powers of the World for the purpose of our function upon this Earth. These Six Powers will be described in detail in a following chapter. Out in the Universe these Six Powers have no function. In my belief system, the Great Mystery made all things upon this Earth, the Earth as well and, of course, all other form and space of which we are aware.

The Sioux believed in one Great Spirit, a Creator whom they called Wakan Tanka (Great Mystery, Great Holy). Wakan means sacred, holy, mystery, unknown, spirit, and a host of other related meanings. Tanka means great, large, much, big or vast. For example, Minnetanka means big water. This is the name of a large lake west of Minneapolis, Lake Minnetonka. Minne means water.

Most older traditional Sioux whom I have known and in particular my teachers, consider Wakan Tanka to be beyond the mind of man or woman. If you ask a traditional believing Sioux who, exactly, is the Great Spirit or who is God?—they will honestly respond that they do not know. It is beyond contemplation of mere two leggeds. If the Great Spirit has made time and space which is certainly incomprehensible, then is not the Creator which made such imperceptible entities even more incomprehensible? How far out is space? When could time begin or end? No human can truthfully answer such queries. Therefore, why should we argue over a vast power that created time and space? "The Great Spirit is a Mystery" might be the best beginning to explore North American indigenous thought.

Most indigenous definitions of the Supreme Being relate to the immediate creation upon which we are dependent. Some tribes refer to these "immediacies" as the four winds or four directions. The Sun and the Earth are also immediate and likewise, observable and foundational. Although undefinable, this Great Creator manifests these major creations. It can also manifest through lesser creations which it seems to control, and this phenomenon will be offered in the course of this writing. In these modern times, we two leggeds are much more aware of space and have even gone out into it. Outer space is beyond the Four Directions and the Earth Spirit but it is obvious that the Creator has this dimension also. It will be interesting when we finally make contact with other entities, other rationalizing beings in space. Sheer math alone tells us they are out there. Such spiritual and religious arguments concerning creation and the human race (which have festered and been fought over for centuries) will be answered rather quickly.

The Creator of all things is Wakan Tanka. Beneath this vast Great Spirit are the differentiated powers which we consider as extensions or manifestations of the Great Mystery Creator. The Earth Mother, Father Sky and the Four Directions (West, North, East and South) are called the Six Powers in my tribe, especially by those adherents who know of Black Elk's vision. Each has distinct influences upon all living things here upon our planet. The sun (Wi) is the heart of Father Sky and gives us the life force—the energy which allows us to function daily. When we die, that mysterious energy force no longer can be found within our inert bodies. The Sun Power has daily communion with our Earth Mother to create all life upon our planet. The Earth is what we are physically made of. Every particle of our bodies is made from the elements and minerals that make up Mother Earth. Upon Mother Earth, the Four Winds—Tate Topa (the four directions) have their influence upon the living entities: finned ones, crawling ones, the four-legged ones, standing ones (plants and trees) and we rationalizing two leggeds. The Indians can see, taste, touch, feel and... "observe their religion or their spirituality."

You, yourself, are made up of the life giving rains of the West. Approximately 80% of your body is fluid. Water allows you to be flexible, to have motion. Mother Earth composition is the rest of you. The energy of Father Sun flows through you. Yes, all of your energy and life force is ultimately from the sun through the foods that you eat which take their life force daily from the sun's rays. Therefore, your physical being is from three of the Six Powers; the West Power, The Earth Power (Mother Earth) and the Sky Power, of which Wi, the Sun, is the heart.

Think about this. It will help you to understand more about being a part of all that is around you. The Sioux have a meaningful phrase; Mitakuye Oyasin (me ta kooh yea oh ya seen) which means, "We are related to all things or; We are all related—We are all relatives."

In an interview by Bill Moyers with Joseph Campbell, Moyers asked what was the best example of this spiritual imagery about which the distinguished philosopher spoke. Campbell replied succinctly—the spiritual imagery found in *Black Elk Speaks*. I believe he meant the powerful imagery offered by the Six Powers which spoke to Black Elk in his vision. Incidentally, that book has been read world wide and has been published in many languages, including Japanese.

Is this religion based on the existence of an immortal being? How does your God manifest itself to humans? Is He always watching? Wakan Tanka, the Great Spirit, would be considered an immortal being. How did the "higher power" become the "higher power"? How It became the Higher Power is impossible to answer. You may as well attempt to count all the sands of the sea.

It will be acknowledged repeatedly that the Great Spirit manifests itself within and through all of that which it creates. Even a tiny spider building its web can be a manifestation if you have the sense to recognize such an example as an engineering and architectural marvel. What placed that ability to perform even into a tiny spider? What about all the rest of the millions and billions of other insects, four-leggeds, finned and flying, functioning and happening? Truly we are all related and existing because of the "Mystery" of this great unseen force that has bestowed so many attributes, gifts and powers even within the tiniest of creatures. Although undefinable, this Great Creator manifests to humans daily through its major creations. What it has created out in space can also be a manifestation.

Is He (God) always watching? I would consider this vast power as all knowing. What makes me offer this concept? Let us simply look at what the Higher Power shows us in this day and age.

Some of us believe that modern technological marvels are reflections of the Ultimate Inventor and are certainly not creations of mere man. We are allowed to discover these marvelous machines; we do not invent them; they have already been invented and made possible by a mind much greater than ours. In this age we can somewhat understand the speed and vast ability of the Creator when we understand a powerful computer. A computer, an almost magically communicative tool, is but an inkling of the capacity which the Immeasurable Entity has invented for human discovery. What allows such a range of performance so far beyond human speed of calculation? Again, this is a mystery that cannot be explained. How silly, how foolish of western and eastern man to think that he invents these things. They function only because the Great Spirit allows them their complexity.

Let us look at electricity before we consider the computer. Look at your electric light bulb which Thomas Edison supposedly invented. Presently there is a piece of coal which is burning. It turns a generator and electricity is transformed over power lines which are connected to your dwelling. Through this wire, the light bulb is supplied energy and shines brightly, somewhat like the sun. The white man calls all of this—modern technology. The indigenous traditionalist says it is a miracle allowed and originally created by the Great Spirit or whatever particular name they have for the Ultimate Creator. Edison was allowed to discover what had already been invented by the Ultimate Inventor. It could not function except for the allowance of function. This is such a complex happening, the sun energy coming through a wire; it is inconceivable that mere human could bring this about without prior design and formation by the Mystery.

Way, way back in time, millions of years ago there existed giant ferns that took energy from the sun. These ferns started out as tiny spores. They grew daily, reaching higher and higher for the sun energy that travelled through space. The larger they grew, the more sun energy they took in. In time these huge ferns fell and compacted themselves upon each other. Eventually they were covered and became black seams of mass called coal. At this point in time, it is apparent the Creator was designing its own purpose. Millions of years later, humans came along and opened the earth to obtain these solidified fern remains because they still contained the force, the energy of the sun. The mystery of this sun force is what is traveling through the wire and actually lights the light bulb. Scientific humans try to explain this with forms of measurement such as volts, amperes and watts, but this explanation is incomplete because it does not include creation mystery. From a tiny spore producing energy we have an incandescent lamp!

The light bulb is an example of energy transformation from energy stored. In its own function it has allowed two leggeds considerable communication. A few decades later, another "discovery," the computer, uses energy but it also has a memory function. A computer has a disk that we can implant much upon or we can choose to leave it basically blank—like the human mind. Is not the Great Spirit subtly telling us to use our minds and seek knowledge of its Creations?

The East Power, the beginning dawn of each new day, tells me to add more knowledge to my Disk of Life. The day will bring me many new experiences if I have the perception to look for them. Technological revelations were never available to medieval man or woman or from time spans earlier where many religions still base their rigid codes, laws and theology. Therefore, is it not obvious that we in these modern times have many more revelations before us if we just take the time to observe and perceive? Furthermore, we are allowed much more access and ability to search and investigate places, depths and outer space which were inaccessible to humans in bygone eras.

Aside from technology, of which modern man claims to be the creator, do we not have a myriad of communicative wave phenomena, infra red, ultra violet, radio, television and other waves surrounding and traversing our planet? What about a tiny electron within the bowels of a computer frame? It too has communicative properties. Its workings are as mysterious as the functions and dynamics of electricity, telecommunication and radio waves when you get right down and admit their mystery. These waves traverse the earth and outer space. They bring a high degree of "knowing" or "watching" to us humans. The television camera can now go into the battlefield and show the actual horrors of war. Consequently, young men are not as easily aroused to become cannon fodder for a false sense of patriotism, especially if they know that the sons of the wealthy are safely tucked away in universities or the National Guard. Courts, legislatures, and even an occasional police beating are open to the public's viewing, thanks to these mysterious forces that the Great Spirit has created for our awareness. In light of these forces and admitting that I am influenced by a scientific aspect, I tend toward the supposition that the Creator may know or "watch" what we are doing.

How much the Ultimate Entity watches our every moment is beyond my speculation. Native Americans did beseech, appreciate and offer thanksgiving to a watching or a listening power. Their Sun Dances, Corn Dance ceremonies and related Wild Rice Harvest ceremonies bear witness to their belief that a supreme power could recognize and was possibly watching over an appreciative people. I have personally observed strong evidence that some force was indeed watching when we were in the annual Sun Dance thanksgiving. After one particular spiritual experience in the Sun Dance, I was influenced that a higher power does watch over us—at least some of the time if not all of the time.

Our own experiences with others become memories. These memories allow us to "watch" each other at least as to what another does to us and indirectly what another observes and relates to us as to their observation. Some terrible tragedies befall many people and the quieter creatures as well. We know that the Great Spirit does not rush to our aid during every calamity or tragedy.

Does your God have a gender? I gathered that my teachers sensed the Mystery more as a Creator than as a manifesting human entity even though they would often use the term, Tankashilah (Grandfather) in prayer. I personally do not refer to It as a male gender. Many tribes do, however, especially those who have historically had a strong dose of

Christianity. Many tribes have been influenced for two to three hundred years under organized Christian religion and refer to God as He. Many in my tribe refer to the Great Spirit as Tankashilah—Grandfather, in their prayers in ceremony. If you are ever fortunate to be in a Sioux beseechment ceremony and you are influenced that you should refer to the higher power in a male gender form, then, by all means do so. That is your prerogative and it is still a free country and hopefully, will continue to remain so. It is a mystery. You could be right.

At my particular moment in time, I have no idea that the Ultimate Power has a gender. Does such vastness of mystery and creation have need for a gender? If it is a male, then is there some great female of like stature out there in space also? To be honest, I really don't care if it has a gender.

What is gender? Is it not more for the procreation of species? Hereinafter, in this particular writing, God or Wakan Tanka will be addressed as It, rather than the dominant culture's customary He. The dominant society has failed to convince me with any degree of credibility that this supreme entity which is also within the vastness of space is a human resembling male. This is my prerogative and I hope that the dominant society including those Native Americans who differ with me in this respect will at least allow me my freedom of religious belief.

Is your religion defined by what one thinks and does? "Spirituality doesn't arrive fully formed without effort. Religions around the world demonstrate that spiritual life requires constant attention and a subtle, often beautiful technology by which spiritual principles and understandings are kept alive."[2]—Thomas Moore

Indigenous Spirituality tends toward observance of what the Creator exhibits. It places a high regard for what the Great Spirit shows us. What an individual thinks and does often enhances or promotes what has been learned from such observations. Yet, I hold this particular question out as especially insightful in revealing the great strength or the utter weakness of a religion. This is where I personally diverge from what one could call "pure" tribal or indigenous thought or practice.

In the past (from my own observation since I have been around for a few years), innovative human influence was ongoing but seldom admitted to. I have seen a tremendous change take place within tribal religion and spirituality, but change is rarely acknowledged, especially by those who are newly "reborn" back into their tribal connections. There are many of those nowadays who know very little but are pretending that they have been observing for a lifetime. I have a term for those who gather together and make pronouncements that their religion never changes or adapts. I call this —"spiritual posturing." I am sure that spiritual change was happening back when the Sioux began to adapt to a new way of life on the plains. This adaptability was a great strength of the Sioux. Not only did they adapt from the woodlands to the plains, they assumed a nomad life in contrast with their agrarian past, if the theory that they migrated from the Carolina area is accepted. Surely, there were detractors in that changing time who possibly complained that spirituality would not work when the first Sioux used a red catlinite pipe in contrast to the clay pipes from the Carolinas. When kinnic kinnick, a tobacco substitute, was used, no doubt more clamor was probably raised by those who thought they had an inside track to God's mystery. Can you imagine when a holy man or a medicine person first decided to cover their sweat lodge with a buffalo hide instead of customary woodland bark or deer hide? "It won't work. He's all wrong!" A century from now, it will be insisted that an often used covering of modern sweat lodges, 4 mil or 6 mil black tarpaulin, must be used over some new covering for a lodge by some detracting know-it-all.

Possibly, the old time Sioux may have been above all of this distraction. Maybe they were so close to the Great Spirit and were so thankful that they were being delivered from the advancing hordes of Europeans coming from the east that they understood such change as necessary. I recently watched a Brazilian chief exclaiming his support of a videotaping of a ceremonial dance which was also viewed enthusiastically by the tribal members. His reasoning was that it will help the young to see how it was done after these tribal members will have passed away. This Brazilian chief was a full fledged, unquestionable traditional who lived in the jungle with his tribe. Maybe these modern day detractors, skeptics, pessimists and attention seekers should consider positive examples of adaptability especially where it makes practical sense .

Learned men and women who have had a track record of close conduct with Nature certainly have left their influence, especially those who were so influential in the spiritual revival among the Sioux. I observed these teachers to be very adaptable when it was necessary. What Fools Crow thought, what Black Elk revealed and what Bill Eagle Feather actually performed definitely left indelible impressions upon my Disk of Life. Each man had different perceptions and had a biography been written on each man, I am sure the divergence would have easily been discerned.

Yes, they had a strong commonality but each was his own person. Each of these men brought significant change to tribal religion even though they are recognized more for their preservation of tribal ways. Bill Eagle Feather did bring back the piercing ceremony but his own Sun Dances, held later, differed from those held by Chief Fools Crow. Bill Eagle Feather was also an ardent influencer regarding the wotai stone—the special stone that many people carry. He did not create this recognition but he was the most outspoken in regard to its recognition or revival. Bill is known for adding a degree of humor to his ceremonies yet when he had to be serious he had equivalent power to commune to the spirit world. Consequently, he received strong answers or directions from that mystery, no less than Chief Fools Crow.

Chief Fools Crow is captured fairly well in the book, *Fools Crow*, by Thomas Mails. I differ with Tom Mails considerably, however, in his attempt to make a Christian out of Fools Crow. Of the many books written by white men about Indians, very few have been able to shed their patriarchy regarding their own religion. Too many have tried to equate Christianity with the spiritual connection power which Native American spirituality commands. In older books, our spirituality was made fun of or was regarded as meaningless by the academics of past eras. I told this to Mails over a friendly meal and yet I also told him that I was impressed with his book which is recommended in my Suggested Readings list. Fools Crow never held me back when I repeatedly took on the local missionaries who were attempting to come into and Christianize the Sun Dance ceremony. I am not against Christianity but I will take exception with any religion that tries to interfere with our own ceremonies for the primary intent of conversion and dilution. Fools Crow was the Sun Dance Chief and could easily have instructed me to be less vehement or defensive. Instead, he defended me when I was to be the lone sun dancer on a Sunday when the Christian missionary had schemed to say his mass at the base of the sun dance tree to make us end the ceremony on Saturday, a day early. In all of the Sun Dances that I was in, and in other ceremonies with Chief Fools Crow, never did I hear him pray to any ultimate entity other than Wakan Tanka. He did recognize the Four Directions, Mother Earth and Father Sky as we all did who participated in his ceremonies. Fools Crow was kind hearted. He did not like to hurt any one's feelings over religion. I believe that too many Christians who knew him took advantage of this trait and tended to make him into one of their own, simply because he did not mind if they prayed together.

Mails is a minister or at least was one, and his interpreter, Dallas Chief Eagle, was an ardent, devout Catholic. Christians have that habit, to make people over into their image. I wish that they would be more careful with their implications when it comes to biographies and writings about our spiritual leaders and indigenous ceremonies.

To this day, writers repeatedly try to Christianize Nick Black Elk, claiming he was a catechist, which he did become after being choked and physically dragged to the mission by the priests at a very disparaging time in the slight man's life. His wife had died, the Sioux were in captivity and the white man's way was all powerful. By being a catechist, Black Elk was issued a pass and allowed to travel to see his relatives in other camps and bands. Such travel would otherwise have been forbidden. So caught up with their zeal, patriarchy and Euro-supremacy, it has been conveniently overlooked by certain authors and writers that Black Elk gave his vision <u>unaltered</u> to Neihardt and made sure that the ever watchful missionaries were not notified of this significant recording event. And when the old prophet prayed on the mountain afterwards, as witnessed by

Black Elk on the mountain.

Ben Black Elk, John Neihardt and his daughter Hilda, the old prophet prayed to the Great Spirit, and only the Great Spirit, in the traditional way. Neihardt took a famous picture of this event that shows Black Elk praying "straight up" to Wakan Tanka. By "straight up," I mean he was looking directly out to the Universe and did not have his head bowed down in Christian fashion. Neihardt recorded his prayer, which was definitely to the Great Spirit and not to the white man's concept. My interpretation is that Black Elk turned back to his traditionalism after looking into the way of the dominant society. I can understand why he could do so. I have done the same.

The facts clearly show that he did return back to the ways of his vision, yet some of these white man writers do not recognize these so-evident observations. The latest attempt is a Black Elk book by Steltenkamp who also attempts to discredit Neihardt. I am sure this author is well aware of my writings. I happen to be an enrolled Oglala who had a direct connection to Ben Black Elk, the actual interpreter for Neihardt's famous book. It borders on the comical to see how Steltenkamp dances around the obvious facts of Black Elk's later life, and ignores pertinent, related writings that offer solid, factual, contrasting evidence. So intense is his zeal to bend what was obvious.

To lie because of religious zeal does not justify the lie. To leave out what was unmistakable observation is as bad as a lie in my estimation. We can learn from our own culture's past mistakes and shortcomings. We certainly should not attempt to alter another's cultural history especially one that has obvious spiritual benefit wherein the people have displayed an honorable record. Steltenkamp's book is a recent publication. The University of Oklahoma Press is very partial to the old practice of missionizing the Indians. Gerald Vizenor, an Objibway Indian who looks like a white man, is associated with this publishing house but his writings criticize modern Indians more so than monitoring this institution that publishes many volumes of Native American books. Indians like Clyde Bellecourt, who have been in the trenches of change and return, have been his targets. Clyde was one who came to my rescue when we were fighting for the return of our Sun Dance ceremony as did Russ Means, Dennis Banks and Lehman Brightman. Another book on Black Elk was written by an author named Rice. It was published by the University of New Mexico Press and for its cover the famous picture of Black Elk praying on the mountain was used. After reading this work, Hilda Neihardt had the cover picture revoked on subsequent issues because she was thoroughly disappointed with the references to her father, the author. If anyone can bear witness to the spirituality, sincerity and absolute honesty of John Neihardt, it is Hilda.

I am often asked if Wallace Black Elk is a relative of Nick Black Elk. Wallace is from the Rosebud reservation and is not an Oglala and not a blood relative. His name used to be Wallace Howard and his book is titled; *Black Elk : The Sacred Ways of a Lakota*. It was written by a white man named Lyon. Wallace never mentions Black Elk's vision or prophecy in any meaningful way in this book or in his travels. From what I have gathered over the years, I often wonder if Wallace even understands or is substantially aware of this great vision. Wallace has had the courage and foresight to share spirituality, however, and has reached many across the globe.

Over and over, traditional respecting Indian people are continually disheartened with these attempts to justify the historic eradication of native spirituality by Christian followers. At South Dakota State University, I viewed with expectant enthusiasm a documentary narrated by Ben Black Elk on Sioux culture. At the end, Reverend Steinmetz, a Jesuit priest in mass vestments comes flowing reverently across the screen, piously holding a peace pipe. If you see the annual enactment of *Hiawatha* at the Pipestone Quarries you will view an interesting depiction put on by the non-Indian townspeople dressed as Indians. The ending is very disappointing to a traditional Indian—a missionary priest standing graciously in a canoe, holds forth a soul saving cross as he is paddled across the water by good little Indians. "We took everything you had, but our religion is superior to yours and you are lucky we saved your souls from hell," is the message implied to me. I don't think this ending to *Hiawatha* was Longfellow's intention.

We two leggeds often receive influence pertinent to our spiritual development either from a particular teacher or several teachers. We are also influenced by what we read from writers who have experienced observations. "Just as the mind digests ideas and produces intelligence, the soul feeds on life and digests it, creating wisdom and character out of the fodder of experience."[3] —Thomas Moore

Quite possibly, were we to be raised separately on a remote island without human contact, we might not consider speculation of the Infinite. For some of us, a specific tribal culture, has influenced us. This present day dominant culture, its ways and norms definitely affects us daily, whether we acquiesce to its influence or not. Of course, there are many, the vast majority, I suspect, who could care less about spiritual influence or any spiritual enhancement whatsoever. These are the Archie Bunkers of life—those who prefer to couch potato along, with little regard for an influencing spirit world. These dense and pithy folks who usually answer serious questions with self-serving one-liners will wind up with blank disks, or with very little knowledge upon them, to take on into the spirit world.

Please bear in mind that for the past century, Native people were constantly told about the European's concepts in a much harsher tone. As children, we were even taken away from our parents to be preached to and converted. So, I think, in the interest of fairness, we native leaning people should be granted some leeway to state our suppositions in regard to our spiritual or religious beliefs.

What is the underlying theme of your religion? One subject was at the base of what exemplary, indigenous people thought and what they did. It proved to guide a pure, unadulterated exemplification of their actions. They were so in tune with Nature, that, as a tribal entity, they did not make major decisions or movements without it. This subject is Truth.

Nature is very, very truthful. Does not a ball always fall toward the earth? Does not the sun rise in the east and set in the west and always on a daily basis? Does the cold come from the north in the northern half of this planet? Do streams flow toward the lower places? Do the animals not always direct their lifestyle toward the direction that the Higher Power has given them? Therefore, Nature can be depended upon as being supremely truthful. Nature does not lie!

What is spiritual or religious truth? It is such a vast, vast mystery and yet two leggeds constantly argue and fight over it. They even kill over the subject. None of us really know. The closest that I can approach the Truth is to admit that I do not know. If I said or proclaimed that I knew the Truth, in the Indigenous Way it would be said that I would be lying. I would be saying that I am claiming to know something of which I am not totally sure. This is a very difficult concept for the dominant society to comprehend. From my observation, it appears that they have had much more of a history of twisting and distorting real truthfulness. In their dealings with the tribes it was certainly so. The modern day legal and judicial system is blatantly reflective of this distortion. The legal system actually twists the truth and makes it difficult to present it directly in disputes, as in the style of tribal review. The judicial system is woefully influenced by materialism which has constantly bought oaths, established its own traditions and perpetuated untruth.

Indigenous thought in regard to truth seeking and application was the exact opposite from dominant society practice. The old time Indian constantly strived to be truthful. We simply have to look at the Indian treaties made by both parties to establish these two points. The Native Americans honored what they bound themselves to and the dominant society did not.

An example of indigenous truthfulness:

In the old days, the old time Indians were very careful not to place themselves in a position where they could be disproven. The Battle of the Little Big Horn may illustrate a point. I heard this story from my parents. My father had a keen memory, one reason was probably the fact that he consumed very little alcohol. He told us many stories of the old west back before the turn of the century. He was born in 1884 and knew many stories. Most of the old time Sioux warriors knew very little about alcohol and had little access to it. Consequently, they had a sense of accurate recall that lasted well into their seniority.

My father told about a writer who came to the reservation to get the inside story on what took place at the Battle of the Little Big Horn. He went around interviewing warriors who had fought there. He was asking a warrior next to his cabin by a creek to describe the battle conditions that he encountered. The Indian told him at length what took place. This warrior happened to fight in an area distant from where Custer, himself, was making his last stand. Probably, the warrior fought against the Major Reno contingent. After the fighting was over, the warrior rode over to where Custer's troops were defeated. The warrior answered the reporter's questions in regard to what he had seen. When the question was asked as to what operational employment the Sioux initially used when they attacked Custer's troops the Indian refused to comment. Perplexed, the reporter asked the warrior's opinion as to what direction and from what draw did the Sioux warriors attack. Finally, the warrior stated that he did not know.

"Come now, you surely must have been told by your comrades what took place against those forces." the reporter insisted. "You were there after the main battle. What did you see?" The warrior shook his head. "You mean you do not know?" asked the reporter.

"No, I do not know for sure." replied the warrior.

"All I want to know is which direction did the Sioux attack from and which bands or tribes attacked first? Surely, you must have been told that."

The warrior shook his head and pointed down stream. "Go to the first cabin downstream. Go see Two Hawks. He was there during the fight. What I might say would not be the total truth compared with what Two Hawks saw. If I tried to tell you what I did not see or do and he can tell you more truthfully—then I would be lying. It will be more truthful if you listen to him."

I have always remembered that story and it conveys the meritorious regard for truthfulness exhibited by such a deeply spiritual people. The warrior was not going to go forward without it. His thinking and action was totally immersed in truth. I believe their truthfulness was the key to the holy person's ability to reach into the spirit world. Certainly the Great Mystery has allowed us these new communicative tools to discover a closer regard for truth. We can now observe more fully the broad scope of created truth that is everywhere. It is much more difficult for truth to be distorted, altered or covered up. The more truth we learn, the more immune we will become toward those who distort, scheme and lie about the truth and who would lead us down some treacherous paths in order for them to acquire more power.

We all have had our experiences, unfortunately, with some individual or a group of individuals who have severely distorted the truth and, consequently, we have suffered as a result. This world is so untruthful that a writer can actually make this statement and expect to be quite accurate. I have had several such happenings and in one particular case I took it to the doors of a state's highest court, but they did not want to hear about it.

I worked for a public corporation. It was supposed to be owned and operated by the state but it was really controlled by one individual who knew how to influence and use favors that he could give out from this public corporation, which was the airport system and of course the main terminal where the major airlines landed. I was a pilot, had flown large and small airplanes, even military helicopters which had been based at the main air terminal, and had a law degree which more than met educational requirements. I was considered quite qualified for the job for which I applied: to become an airport manager. The end result was that my immediate superior's son wound up with my job and the Airport Director's son-in-law and other relatives were hired into positions and unscrupulously promoted, against all manner of affirmative action federal policies. His daughter was given choice employment within the passenger terminal. The son-in-law was immediately awarded a take home vehicle and rapidly promoted. Along the way, relatives of friends and politicians were also selected and promoted. I was a minority and was assigned to promote fair employment policies. I simply asked some questions: whether or not such a policy would jeopardize millions in federal grants for airport construction which supposedly required affirmative action and fair hiring demands in the federal grant requests.

Immediately, since there was too much truth in my questions, a severe discrediting procedure against me was initiated. Some extreme lies were spread. White man's old tactic against Indians,—"untruth"— was skillfully employed to cost me my job. Naturally, I fought back and it resulted in my taking the case to the state supreme court with no results. This whole experience revealed and exposed the American judicial, legislative and legal system as being extremely corrupt and so easily manipulated by those who can extend favors, even if it is free airport parking for a well paid judge. The airport system even hired the law firm I had hired first. I could no longer use their services after much effort and time was expended. Unethical, it certainly was, and against the legal profession's supposed guidelines, but big money controls the legal system when you get right down to it. The law firm knew they, themselves, were selling out and I did not have to pay for their services rendered when I refused to do so.

All of this happened, I now believe, to teach me how rotten to the core, organized society has become. I am convinced that the dominant system is very corrupt and utilizes untruth to keep itself in its present form. Dominant society religion has little influence as to enforcing real truth and consequently all manner of subtle or overt distortion of truth is allowed. The result is where we are all at today; a higher crime rate, waste of resources, demoralization of honest people and too many bureaucrats, politicians, judges and lawyers who are so easily corrupted. They think nothing of the tribe or the nation they should be representing. Am I simply a former disgruntled employee? Go out to the airport and count the relatives. Then discover how they got there and what were their credentials.

I believe that unless modern day two leggeds can learn that high state of truthfulness, eventually we will lose the planet and we will suffer a great amount of disharmony before we arrive at that fateful destiny. We really do not deserve this planet unless we can return to that state. I have a strong supposition; all that Nature exhibits is pure, unalterable Truth. I also believe that Nature will exact some severe, corrective measures if we humans cannot take charge of our errant conduct and destructive values.

Where does the Great Spirit exist? This question is rather easy. The answer is—everywhere.

* * * *

How Did You Become Involved?

I love a people who worship God without a bible, for I believe that God loves them also.

* * * *

How did you become involved in this religion?
Does your God control all your actions?
Is there a book in your religion that is supposedly dictated directly as the word of God?
What is the authority for your beliefs?
Where did the religion originate?
What is the history of your religion?
Has your religion changed over time? How?
How does your religion view other religions?
Does your religion have any God living on earth as a human?
Do you believe in a savior?
How does your religion view Jesus?
Does scientific evidence support your religion?
What are your fundamental beliefs?

* * * *

I have no idea when I became involved in this religion. At this point it is too confusing to answer questions as religion. Henceforth I shall use the term *spirituality*, instead of the word religion when I am speaking about my own particular belief system. I think of denomination, institution, church, affiliation, congregation and even hierarchy when I visualize religion. Spirituality is more individual, celestial, intangible and accepts mystery. There are many people not of immediate native or tribal descent who prefer the term spirituality. Native Spirituality discerns the influence of God through Nature as the Natural Way.

Because all humans could be traced back to a tribal or "native" lineage, everyone is tribal descended hence the term—not of immediate tribal descent.

I was just a little boy when I first came in contact with my native culture. Was it fate that brought me to a particular place at a certain time which would forever leave me deeply impressed with the way of an indigenous people, a tribal people who expressed their reverence, respect and acknowledgement toward a higher power? It wasn't a religious beginning for me when I viewed my first ceremony. I was just a social dancer curiously looking on. I was even afraid of what was taking place yet some inner force (was it my tribal connected DNA?) kept me watching a powerful ceremony, the Sun Dance. I had been programmed to fear such tribal "things" by the Christian missionaries who had been over me, in a religious sense, ever since I was quite young.

Somehow this fate, the spirit world, or whatever mystery it is that seems to influence our lives (if we let it); this mystery force made sure that I was there to watch Bill Eagle Feather dramatically bring back our Sun Dance ceremony after over a half century of repression. Chief Eagle Feather brought the Sun Dance ceremony out into the open. By out into the open I mean that the tribe could actually stand and watch the ceremony take place without the government stopping it. This was a very brave thing to do because the tribe was strongly influenced by Christianity. Traditionalism that held sacred the old ways of belief in Wakan Tanka suffered serious ridicule by our own people who were brainwashed by the dominant society. At that time, in the middle of this century, the reservation missionaries were in the flower of their power.

Peter Catches, a younger Oglala holy man than Fools Crow and Bill, had gone out into the badlands and secretly performed the Sun Dance several summers earlier. The Catches Sun Dance was not a secret to some traditional believing families but for the entire tribe it was not given widespread publicity. Years later, Peter Catches was a sun dancer when I first danced. My lasting impression of him was that he was a very sincere and devout man. He was mild mannered and soft spoken, and had some strong visions in those later sun dances. I heard him speak about one vision in particular and it influenced me deeply in regard to how I should conduct my life on this Earth. It actually scared me at that time, his message was so powerful and practical. That vision and his words will be addressed in line with the subject area of punishment, reward and retribution in a later chapter.

A Sun Dance is the annual coming together by the tribe. Most North American tribes annually acknowledged to their higher power. They offered thanksgiving for all that the Great Spirit had given to them. Among the Sioux when they were free on the Great Plains, this celebration took place after the summer buffalo hunts. Most thanksgiving celebrations were held during a time of plenty when many people could comfortably gather. A plentiful food supply was essential for such a gathering. The Objibway had their annual wild rice harvest thanksgivings when this grain was plentiful as did corn planting tribes that held corn harvest ceremonies of acknowledgment to their Creator for all that it had provided. The southwestern tribes of North America hold these corn dances to this day.

A more detailed description of the Sun Dance will be offered in a later chapter dealing specifically with those questions related to forms of beseechment within Indigenous Spirituality. Suffice for the moment, I was just a young pow wow dancer when I saw my first Sun Dance. In those days, to draw a crowd, Chief Fools Crow, the Sun Dance Chief, allowed social dancing to take place when the Sun Dance was not being performed. Several hundred dancers would come to the Sun Dance circle and camp. Colorful dance outfits would be donned and we would enjoy ourselves dancing before the crowd that would gather to watch us in the evening.

Pow wow dancing is social dancing. It is not religious dancing on a par with the Sun Dance. I danced for sheer enjoyment in my early days as a pow wow dancer. The steady drum beat kept us in rhythm as we danced around in a circle. Women and men often danced together but seldom as partners. You were allowed your own freedom of movement as your body seemed to pulsate to the drum beats. I would dance in the afternoon and long into the night, whirling, spinning and keeping my feet in time to the drumming. Bells were attached to our ankles over furred padding. The bells added to the sound of the drums. At a young age, I did not seem to tire. The flow of the rhythm seemed to add to your energy. My sister danced also. She wore beautiful, beaded dresses and a lighter, buckskin dress for dancing. During a grand entry she would wear a heavily beaded dress but would change for the evening dancing which usually was quite lively. I wore a porcupine head roach with two swiveling eagle feathers, a breech cloth under an eagle feather tail bustle and a breast plate made of cow bone hair pipe beads. My back was bare and my arms were adorned only with a matching pair of beaded arm bands several inches wide. In those days, pow wow dancers did not have the elaborate dress that is now in the dance arenas. I would sleep soundly in my sister's camper trailer after we were through dancing. Early in the morning I would hear the different drumbeat of a sweat lodge song and my curiosity would rouse me or was it that strange fate associated with the spirit world that drew me to look on at the sun dancers emerging from a tarpaulin covered sweat lodge the size and shape of an igloo?

After the morning sweat lodge, the dancers would towel themselves dry before dressing in their ceremonial attire in a large tipi. For four days the ceremony would be held. At that first Sun Dance, Bill Eagle Feather was the only dancer who was pierced in the chest by Chief Fools Crow. Many detractors said that it was illegal to do what the old time sun dancers did decades before but Bill was defiant. Several plains tribes further west also performed the Sun Dance. They did not pierce themselves and lean back from an implanted tree. I looked on in awe while Bill was attached to the "Tree of Life" that stood alone in the center of the arena. It was not gory or overly dramatic as in the movie, *A Man Called Horse*. That was not a Sun Dance which they were claiming to depict. It was a Mandan Okipah ceremony and not an annual thanksgiving by a tribe, but such is Hollywood with its history of untruth in regard to their portrayal of the Native American. Every movement that Bill made was gracious and sedate. The scene is etched into my memory. To this day, my Disk of Life—my memory, portrays that momentous happening for our tribe's spiritual revival.

If I had to make a statement regarding what influenced me the most in my beginning with my spirituality, then it was this event, the first Sun Dance by Bill Eagle Feather and his intercessor, the Sun Dance Chief, Frank Fools Crow.

My personal experience in regard to the spiritual, could be considered rather unique in this day and age. Besides Ben Black Elk as a mentor, I have had two profound holy men as my main influencers. I also come from a tribe that managed to keep a considerable amount of its culture alive despite the relentless oppression of the dominant culture. Black Elk had his great vision within that tribe. Chief Fools Crow, Chief Eagle Feather, ceremonies, the Sun Dance, Vision Quest, Sweat Lodge and

observing Fools Crow's and Eagle Feather's Yuwipis; they were all significant factors toward my personal conviction that there is a Supreme
Being of unknown mystery and that, for me, a rare, definite conviction,
that a spirit world does lie beyond. I usually avoid definite convictions,
such is my regard for the infinite of mystery.

I have learned much from this culture and these teachers and yet I
have gone on; on to another but yet a very related dimension because I
believe that all things are related as long as we have this one Creator
which seems to have passed a commonality down to all.

Does your God control all your actions? On the contrary, we, not
God, we control and are responsible for our own actions. That seems
pretty obvious. Humans deal themselves into some terrible tragedies. If
God controlled our actions I do not think that we would be allowed to do
so many of these things to each other. Look at all the wars that have happened and so many in the name of religion. In medieval times there were
the crusades, holy wars and the Great Inquisition. They were all created
and occasioned by man and not by God.

I have made a personal discovery that affects me daily. I believe that
we shape and form ourselves every day of our lives and that this freedom
of action or inaction develops, molds and actually creates our spiritual
entity—our individual spirit or what some refer to as the soul. Yes, what
we do today, what we did in the past and what we will do in the future
will create, reshape and re-shift our spirit. And then (it is my mere two
legged supposition) we will carry that self-creation on into the spirit
world. Inside of us, within this great Disk of Life that each and everyone
of us has been bestowed with; within that creation, therein lies our character, our record, our background, our reputation, our knowledge; this
mysterious spirit that the dominant culture refers to as the soul. I call it
the Disk of Life because I believe that this term makes it easier to identify and understand from a perspective of ongoing change, development
and self creation. You expand, alter and transform this disk, this circle of
growing knowledge and related experience.

The human body itself; its physiology, anatomy, neurology and so on,
are symbolic of a limitless, vastly intelligent Creator. I often wonder if the
Creator is not more pleased with us if we try to increase our knowledge
of what it has created and how it works in harmony, than to observe us
learning little of its creation yet mouthing praises. We are advancing
more toward the direction of this great entity when we at least attempt to
probe, investigate, ponder, wonder and learn from its creation. We cer-

tainly are not retreating away from this Creator by learning more of its creation. To go out and explore the Creator's created nature has a much healthier ring for me than sitting in a church and constantly saying, "Praise you Lord. Praise be to you God. Hosanna in the highest." I thank the Great Spirit for allowing me to observe but I have to get out into this vast world and do the observing. I also intend to question what learned men tell me and am uncomfortable with just accepting teachings with an attitude of "blind faith." A good teacher welcomes a questioning attitude rather than condemning you for your own investigation or searching.

Our life experiences, our daily experiences and observations mold us continually. With the exception of Siamese twins, let us visualize two people who profess the same philosophy, the same interests, same tastes, same backgrounds, etc., and yet when they walk away from each other they will have different life experiences that will enter their Disk of Life. These experiences and observations will affect their thought processes, their opinions, suppositions, questions, conclusions, theories, prejudices, stereotypes, ideas and, yes, even their spirituality or religion to enough of a degree of influence, that they will no longer be in total unison or agreement with one another in reference to some major or obscure point of life.

How often have we proclaimed that we have finally found an individual with whom we share complete agreement? We are so overjoyed when we finally find such a person. "At last, we now have a friend or a mate that is in complete, total agreement," is what we often tell ourselves. But it is usually a short span of time when our cloning pronouncements prove otherwise. Has there ever been a couple existent in life who has not had a disagreement upon some matter? I doubt it. I do not believe that a single cardinal or a bishop has agreed totally with every precept and concept, every pronouncement or statement made by the Pope himself. Do all monks or mullahs agree totally with each other? That would mean that they have never had any arguments, disagreements or even doubts. I doubt if any monastery or convent was not without its disagreements down through time and yet they all vowed to obey definite dogma and established rules when they were novices entering the portals. In time, the rules and the dogma changed. Many such places have faded into oblivion. There must have been some change, some new thinking and an exodus by dissenters. I can carry this example further. Let us imagine two of the most radical fundamentalists within the far right wing of the Christian religion. Would they agree to every religious thought, precept, concept, pronouncement or statement made by the other? Certainly, two competing televangelists would never do so. We are all different because we all have different experiences and influences daily.

Sooner or later, the daily circle will bring totally new experiences into our lives. Many of these experiences will be deeply profound and some may bring shattering change. For some, little change will happen. The sum point will be that our spirit, our soul if you prefer such a word, will be changed in our thought process and our spiritual outlook. Maybe spirituality is like a fruit tree. It blossoms and bears fruit. Other trees have their purpose too but they do not blossom.

A tragedy is usually buried and avoided in thought if it is at all possible yet the knowledge of the happening is forever imprinted deeply within. Conversely, in a joyous manner, a grand revelation will be nurtured by the bearer. But each, tragedy or joy, will affect us to a lasting extent.

There is some entity, a created entity, that reflects back upon that which has been experienced. What is it that allows us to recall, to remember, to visualize a happening within one of the new days that come from the dawn? That entity of mystery, recall or remembrance we call it, is integral to the Disk of Life. It is that which records and retains a happening or an influence. Of course, it is much more than that, for it is a mystery like time and space, well beyond our total comprehension. Pride, honor, guilt or shame can accompany this mysterious recall giving it much more than just a cold, impersonal video view. We can feel the horror of the pain or still taste the sweetness of the joy. You will never be the same once such imagery enters into your Disk of Life. Of course, a loss of a loved one will cause you to grieve deeply, remembering forever, but each experience, joyous or miserable, will alter one's Disk of Life.

What of other experiences, those which vicariously affect our thoughts? You may pick up *Black Elk Speaks* or *Indian Givers* and your life will have so many rich and new thoughts. You will visualize and comprehend history from a totally new perspective, one that is close to creation. We are borrowing from another being's knowledge when we read of Black Elk's experiences. We can witness Jack Weatherford's knowledgeable probing, his researching and exploration which became *Indian Givers*. This author's research, investigations, findings and discoveries pass through us and become retained. The pain or the joy is more subdued and less personal but so much of what we listen to through another will shape our destiny. We are still in command as we reach out for this form of knowledge. In most cases we are in good hands as our spirit ship steers its course. We have made the choice to select this momentary company. In the sweat lodge, just before the ceremony is over I always ask those participating to thank themselves for bringing themselves to ceremony. It was their decision to do so. "Honor yourself, that you are reaching for a high plane upon this great circle of life," I usually say, "Be proud of yourself for bringing your spirit to ceremony to beseech, acknowledge, respect or to simply seek knowledge through the words and beseechment of others who have gathered in this humble little lodge." So, maybe you can be proud of yourself if you read and reach out to other forms of knowledge to bring into your Disk of Life.

We are all distinct entities. We are what our minds perceive and these perceptions are honing experiences and influences. In some manner all of these mysteries have an effect on us, even the illusions that remain undefined including vague dreams.

Is there a book in your religion that is supposedly dictated directly as the word of God? There is no special book on the Natural Way or indigenous thought. No such a book is recognized as a solitary, authoritative "voice." The "authority" of indigenous approach to spirituality would be the tribal honing of a people who had proven their virtues, values and environmental conduct. A book would have to be written by a human or many humans as all religious books are written—all by humans. I do not think that spirits have some magical typing machine or a scribing place in a hidden cave out on a lonely desert and therein do they scribe away great spiritual truths, bind them and then leave them for humans to find. I think that all books, regardless of cover or color, have been written by a two legged or many two leggeds.

My book, this book which is now your book, was written by me, every page except where I have included material from a contributing writer or quoted another's works. In the spirit world, I am confident that you will discover I was telling you my truth on this matter. So many clamor that their religious books are written by God but most indigenous people whom I have known do not believe that any one human or several humans grouped together could come up with such a book.

A book of real Natural Truth is beyond the mind of any human. It would be impossible to convey in totality. Yet there is abundant authority for nature based beliefs. I see this authority every day and was blessed as a child in that so much of unblemished nature was available for my spiritual education. I was raised in the Black Hills at a time when it was uncrowded and the streams ran clean except for the cyanide creek that came out of the Homestake gold mine. We stayed away from that stream which was black and deadly.

Lately, especially since advocates of religious persecution and repression have been severely curtailed, more books of experience have been written that shed considerable light on indigenous thought. Many of these books are the stories of people who have been close to the Natural Way. None of these books claim to be the "only way," however. They are merely books that shed light on particular experiences or they explain how the writers, themselves, became involved with the Natural Way. This book has no intention incorporated or lurking within that it is an "only way" book. It is the opposite. We are all distinct individuals with so many different experiences that shape and influence us.

Many books in this age of communication tell about teachers and influencers. More and more, these books are coming to the fore. For those of us who believe in this Natural Way, I think we have a so-called "book," which we go by. This "book," however, will never be found in a hotel room or brought to your door, because it is too big to be carried or placed in a drawer to proselytize to you. It is not written. In the philosophy of the Natural Way, it is generally concluded that native or tribal peoples who lived within Nature, usually based their spiritual beliefs to a considerable degree upon the actual portrayal of Nature itself. This, then, was their unwritten "book."

What does Nature reveal to us by her own actions? How does she react to a happening? What does she show us from each, distinct creation, each species? I consider the flora and the fauna as a part of Nature, and like many of the old-time tribal people, I have a strong tendency to check out my thoughts and beginning belief patterning with the various identities that are found in Nature. How did the species react to a climatic, seasonal or an unexpected happening? Maybe this philosophy of nature observation is rooted in my DNA.

I will attempt to illustrate an unwritten "book"; a book of created nature which is our teacher.

I was fortunate to have Nature all around me when I was a growing child. The four-legged, finned and winged ones that resided within the Black Hills of Dakota where I was raised as an Indian youth were very much alive and in their natural setting. I did not view them as captives in a zoo. I have stored many mind stamping scenes as a child and on into adulthood that could look quite impressive if they were placed on canvas or if a moving video could have captured them.

There was a big brown trout who lived in a pool among the roots of a towering cottonwood. I would sneak up to the old tree by Rapid Creek and peer down into that shaded hole before joining my friends for a swim farther up stream. The scene was more than just a painting, the fish was the largest trout I had ever seen. I noticed every movement of his fins as he waited for quarry to come by. There was an eerie feeling as I stared down into that shaded hole. It was almost as clear as wearing a diving mask in the coral reefs of the ocean. Maybe the trout sensed my innocence, my awe, and respect that would do no harm. To this day I am impressed with these clean water fish. I fly fish often and release most of my catch.

I once viewed a pair of golden eagles teaming up on a wily jackrabbit in the Wasta cedar breaks close to where Rapid Creek emptied into the Cheyenne River. My brother motioned for me to crawl up to his vantage point behind a clump of sage on the rim of a bluff to watch the eagles slowly drive the jack from one cedar tree to another. The rabbit was too wise to make a run for it in the open and instead dashed from tree to tree. How clumsy the eagle looked as it waddled in under the low branched cedar tree while its mate fanned its wings in the open ready to take after the prey.

My father found an eagle starving to death in a coyote trap. Its leg was badly mangled. He took a blanket out of the car to capture it with the least harm and received a life long scar on his forearm from the eagle's claws. We attempted to nurse the eagle back to health in the chicken coop. We had a big orange-colored rooster which was so mean that he would even chase us kids. This rooster never lost a fight and was not even afraid of dogs. The eagle sulked in the chicken coop looking out at us through an iron gate that covered the opening. A smaller hole was beneath the gate which we used to place jack rabbits through. Chickens could pass through this opening which we kept covered although they stayed away from the chicken coop because of the eagle. My father was worried about the eagle losing its strength. Then one day the big rooster went through the opening. I guess he must have thought that he could whip the eagle. Some people, even some countries have been like that, making some ill advised decisions to go off and fight a force much larger than themselves. All of a sudden, there was nothing but orange feathers in that chicken coop. The eagle ate the rooster and from then on devoured our rabbit offerings. He became so healthy and strong that the Hill City zoo offered one hundred dollars to my father. This was a large sum of money in those days. Most people would have taken the offer but not my father. We were poor but he took the eagle back to the badlands and released it. The eagle circled high above my father before it flew to some distant buttes. At times my Dad would go back to that place and hold up his big cowboy hat, waving it at the buttes. Often the eagle would come and circle over my Dad. He was proud of his scar and the fact that money could not buy the eagle.

A pair of eagles hovered over us as we built a sweat lodge. It was at a time when they usually were out hunting fish along the Mississippi River. When we went down below to gather more saplings for the frame, there they were, hovering closer to the lodge site in our absence. The manner in which they flew and interest that they seemed to display imparted to me an approval that we were doing a good act. Since then, that little lodge site, a small church place, if you will, has had some strong and rewarding ceremonies.

Have you ever come to a corner of a corral and there met face to face with a bobcat out for its evening hunt? His eyes or her eyes wide and open, looking straight into my soul, my spirit, my Disk of Life. A very frozen moment in time. One look. They are so fast, it seemed to vanish in thin air. This experience will never leave my memory.

Have you ever had a close brush with death? Life for all ends in death whether we want to think about it or not. Nothing can give you such a scare than to leap across a fallen log and land beside a coiled rattle snake while out cotton tail hunting. Fortunately it was autumn and just a little too chilly for the snake to be aggressive, the time I had this experience. Instead of striking, he could barely crawl back into the rotting hollow of the log. Deer, buffalo, coyote, elk, and even the spooky antelope; I have seen them all at close quarters in vivid scenes that are forever painted beautifully upon my own Disk of Life.

Scenes still continue to be painted annually within my memory as I fly fish those clear Black Hills streams where you can still safely drink the pure water. There is no industry west of the Black Hills. No acid rains fall on these streams as they do in the east. It is sad to fish eastern streams where the stocked trout can not reproduce and feed sufficiently. You can lift up a simple rock in the Black Hills streams and smell cool moss. You see life, a whirl-a-gig or a rock worm nymph scurry and wriggle or watch the flies dance up from the waters when the temperature reaches the mid-fifties due to a winter Chinook. Trout leap and splash when the flies dance.

A heavily racked deer poked his face out of the edge of a Dakota corn field while I was walking a dry creek covered with pheasant tracks. Somehow, he knew that I was only pheasant hunting. He stood there for some long moments and simply stared at me when I stopped to admire such an enrapturing scene. A starling flock cackled, and the sound of changing fall blew down from a railroad embankment in the background to rustle drying corn with hanging ears, while my regal friend bearing such commanding horns surveyed me so handsomely. I see so many big racked bucks in the fall, no doubt because I always try to get "way back in there" when I pheasant hunt—about the only hunting sport that I do anymore. In the Dakotas, there are thousands of acres which have been returned to their natural state. Often these lands cover several miles. Pheasants, songbirds and related wildlife abound. I hope the government does not change this program which returns the land to the Natural Way.

For a worldview, several Arctic terns come back each year when I look out on a favorite pond in the spring. They "dive bomb" schools of bull heads and rest for several weeks or often a month before going on toward the top of this planet. They are so streamlined and effortless in flight, I can understand how they can cover such great distances in their travels.

I hope the Great Spirit, the Great Mystery, lets me take all of these pristine memories of its magnificent creation on into the spirit world when I depart. Better yet, maybe it will let me be an eagle and I can fly so freely to watch these scenes which have been described. It is comfortable to be an American Indian in this respect because many of us believe that you take with you that what you have earned, learned or what you have put into your own Disk of Life while you walk your earth path journey.

Such scenes allow a more vivid and knowledgeable portrayal of a rich culture. I meet so many people who have so many misconceptions and just plain lack of knowledge about such a rich past that revered and respected the wildlife, our animal brothers and sisters as relatives. In fact, an Indian would consider these memories of the Creator's direct creations—the Wamakaskan, the animal world—as spiritual paintings because they are revealing a deep, living depth of Creation. Each animal has its own power or gift to convey because they were so endowed by Wakan Tanka. Does not a mountain lion tell us that we can become independent and walk those lonely chasms of change undaunted? Doesn't a portrait of the owl, the eagle of the night, tell us not to fear the dark or mysterious places? Surely the beaver conveys a serene security and pace brought forth by a steady endeavor if we can be so fortunate to find our own bliss. And yes, we all need endless scenes of the freedom of hawks, eagles, wolves and the great orcas of the seas to forever implant a resolve that we must never lose our connection with the vast soothing solitude of Nature. Each winged, four-legged and finned has a meaning to convey that can be beneficial to our intricate two legged lives. Yes, even a common field mouse or a disciplined, dedicated badland ant has a message to convey if we will stoop to study and look for it.

Animals are the innocent ones, the truthful ones who follow obediently as the Creator has intended. Is the Great Spirit telling us something for our own good? "See, here is what I have made. Notice well that all these truthful ones live in harmony among and within themselves." Maybe God, the Great Spirit, is telling us this. "Notice well that my creations do not take more than they need. Notice that they care for their young and do not abandon them. Notice that they do not over populate and in the rare cases that this happens, Mother Earth steps in to severely curtail that species. No species controls this world of the Wamakaskan." These are teachings that I have learned by simply watching and observing. They reveal much of the Creator's Natural Way, a way that takes a nature oriented, yet attainable intelligence to look for it; one that can throw aside ego, greed and the foolish supposition that human is superior over Nature.

The actions and the characteristics of the Wamakaskan offer a penetrating insight into Nature because we have so much in common. The greater entities also have made their influence upon my Disk of Life especially as I have become older and think more in philosophical and spiritual wonderment. The Six Powers, the Four Winds, air, fire, earth and water,—these are the four elements—and on out beyond to the heavens, galaxies, black holes, unfathomable space. Oh such mystery leads one to unanswerable thoughts but yet one can think! Adventures and revelations from ceremony also have influenced my speculations. This knowledge, coupled with the idea that Great Spirit will teach through its own, direct creations has become my "book," but it is too vast to ever become fully attained in printed form.

What is the authority for my beliefs? The authority for my own personal beliefs lies within created nature. Within those stories and teachings of learned and wise two leggeds who have crossed my trail of life, there has also been some authority, and usually more so, when their predictions and teachings harmonized with unfolding events brought by the dawn of each day. John Fire, a Rosebud Sioux holy man (wicasa wakan) tells us:

"The wicasa wakan wants to be by himself. He wants to be away from the crowd, from everyday matters. He likes to meditate, leaning against a tree or a rock, feeling the earth move beneath him, feeling the weight of that big flaming sky upon him. That way he can figure things out. Closing his eyes, he sees many things clearly. What you see with your eyes shut is what counts.

"The wicasa wakan loves the silence, wrapping it around himself like a blanket—a loud silence with a voice like thunder which tells him of many things. Such a man likes to be in a place where there is no sound but the humming of insects. He sits facing the west, asking for help. He talks to the plants and they answer him. He listens to the voices of the Wamakaskan—all those who move upon the earth, the animals. He is as one with them. From all living beings something flows into him all the time, and something flows from him."[1]

I guess that I would have to say that visible created nature is the ultimate authority for my beliefs. I have not seen the Great Spirit yet.

Where did the religion originate? My spirituality originated whenever the Creator decided to create all of which is now before us. The religion probably originated back in time when indigenous people first began to wonder about their surroundings and their lifestyle.

What is the history of your religion? The history of each tribal religion would be the tribe's ability to reach back into their past and be able to bring forth spiritual or religious significance. Important accounts for my spirituality are the stories of the Buffalo Calf Woman who enhanced the Seven Ceremonies with the Red Pipe and Black Elk's spiritual message and spiritual imagery.

Written accounts of Sioux history reach back to the sixteenth century. The Crow, who are Siouan in linguistic classification, trace their roots back to 1550 when they began their western migration. Tribal historian, Joe Medicine Crow was interviewed and contends that the Crows lived south of Lake Superior and east of Lake Michigan.[2] Before that time and following, oral history recorded Sioux and Crow events. Winter counts, symbolic recording on hides, was a form of written history used by these tribes. Radisson reported meeting the Sioux (Naduesiu) in 1660 in what is now eastern Minnesota or northwestern Wisconsin.[3] The beginning of that century finds the Sioux at the headwaters of the Mississippi River. Siouan linguistic based tribes were also established upon the Missouri

River (Omaha and Mandan). The Kansa and Arkansa tribes were settling further south.

"Ethnologists have long considered the Crow as part of Siouan linguistic stock. If the classifications are correct, then the ancestors of the modern Crow were part of the great migration of Siouan peoples who began to move from a homeland on the Atlantic coast sometime before the coming of Columbus.

"...The ancestors of the modern Crow were part of this migration which took place over centuries. It seems reasonable to assume that as the migration began it was little different from other prehistoric migrations, that there was no specific objective in mind, and that the journey was interrupted from time to time as the tribe found new agricultural and hunting areas."[4]

The Sioux were an extremely spiritual people. Enough evidence in the findings of many writers of Siouan history and culture (Mails, Erdoes, Walker, Powers, Ohiyesa, Neihardt) can substantiate that the Sioux seldom entered into a major undertaking without calling upon their concept of the Higher Power. They also had the ability to communicate into the spirit world—the foretelling power. This ability to predict a future event is clearly illustrated in the Yuwipi ceremonies that were held and told about in *Mother Earth Spirituality* and *Rainbow Tribe*. I do not think it would be a preposterous supposition to assume that the Sioux people, in fact, were forewarned of the coming danger of migrating Europeans to the eastern shores. Maybe the Iroquois chose to remain and fight and the Cherokees decided that they could feed and grant prosperous lands to any potential threat of an invading force. I do not believe that the Siouan speaking people were alone in foretelling power. No doubt the other successful tribes also had attained this ability through their Natural Way spirituality. The foretelling power will receive considerable focus in a following chapter.

The dominant culture has condemned all manner of spiritual concepts except their own when reviewing history, especially indigenous spiritual influence. In the Sioux situation, a tribe that strongly evidenced their spirituality was on the move in what could be considered a relatively abrupt dispersal, before the arrival of a significant number of European immigrants. It is possible that their spiritual foretelling communication issued a serious warning, telling them to exodus westward.

Change became a part of Sioux lifestyle when they left a woodland environment to adapt to prairie life and become pure nomad, buffalo hunters. In Minneahtah (Minnesota), they were hunter/gatherers. Villages were often set up along waterways. Mdewakanton, a tribal group of the Santees, means people or village by the holy or sacred water. From canoes to the horse, as the main mode of travel, this adapting involved tremendous contrast. Earlier in time, if the theory of migration from the Carolina area is correct, the Sioux were primarily agricultural people. If the Kansa tribe claims are correct they were coastal dwellers around Long Island prior to their establishment in the Carolina piedmont. "On the other side (of the Mississippi) by the tciyeta (ocean) which is at Nyu Yak (New York), dwelt the people at the very first." Interview of Alikawahu, Kansas Indian. Interview in 1880 with Dorsey. Waqube-ki, a Kansas Indian in latter1800, stated that the tribes sacred objects including the medicines, the pipes, and the clam shell, "were brought from the shore of the great water of the east."[5] These shells trace back to the Atlantic coast. Adaptability played a key role for Sioux cultural survival to become the last of the major tribes to be finally forced to come in from their natural freedom in the late1800s..

When the main body of Sioux left Minneahtah (Minnesota), they were the Teton or "L" dialect Lakota Sioux. Teton means prairie dwellers. The "D" dialect Dakota Sioux remained in Minnesota or traveled only as far as what is present day eastern South Dakota and North Dakota. The Yankton Sioux group occupied the middle ground and are presently reservationed in central South Dakota, east of the Tetons and west of the Santees. The Tetons are the Oglala, Sichangu (Brule), Hunkpapa, Minicoujou, Sihasapa (Black Foot), Oohenunpa (Two Kettle) and Itazipco (No Bows or Sans Arcs) tribes.

Has your religion changed over time? Some examples of spiritual adaptation: The Vision Quest would have new locations, new hills, buttes and mountains. The Sweat Lodge would have a new covering, from bark to buffalo hide. Abundant Carolina tobacco for ceremony would become short in supply. Substitutes such as red willow bark or dried sumac leaves would be found. Was the Sun Dance discovered out on the plains? A new pipe, a red catlinite, would replace clay pipes. The warm springs of the Black Hills would be discovered along with new stones that would contain myriads of pictures and images. The Buffalo Calf Woman would enhance certain ceremonies. New foods and new medicines would be discovered as well.

There will always be adaptation in a religion especially when new technology makes a profound impact. A tribe or a people move to a new locale and new knowledge is gradually digested and pondered, especially by the younger generations. Many other factors will also bring about change. This change may be so slight as to be unrecognizable but as generation follows generation change will surely become evident.

How does your religion view other religions? Historically, indigenous people were always polite and would listen to another's point of view, especially when religion or spirituality was being discussed. One might learn something to bring them closer to the Great Spirit, it was thought. I have observed the Sioux holy men talk to others of differing tribes and they all respected each others' points of view. There was no arguing about what was mystery. When the missionaries first came to the reservations they were listened to by traditionals who had their own ways and an extremely different lifestyle. In the Indian mind, it seemed that something must have blessed these new people because they were so powerful to conquer all tribes. Naturally it was assumed that it was their religious beliefs that gave them such an advantage. Even Black Elk, himself, became a catechist to the Jesuits for a period of time. When the Indians wanted to speak of their connection to the Ultimate, however, the missionaries had no ears and would not listen.

My personal spirituality has taught me to respect all of those religions and other spiritual ways that allow me to respect mine. I cannot respect a religion that attempts to subvert and destroy other religious faiths. Naturally, I have little respect for that part of a religion that has historically attempted to eradicate the Natural Way, especially when there now exists severe and dangerous environmental problems, even resulting warnings of the disappearance of two leggeds. Should this religion learn from its past history and allow us to go back to our way, then I would like to respect them. I also want to see them admit that their "black book" says little about this environmental calamity that is before us. They need to look spiritually at Nature to approach it. It is their move now. I will have to see what will happen.

Does your religion have any God living on earth as a human? From what I have observed and from what I have learned over the past decades since I have been involved with the Natural Way, there is no God that lives here on this earth as a human being. Its (God's) force is within every entity, organic or inorganic, rock or animal, field or stream. Maybe this question can be answered both ways. Yes, it lives here, in a sense. It lives in everything.

Do you believe in a savior? I do not. I dearly respect Native Spirituality because we do not hold ourselves out as able to grant entry into a spirit world that would otherwise be closed to other two leggeds. My experience with indigenous thought has been one where native peoples did not have this concept that others needed to be saved. They seemed to get along pretty well down through the centuries without knowing about "salvation." Furthermore, they stayed very ethical and honorable without it! How am I going to be saved? How can a human save another human? Did the Great Spirit create us to be saved from something? Two leggeds are about to lose the planet, let alone save themselves. We had better start concentrating on saving the planet. I do not believe that I could ever have power to save some one. What would I save them from?

The Great Spirit has indicated to me that it is extremely beneficent. It gives everything. When it creates such tender and soothing entities such as a beautiful flower or a fish glowing like a neon sign within a tropical reef or paint a sun set for me as the day ends, it is very difficult for me to believe that this is a harsh, punishing God. Is God such an ogre that my mere ignorance offends it even though I was given a fairly blank disk as a baby? Am I to be saved from this great, creative Higher Power as I enter forth into a hopefully higher realm of thought? Why was I allowed here to view, visualize, comprehend and experience so much of its creation? I do not think that this Great Mind that paints, gives, and creates is into punishing us. We will do that to ourselves. We will also reward ourselves accordingly.

How does your religion view Jesus? Some from the Natural Way walk two roads, others only walk one. Some incorporate Jesus into their spirituality and others do not. That is one's own personal preference and should be respected. I have no problem with any one who wants to pray to Jesus while in a ceremony I conduct although this rarely happens. I wish that the Christians would be as equal in their respect towards those who simply wish to pray to the Great Spirit without incorporating Jesus.

I was raised under Christian tutelage and was taught that Jesus was God. Others have told me that he is the divine son of God. Most Christians that I know deify Jesus as God or part of God.

What are my views on all of this? I do not think of God as other than the Great Mystery and I am no longer in any fear of what the missionaries have threatened if I do not believe their way. They do not know any more about Mystery than I do. I think as time rolled on, they (Christians)

deified Jesus and made him into a God. For a long time mo
controlled and recorded the Christian religion. Recording,
and communication of the religion came under their comp
The teachings of Nature and God's connection with Nature were gradually eradicated from this new thought which was to create a deified
human. The deification allowed a controlling power base for the priests
and the monks. The church became extremely structured and was able to
operate through religious fear and the fostering of a wrathful and punishing God contrary to what Nature exhibits. The people's lives came
under the control of the church and they could even be put to death for
suspicion of questioning the church.

I am more comfortable in thinking that the Great Mystery, Wakan
Tanka, is God or the Creator and as explained earlier, I think that this
Highest Power is just way too vast for any specific attempt at definition.
I have to put my being into a center where it is more comfortable for me
to comprehend such mystery.

I also have to look at the track record of a people when they come
before me with their religious and spiritual pronouncements. This is a
very important part of my spiritual reasoning—my looking at what I can
observe. What have they done in the past is far more important to me
than all of the proclamations that they make. I also have to look and compare that past with what I perceive as the past of those indigenous people who truly demonstrated a love for humankind, the Wamakaskan (the
animal world), the Standing Ones (plants and trees) and of course, our
Mother Earth.

When the Pilgrims first arrived, how had their spiritual beliefs, how
had their religion influenced their values, conduct, perceptions and outlook toward all that had been created? If it was not as exemplary as the
actual conduct, worldview and lifestyle of the American Indian, then
why should I embrace their belief system now that religious freedom and
knowledge has allowed me to return to my ancestor's ways?

Truth is a very important standard to estimate how close I wish to
get. How do these people's past dealings with other peoples measure up?
How truthful are they to each other? This is a highly important question.
It is what I call their spiritual track record. How does the Christian track
record compare to other world religions? How do religious people of
other countries and continents compare? What has the beliefs of others
(Muslim, Shinto, Buddhist, Confucian, Hindu, Bahai, etc.) done for their
humanitarian and environmental values? How amenable are they to

adaptation and change? When I compare Christianity to some of those concepts, I seem to prefer Christianity. But then I caution myself and ask if I have received adequate information before making such a judgement. I need to hear more from these other views and beliefs before I can make a higher degree of comparison. Hopefully we all have a basic enough commonality to dance together in harmony around the Great Tree of Life, someday, as in Black Elk's vision.

In regard to Christianity, what is the present track record of these religiously professed people? What are they doing now? Are there any wars going on that are religiously connected to these people? Why are they fighting and who are they fighting? Are they fighting over their belief in Jesus? How are they recognizing all of this new technology that the Ultimate Inventor has allowed us? Do they want to add to their Disks of Life or do they want to be bound totally to the past? What are their religious leaders telling them about all of this change that is happening? Do they recognize the danger of over population? Are they recommending positive measures? Are they talking to stay in power or are they recognizing that people are seeking new freedoms, especially to think freely? Do they bend the truth when they are asked a direct question? Where is the role of woman within their prophecy, standards, stories and leadership? It is she who is, at least, one half of the world's population and quite obviously the Creator's creation. It is highly important as to where and how well she is regarded. All of this tells me how strong or how weak a religion is, at least, in relation to humans living in harmony.

How does this Jesus fit in to what these Christians profess? If he is as powerful as they profess, then why is it that their ministers, their priests, popes and bishops have exhibited to me that they do not have the spiritual connection that I saw in Fools Crow, Bill Eagle Feather and the words of Black Elk? Why do some of these people claim and tell our youth that Bill and Fools Crow were actually in contact with the devil when they had such power or communication?

I would like to believe that there once was a man who professed love as he walked about upon this planet several thousand years ago. I hope that there were many others like him that also professed for their fellow humans. If love came from this person and also was professed by his followers and they developed a very worthy and distinct track record of love and good works then I hope that he will be sufficiently honored. If it was side tracked along the way and his words and teachings were diluted then that would not be his fault. It is too bad this present day technology of recording was not available in those days. It would have saved many arguments.

A close friend, Brad Keeney wrote in his book, *Shaking Out the Spirits*, about another person whom I have met and was quite favorably impressed with, Ram Dass. After being a professor at Harvard University, Ram Dass went to India to find his guru. The man he found in India had a blanket, sat on a wooden table, had no possessions, was not interested in having anyone around him all the time, and would often disappear into the jungle. For a period of five months, Ram Dass saw him only three times for about thirty minutes. After a year, he came back again to see him. What surprised Ram Dass was that his guru spoke repeatedly about Christ. In his own words (Steindl-Rast, Brother David and Ram Dass, "On Lay Monasticism," The Journal of Transpersonal Psychology, Volume 9, 1977, pp.132-133), "I had gone to India, a Jew, had gone to a Hindu Temple, to be introduced to the New Testament, and when I came to India my guru talked about Christ."

Maharaji said to him, "Christ is your guru... He never died. He lives in everyone's heart. Be like Christ... Christ told the truth. They killed him for it, but he told the truth. Be like Christ, Christ died for love... They slandered him but it didn't matter." When Maharaji was asked how to meditate like Christ, he closed his eyes and tears ran down his cheeks and he opened his eyes and said, "He lost himself into the ocean of love." When asked how one can know God, he answered, "Feed everyone." When asked how to awaken Kundalini, he said, "Serve everyone." When asked again how one can know God, he answered, "Love everyone."

"The great traditions of shamanism, with their emphasis upon direct communion with the spirit world, teach us that the boundaries imposed by religious institutions and their texts are artificial. Siberian shamans may commune with the Virgin Mary, Native American medicine people may converse with Christ, and Christian shamans may fly with the eagle. There is a sacred circle connecting everything that is holy. Independent of which tradition one enters, the ascents and descents of an impeccable spiritual journey will always lead one to that center of great stillness. There, the strongest medicine of earth, love, will break our hearts and open our minds to be free of our own self-imposed limitations. There we surrender and die to be reborn to the hope that a meaningful life is made through the action of being a good steward. We truly receive all we need when we give all we have. That is all we need to know.

"We live in a time when Mother Earth and her many children are struggling to survive. Our oldest custodians, the ancient cultural healing traditions, face the danger of extinction. Our stewardship must immediately address these traditions and custodians of life. We cannot afford a future without them. We cannot wait any longer to act. We must return home to the calm center of the sacred circle of healing."[6]

Okiksapa is a good Sioux word. It means to have gained wisdom from experience. You can become wise in respect to wisdom that you have gained by experiencing it. Brad Keeney had a fascinating personal odyssey across this planet interconnecting with indigenous spiritual people and in turn has become "Okiksapa."

"In the world of spirit, there are no ruling powers granted to human beings. Social hierarchies and textual interpretations are the inventions and devices of social institutions. They serve to maintain the social institution that created them and have no necessary connection to spirituality. The old ways, which have not been lost to indigenous people from around the world have all but been extinguished by the Christian churches, Catholic and Protestant. Followers of Jesus need to learn again how to learn from sacred places in the wild, to sweat with the breath of God's sacred stones, to fast and cry for visions, and to live for one's brothers, sisters and all living creatures of our creator rather than live for oneself. These old ways can be taught to us from other spiritual cultures. We must learn to respect and learn from another's visions and prayers. The coming together of the four colors of people to make a prayer is also a metaphor for how we must learn to learn from one another."[7]

After a brief dissertation explaining the four directions in the tradition of the colors exemplified by Black Elk, Brad Keeney continues. "All spiritual traditions embody each of these four spiritual directions, although it may be argued that each has developed a particular direction more than the others. Followers of Jesus can therefore learn wisdom from Native Americans, learn about activating energy from the Orient, and learn about communication with the spirits from Africa. All of these traditions in turn, can learn about sacrifice and service to others from Christians exemplified by Mother Teresa and Martin Luther King, among others.

"Some Indian legends prophesy that Jesus will return as a red man. There is truth in this metaphor. Christians may have to learn wisdom from their red brothers and sisters in order to fully meet Jesus again. Other legends from both the Southwest Indians and the Himalayan

Tibetans predict a time when East and West will meet. Hopi elders have already met with the Dalai Lama and exchanged wisdom. The time has come for us to appreciate, value, and honor our differences. In this way we may learn to make prayers together."[8]

I had an experience with a major church group a while back. It was interesting for me as I am sure it was interesting for this group that brought me to them. This was a good experience, from my point of view, a good "Okiksapa." Maybe what happened will shed some light on the concept of Jesus which has always been put before me by Christians it seems, since I was born.

I was contacted by an elder of a synod of a particular church which is nationally known. They have been in this land since way back in colonial times. A group of these elders were in a meeting and in a conference call they had decided that I should be invited to an important meeting which they were going to hold. One of the elders had read my book, *Mother Earth Spirituality* and had somehow talked the other members of this governing board for a four state area into having me attend and discuss my view point on some important matters in regard to this particular congregation's progression within modern society. This is my point of view, as to why they called me. Maybe their point of view might be expressed in a different manner.

I listened to what they had to say as it was a conference call and introductions had to be made before each board member spoke over the phone. There was even an Indian at this meeting who was a member of this church and I gathered that his position was somewhat like a mission-to-the-Indians type of person. He spoke to me also. Everyone seemed fairly friendly and sincere so I agreed to meet with them.

Life can be a strange experience at times, at least facets of it. When I showed up in the dark of the night, where I was supposed to meet with these people the following morning, I was somewhat bewildered that the address was a somber structure within a huge, isolated estate. A very large building was in front of me and no one was around when I arrived from the airport. Big spacious lawns reached down to a miniature valley of trees with a creek running through it. The wind was blowing and moaning and the scene was sort of eerie and spooky. I thought I had the wrong address because the place I was at was a Catholic diocese headquarters. I rang the door bell and was led to a room. It was a dormitory type of room. I placed my bags down and sat, somewhat puzzled as to why a Protestant church would be using a facility owned by the Catholic

Church. Later, I learned that because of the meeting rooms and cafeteria within this diocese building, it was considered a convenient place. Of more importance, the secluded space afforded by the creek area was something that a hotel with meeting rooms could not offer. This feature was the main reason my sponsors chose this facility. Such a good example of ecumenicalism, that a church group of differing views could offer a service to another.

That morning I met with the synod members at the first meeting which began somewhat formally. I was told matter-of-factly that these committee members were aware that the Natural Way appeared to be growing in numbers and that people seemed to adhere to it. They openly admitted that they were losing membership. There was also some concern that Indian members within this group were also going back to tribal ways and beliefs. The Indian who was a member of that group seemed ill at ease in front of me but he also conveyed the impression that he was sincere. I could understand the predicament he was in as most of the tribes in that area had pretty much gone over to the Christian Way and most had given up or abandoned the old traditional beliefs. Now it was a new time and even these tribes were starting to take a serious look at the older tribal spirituality. I had a good feeling for this person and began to feel comfortable with this group that was being so open and honest.

To begin, a panel started out consisting of the Indian member, myself and one of the board members who was somewhat knowledgeable of some of the local tribal customs. A review of the church mission activity was stated and the Indian member talked about his work within the church. I spoke about my recent involvement with non-Indian people relative to spirituality and also about how I became involved at an earlier time in the return of the Natural Way to my particular tribe. A recess was taken after the panel presentation and afterwards I was called upon to elaborate further on Indigenous Spirituality until it was time for lunch.

At lunch time we went to a cafeteria within the diocesan building which was mostly staffed by Mexican workers. They were obviously Catholic because when the Bishop walked in, most came up to him and kissed his ring as a form of greeting. This is a custom that I am quite familiar with because I used to see my mother and other Indian women do it when the Bishop would come to the Indian center where I played basketball as a youth. My mother would kneel on one knee and kiss the Bishop's ring. The Mexican people did it in the same manner. The Bishop said hello to us but we did not kiss his ring. I looked at the Mexican people and thought of them as Indians. I always think it strange how a whole nation of people seem to downplay the fact that they are mostly Indian when I think of Mexico. Aztec, Inca and Mayan were their major tribes and they did have a rich history but it seems that they would rather identify with European values and European based religion.

After lunch, again I was asked to state my views on Indigenous Spirituality. I projected Black Elk's vision in depth and much of the material that I had written about in *Mother Earth Spirituality*. Another panel was held and we were through for the day. I was told that several Indian people from one of the local tribes would arrive the next morning and a sweat lodge would be built. I was asked if I would lead the sweat lodge ceremony.

The following day I spoke about ceremony. A panel meeting followed, allowing me some free time. I went over to the creek area where several Indian people were building a sweat lodge. It was an unusual sight. They had a large U-Haul van holding freshly cut saplings parked in a spacious area bordered on one side by trees. Also in the van was an ample supply of firewood, many tools, tarps, blankets and a pile of rocks. The older man in charge seemed to know what he was doing and was congenial once we greeted each other. They proceeded to build the lodge and began to mark off and estimate its size upon a comfortable piece of ground covered with soft grass. In time they dug some holes and placed some of the saplings into the holes. When it came time to bend them over to make an igloo shape, the saplings either snapped or came out of the ground because they were fairly thick and difficult to bend.

At that point, I offered a suggestion and demonstrated a method to bend the saplings between the crotch of a nearby tree. You can employ quite a bit of force for bending by this method because the long saplings are like a lever. This technique solved their problem. They proceeded to build the lodge with the pre-bent saplings when I glanced at my watch and realized I had to be back before the synod committee to make another presentation. Before I went back into the diocesan building to conduct a lecture on the sweat lodge, I turned to survey the scene before me. There was a U-Haul truck with its big back door open exposing the saplings, rocks and tools which covered the floor of the cargo area. The sweat lodge frame was just beginning to take form as the Indians bustled about. I thought that someday in the future, maybe within a thousand years, there would be a great anthropological painting or a mural titled,

Indigenous Americans Building Ceremonial Lodge. The U-Haul truck would have to be in the painting.

I can't help but to tell about a small joke that we played on a woman who drove up in a new car to the lodge site. While we were progressing with the lodge, this lady asked us what we were doing. She was kind of official acting so in order to bring her back down to earth, I told her we were going to dig a hole in the ground for a fire pit and we were also going to dig another hole and put some heated rocks in that hole. She asked who said we could do this and I answered that we thought this was a nice place to do it being the trees and the creek was so pretty and all. Just to add a little, I told her we would probably cut down some of the saplings out by the creek if we figured we didn't have enough for this lodge we were building. She didn't look like the type who would understand what a sweat lodge was so I didn't bother to tell her about that. She let us know that she was the Bishop's secretary and drove off somewhat in a huff. Later on a Monsignor or maybe he was just a higher-up priest, came by and he thought it was all pretty funny and told us to carry on with what we were doing. I should have invited that priest to our sweat lodge because he seemed to have a sense of humor.

I had so many serious questions put to me in two days, maybe that was what made me go into my humor role, which I do at times.

At lunchtime the Bishop walked around again. As I watched the Mexicans kiss his ring, I thought about inviting him to attend our sweat lodge that evening but he just didn't seem like the type who would be interested. It probably would have opened his eyes to what spirituality is about but I just did not get a feeling that he would appreciate what we were about to do.

That evening we held a sweat lodge ceremony and all of the elders at the meeting took part including the Indian missions Indian. A Natural Way friend of mine, Sondra, came that evening also. There was one exception among the elders, however. One of the elders told me about his weak heart and asked for advice. I told him that maybe he should just observe and not go into the ceremony.

The Indian people who built the lodge made it smaller than what I am used to, so I conducted two ceremonies to allow all to take part. It was an ascetic setting and also an unusual setting. Can you imagine having an indigenous ceremony on diocesan grounds? As I said earlier, life can be unusual at times. The spirits of Indians of long ago must have appreciated what we were doing because they seemed to be present. Sondra felt their presence as well. She has exhibited a deep spirituality in these matters and walks her talk. When she also felt their strong presence, this was enough acknowledgement for me. She was a good person to have in the lodge. Earlier, she opened the lodge right after she smudged everyone with sage that was provided by her fiancée, and after we initially beseeched to the Six Powers outside of the lodge. She sprinkled tobacco around the fire while I drummed and then made a trail into the lodge and around the stone pit in the center. When she emerged from the lodge she stood up erectly and spoke out in a very commanding and dominant voice, "Behold, I am woman. Let it be known that this ceremony has been opened by woman." I will always remember her striking presence. Sondra is a spiritual woman who is in command of her own spirit.

I believe that many of the female members present appreciated this teaching which I had learned from Chief Eagle Feather and Chief Fools Crow. Bill Eagle Feather told me this: "We come from woman and we come from Mother Earth. When you do ceremony and a woman is present, have her open the ceremony in honor of our beginning."

If there was one issue to remember during our meeting it was that matriarchy should not be excluded from religion or spirituality.

The following morning we had one last meeting. The Christian elders informed me that they considered the ceremony they witnessed in the sweat lodge to be a positive reflection of spirituality and that all had received positive benefit by attending. I asked them what were they going to do with this new knowledge which they had experienced—Okiksapa. They surprised me with their reply. "We are going to attend a national church meeting. And we are going to tell them what we have experienced."

I shook my head at my new found friends. "You will be kicked out of your church."

They replied back and without any remorse or worry. "We are truthful. We cannot deny what we experienced or how we feel about it."

I said goodbye and went on to my journey. I learned a lot from these people and now am even writing with good thoughts of this happening. If these were true people of Jesus then they are a good reflection. They were not afraid to observe another culture's spiritual resources which definitely could allow or project a closeness to the Creator.

Does scientific evidence support your religion? Dominant society has allowed science to be separated from the sacred. Indigenous thought does not separate science from the sacred. They are one. Science is but a means for human to explore into the sacred with forms of measurement and each and every discovery is but a newer look at what the Creator has already perceived, designed, invented and created.

Science could take greater strides toward discovery if it would recognize that the Creator has established forms, certain patterns and offers numerous clues regarding its creations. Science has recognized that creation does react in set form. Whereas the indigenous scientist would call these happenings as truths, the modern scientist has published laws. Botanist scientists with some pharmaceutical companies are recognizing indigenous knowledge in regard to medicine from specific plants.

I believe that any natural evidence supports indigenous thought or my particular spirituality which is so strongly influenced by observed nature. A happening within a test tube, a computerized observation, a microscope allowing me to peer into small spaces, the laws of physics, natural selection, genetics and outer space exploration, are simply varied probing, measurement, and verification of what has already been created. All scientific discovery would naturally support my beliefs.

Unintentionally, science is an avid support basis for the Natural Way in these modern times. What is happening upon, beneath and above the planet is revealed by science. The ominous warnings occurring are not found in the black books of world religions. Whereas science is warning humanity about world population explosion, the ozone layer, resource depletion and threat to the earth itself, the black books encourage "increase and multiply," "subdue the earth" and some even claim that certain races are chosen. Science discredits these statements. Some people are realizing the warnings of science and are turning toward a spiritual mode where they can feel that the forthcoming calamities predicted by science can at least be philosophically addressed.

Science has been reaching farther and farther out into space. If and when other rationalizing beings are contacted in outer space, I will not have to alter my beliefs nor will I be confused regarding my concept of the Creator. When this occurs, science will make a tremendous contribution to the Natural Way.

What are your Fundamental Beliefs?

There is a Creator.

The Creator reveals itself through what it has created.

I am a spirit, an entity of mystery and I have received a life upon this planet.

I am a spirit within a human body as all free reasoning two leggeds are.

While I am here, I am allowed a vast amount of freedom.

We can shape our spirit everyday and every time we take in new knowledge.

There is a spirit world that lies beyond and I should live this life in such a manner so as to earn harmony in that world which might last for a much longer time.

All attempted explanation of this mystery is but mere speculation and supposition. No one knows.

* * * *

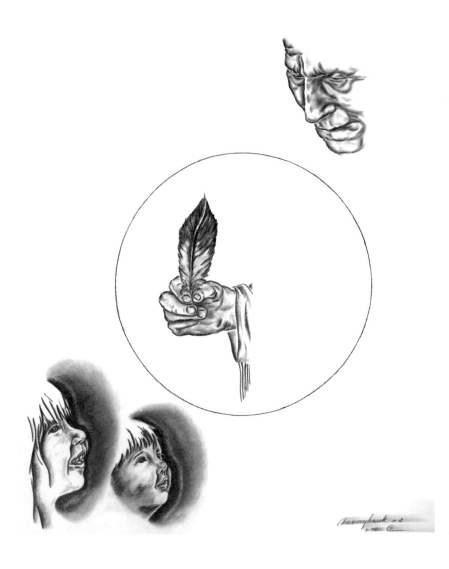

Worldview Philosophy

I love a people who never swear, who never take the name of God in vain.

* * * *

Is the religion a "worldview" religion, or is it concentrated more on itself and its members?
Who are your religion's prophets, if any?
Does your religion teach a view of the end of time?
Do you believe this world will end?
What is the purpose of humans on Earth?

* * * *

Indigenous tribes were content to remain as distinct tribal entities. With the exception of the Iroquois Confederacy, most tribes did not form a union or leagues with other tribes other than becoming occasional allies. As the Sioux increased in numbers upon the Great Plains, their bands became larger and took the form of new tribes with separate chiefs. They were held together by a common language along with their religious and spiritual ways. Hunkpapa, Oglala, Minicoujou, Yankton and Sichangu are examples of these tribes that made up the Sioux Nation. During the annual Sun Dance these former bands, now designated as tribes, camped on the Great Plains for the annual thanksgiving ceremony to their higher power, Wakan Tanka—the Great Spirit.

When the Sioux left Minnesota and went out onto the plains, they concentrated on finding a safe place to live and simply wanted to be left alone. When Chief Red Cloud signed the Treaty of 1868, that treaty stated in effect: "All of the land west of the Missouri River, continuing past the Black Hills, and between the Nebraska Sand Hills and the Cannonball River in present North Dakota, would belong to the Lakota/Dakota Nation for as long as the rivers flow, for as long as the grass will grow and for as long as the Sioux dead lie buried." That is forever, in my estimation. Red Cloud envisioned that the Sioux people would make their existence within this territory. Judging from their conduct, and had they not been influenced by the missionaries' total disregard for population control, I believe they would have set an excellent environmental example, if the dominant society would have honored this treaty commitment to which they bound themselves. Instead, the white man, the Blue Man of deceit, greed, dishonesty and untruth, lied and did not keep his word. The rest is standard dominant culture history; gold was discovered in the Black Hills, choice agricultural lands were coveted by settlers and the treaty was broken. Today, Sioux people live on the least productive lands in western South Dakota. The largest gold mine in North America operates in the Black Hills, a land which is presently strewn with advertising signs beseeching to tourists.

European immigrants came to these shores and in only a few short centuries we have what we see today. Because of materialism, power acquisition, ego, patriarchy, and an actual cutting off of the old tribal influences, dominant society shut down the cosmic worldview of universal harmony.

Thomas Moore tells us in *Care of the Soul*, "We have a spiritual longing for community and relatedness and for a cosmic vision, but we go after them with literal hardware instead of with sensitivity of the heart. We want to know all about peoples from far away places, but we don't want to feel emotionally connected to them. Our passion for anthropological knowledge is paradoxically xenophobic. Therefore, our many studies of world cultures are soulless, replacing the common bonding of humanity and its shared wisdom with bites of information that have no way of getting into us deeply, of nourishing and transforming our sense of ourselves. Soul, of course, has been extracted from the beginning because we conceive education to be about skills and information, not about depth and imagination."[1]

"The soul, for example, needs an articulated worldview, a carefully worked out scheme of values, and a sense of relatedness to the whole. It needs a myth of mortality and an attitude toward death."[2]

"Worldview: the way a people characteristically look outward upon the universe."[3]—Robert Redfield

"In Tsalagi (Cherokee) worldview, life and death, manifestation and formlessness, are all within the circle, which spirals out through all dimensions. The teaching expresses that expansion of the spiral. The same story can be understood in various ways as one is exploring vaster dimensions of mind."[4]—Dhyani Ywahoo

Ake Hultkrantz stated in *Native Religions of North America* in relationship to worldview: "Indians value highly life on earth, and their religion supports their existence in this world. The whole spirit of their religion is one of harmony, vitality and appreciation of the world around them."[5]

"What some scholars describe as "nature rituals," Indians view as affecting the whole of the universe. The Sun Dance is not just a ritual that promotes the vegetation and animal life during the new year that it introduces, it is a recapitulation of the creation; in fact, it is creation and its effects concern the whole evolution and sustenance of the universe."[6]

The spiritual revealing the true nature of our observed world surroundings; this inference will be strongly emphasized in these writings because it is key to indigenous apotheosis and promotion of the balanced system exhibited by the universe. The stars have not fallen in on us yet! From the many ceremonies that I have been in, and many were led by some knowledgeable Sioux holy men, the prayers and ceremonies indicated a constant emphasis for cosmic harmony.

Did the Sioux have a "worldview"? Their Sun Dance should be proof enough. They definitely had a philosophical and theological worldview. Their concept of the Great Mystery was all encompassing. They recognized its unwritten laws existed for the entire world. Since they were so close to their Great Spirit, it was difficult for them to believe that the Great Spirit would not intervene into the deceit, greed and lies that the white man displayed so carelessly. I believe that this was the main reason behind the frustration that led to a brief belief in the Ghost Dance, which was created by those who needed to rely on a "Messiah." Because the white man had nowhere near the principles and honesty as had been displayed by the red man, the Great Spirit was expected to intervene. A Sioux named Kicking Bear brought the Ghost Dance to the Sioux reservations from the Christian influenced Wovoka, of the Paiute Tribe. The awaited spiritual intervention was desperately called out to by the ghost dancers. Chief Sitting Bull, a brave and honorable chief of the Hunkpapa Tribe, was shot to death as a result of over-reacting Indian officials due to the Ghost Dance craze. Sitting Bull, himself, wanted no part of it, but in respect to individual freedom, he did not restrict any of his tribe from taking part, if they so chose.

The end result of the Ghost Dance was the carnage and death dealt out by the Seventh Cavalry at Wounded Knee on the Oglala Reservation when Chief Big Foot's innocent band, hungry and cold, was attempting to return to their own reservation under a flag of truce. They were surrounded by the Seventh Cavalry; Hotchkiss guns were set up overnight. At dawn they were indiscriminately murdered. So eager to kill, the cavalry shot some of their own troops who were checking the Indians for weapons. Thus the Ghost Dance appeal to the Great Spirit was ended and many lives were lost. The soldiers were rewarded with Medals of Honor.

Do Indians have religious prophets? I have a religious prophet. His name is Black Elk. His vision has a worldview. I will relay the story of his vision which I have taken considerably in part from *Black Elk Speaks* and combined with the influence of the interpreter of that book, Ben Black Elk. Ben was a personal friend and influenced me as a child. Even when I was a Marine pilot I would stop and see him when he worked at Mt. Rushmore. At the University of South Dakota I helped bring him to the campus and offer several lectures. As mentioned earlier, Ben was the interpreter between his father, Nick Black Elk and the writer, John Neihardt when this great revelation was written.[7]

In a time when the tribe enjoyed the freedom of the Great Plains, a powerful vision took place. This event occurred several years before the famous Custer battle when the Sioux defeated General Custer. A young boy named Black Elk had a vision that took him into the Rainbow Covered Lodge of the Six Powers of the World.

Two spirit men carried this young boy upward to the spirit world. On a cloudy plain, thunder beings leaped and flashed. A bay horse appeared and spoke: "Behold me!" Twelve black horses appeared showing manes of lightning and nostrils that rumbled thunder. The bay horse wheeled to the white north and there Black Elk saw twelve white horses abreast. Their manes flowed like a blizzard wind and their noses roared. White geese soared around these horses. The bay wheeled to the east and there, twelve sorrels (red horses) appeared abreast. Their eyes glimmered like the day-break star and their manes were like the red dawn of morning. The bay wheeled to the south and there, twelve buckskins (yellow horses) stood abreast bearing horns and manes like living trees and grasses. The horses went into formation behind the bay horse. The bay spoke to

Black Elk: "See how your horses all come dancing!" A whole sky full of horses danced and pranced around him

Black Elk walked with the bay and the formation of horses marching four abreast in ranks. He looked at the sky full of horses and watched them change to other animals and winged. These fowl and four leggeds then fled back to the four quarters of the world from where the horses had come. He walked on toward a cloud that changed into a teepee with a rainbow for an open door. Within, he saw six old men sitting in a row. He was invited to go into the rainbow door lodge and told not be fearful.

He went in and stood before the six old men and discovered that they were not old men but were the Six Powers of the World. Of the powers, the West Power, Wiyopeyata, spoke first. When the West Power spoke of understanding, the rainbow leaped with flames of many colors over Black Elk. The West Power gave him a wooden cup filled with water and spoke. "Take this, it is the power to make live." The West Power gave him a bow and spoke. "Take this, it is the power to destroy." The West Power then left and changed to a black horse but the horse was gaunt and sick.

The second power, Waziya, the Power of the White North, rose and instructed Black Elk to take a healing herb to the black horse. The horse was healed and grew fatter to come back prancing. The horse changed back to Wiyopeyata and took his place in the council.

The North Power spoke again. "Take courage, younger brother," he said, "on earth a nation you shall make live, for yours shall be the power of the white giant's wing, the cleansing wind." When the North Power went running to the north, he became a white goose wheeling. Black Elk looked around and saw that the horses to the west were thunders and the horses to the north were geese.

The third power, the East Power, Wiyoheyapata, spoke. "Take courage, younger brother," he said, "for across the earth they shall take you." Wiyoheyapata pointed to two men flying beneath the daybreak star. "From them you shall have power," he said, "from them who have awakened all the beings of the earth with roots and legs and wings." The East Power gave Black Elk a peace pipe that bore a spotted eagle. "With this pipe," the power said, "you shall walk upon the earth, and whatever sickens there you shall make well." A bright red man appeared standing for good and plenty. The red man rolled and turned into a buffalo. The buffalo joined the sorrel horses of the east. These horses then changed into fat buffalo.

The fourth power to speak to Black Elk was the yellow South Power—Itokaga, the power to grow. "Younger brother," he said, "with the powers of the four quarters you shall walk, a relative. Behold, the living center of a nation I shall give you and with it many you shall save." In Itokaga's hand, the power held a bright stick that sprouted and sent forth branches. Leaves came out and murmured and birds sang in the leaves. Beneath the leafy stick, in the shade, Black Elk saw the circled villages of people and every living thing with roots or legs or wings, and all were happy. "It shall stand in the center of the nation's circle," Itokaga said, "a cane to walk with and a people's heart; and by your powers you shall make it blossom."

Then when he had been still a little while to hear the birds sing, he spoke again. "Behold the earth!" Black Elk looked down and saw the earth and in the center bloomed the holy stick that was a tree, and where it stood two roads crossed, a red one and a black one. "From where the giant lives (the north) to where you always face (the south) the red road goes, the road of good," the South Power said, "and on it shall your nation walk. The black road goes from where the thunder beings live (the west) to where the sun continually shines (the east), a fearful road, a road of troubles and of war. On this also you shall walk, and from it you shall have the power to destroy a people's foes. In four ascents you shall walk the earth with power."

Black Elk thought that an ascent was a generation and that he was seeing the third ascent (generation) when he revealed his vision in the fourth decade of the twentieth century.

Itokaga rose and stood with the buckskin horses (yellow horses) at the end of his words. The South Power became an elk and the buckskin horses changed to elks.

The fifth power, the Sky Spirit, which was the oldest of the Six Powers, was the next to speak. Makpiyah Ate, Father Sky, became a spotted eagle hovering. "Behold," he said, "all the things of the air shall come to you, and they and the winds and the stars shall be like relatives. You shall go across the earth with my power."

The sixth power, the Earth Spirit spoke, "My boy, have courage, for my power shall be yours, and you shall need it, for your nation on the earth will have great troubles. Come."

The Earth Power rose and went out through the rainbow door. Black Elk followed, finding himself on the bay horse that had appeared at the beginning of his vision. The bay faced the black horses of the west, and a voice said: "They have given you the cup of water to make live the greening day, and also the bow and arrow to destroy."

The bay faced the sorrels of the east, and a voice said: "they have given you the sacred pipe and the power that is peace, and the good red day."

The bay faced the buckskins of the south, and a voice said: "They have given you the sacred stick and your nation's hoop, and the yellow day; and in the center of the hoop you shall set the stick and make it grow into a shielding tree, and bloom."

All of the horses now had riders and stood behind Black Elk, and a voice said: "Now you shall walk the black road with these; and as you walk, all the nations that have roots or legs or wings shall fear you."

Black Elk rode east, down the fearful road and behind him came the horsebacks (horses with riders). He came upon a place where three streams made a river and something terrible was there. In the flames rising from the waters a blue man lived. Dust floated all about him, the grass was short and withered, trees were wilting, two legged and four-legged beings were thin and panting and the winged were too weak to fly.

The black horse riders shouted "hokahey!" and charged down to attack and kill the Blue Man but were driven back. The white troop riders shouted "hokahey!" and charged down but were driven back; then the red troop and the yellow. When each failed they called to Black Elk. Black Elk's bow changed to a spear and he charged on the Blue Man. His spear head became lightning. It stabbed the Blue Man's heart and killed him. The trees and grasses were no longer withered and every being cried in gladness.

Black Elk thought that it was drouth that he had killed with the power that had been given to him. At the time that he related the vision, he was probably unaware of the great environmental dilemma that the Blue Man was symbolizing.

The Six Powers:

West Power. We acknowledge the life-giving rains as the power to make live. The thunder and the lightning are the power to destroy but we realize more life than death transpires with each rain. As the sun goes down in the west, darkness comes to the land. The color for the west is black. The spirits who enter ceremony appreciate less distraction in the darkness when two leggeds seek to communicate with them, therefore the spirit beseeching ceremonies are usually held when the west power has allowed darkness to come forth. The spirit world is associated with the west power in this regard but are not confined to a direction. Spirit Beings seem to be called with less distraction when it is dark.

North Power. We think of endurance, cleanliness, truth, rest, politeness and strength as associated with the North. The cold north has Mother Earth rest beneath the white mantle of snow. She sleeps and gathers up her strength for the bounty of springtime. When the snows melt, the earth is made clean. When native people wintered over, often confined to a small area for a lengthy time while they waited for the spring thaw, they learned to be extremely polite, to be truthful and honest with each other. They kept clean by using the sweat lodge to take winter baths and to beseech to the spirit world. The power of the cold white north taught them to endure. The cleansing white wing within Black Elk's great vision emphasizes endurance and cleanliness.

East Power. The third power brought him the red pipe of peace. Peace begins with knowledge. To have peace, one must first become aware of knowledge, which comes forth out of the red dawn, the east, with each new day. When you have knowledge and it is discussed and considered, it can become wisdom. Others share their thoughts, their observations and their needs. A widow can add much wisdom to a council that is deciding to make a war, or planning to send out a war party. She can tell of the loneliness of the children and her own grief when they learned that their father and her husband was slain on the last war party. When lands are to be taken from a people by financiers or politicians the peoples voices should be heard. Communication and knowledge of what is happening can lead to the wise decision that the people's interest must be seriously considered and they must be adequately compensated, or the project may be halted. Especially when sabres rattle and threats are being made, wisdom can lead to understanding and understanding can bring peace to the land. The pipe of peace and the red dawn that brings new experience each day is symbolic of knowledge, wisdom and communication coming together in this day and age.

This is the beginning of the age of communication. We have seen great progress from communication that allows new knowledge to come into people's lives. The red dawn rises to bring a bright new day in which we can add knowledge to our lives on a daily basis as long as we walk this planet. Now we have modern communication that is allowed by the mystery of the radio waves, the television waves and other mysterious gifts. These created and allowed forces, put here for our use, give us optimism that our planet can be saved from past practices of destruction. We have no choice. We have seen in Rawanda and the "ethnic purity" cleansing of Bosnia what can happen when humans refuse to communicate.

South Power. Medicine from roots, stems, herbs and fruits are associated with the south power. Today, many species are beginning to disappear and these medicines can soon be lost. The sun rises higher and higher as the South Power advances with summer. Eventually plants such as corn and wheat will bring forth yellow or golden kernels that will sustain much life through the long winter. Abundance is the primary gift from this power, for it makes all things grow and we are allowed to take that which grows. In the summer, buffalo fattened on endless grasses. During the heat of summer, buffalo hunts provided meat to cure in the hot, blowing wind for long winters. During this time of plenty, dances and gatherings of thanksgiving would happen. To be thankful for what you receive adds strength to your search for sustenance, provisions and shelter.

Sky Power. Father Sky spoke and said the things of the air would be with Black Elk to help him in his struggle. Could these "things of the air" also be the open space of communication which now can transcend across the globe? Can it also be the satellites—"things of the air," beaming back video and radio waves so we may see and talk directly across the skies? If so, Truth will be more difficult to distort. I perceive that what the Sky Power said could be closely associated with the advance of more peaceful people upon the earth because the things of the air are helping to promote peace and harmony. It is happening right before us.

Earth Power. Mother Earth, the Sixth Power, spoke and took Black Elk to the danger that was confronting the earth. This danger was the Blue Man of greed and deception that was already harming the living things. This Blue Man symbolizes the corruption, insensitivity, greed and ignorance which is upon the Earth. The Blue Man would wreak great destruction using lies and untruths and would have to be addressed or else all creatures including two leggeds would perish. Untruth is the Blue Man. Every day we observe much deception by those who lobby our political leaders in Washington with disregard for the environment and the ongoing dilemma. As the situation worsens, more eyes will be opened and eventually the old ways of real Truth will have to be accepted in order to finally destroy the Blue Man. Hopefully, it will be in time for the planet to have a chance to regain the old harmony. Two leggeds will discover that there is no other choice. Religious fundamentalists will no doubt keep on praying and waiting for miracles but the realistic and workable solution will be to return to the values that actually worked. The ozone layer and the population spiral will not wait for miraculous curing. Some tragic consequences will be learned along the way.

The Blue Man. The Six Powers attacked the Blue Man but were beaten back. They called on Black Elk for his help, which was the knowledge he had received and had the power to communicate, now that he had learned of the Six Powers. His bow changed to a spear and when he attacked, he killed the Blue Man. The Six Powers demonstrated the need for two leggeds to destroy the corruption, lies and greed of humankind which in turn is destroying our environment. His bow changing to a spear and thus giving him the ability to destroy the Blue Man, I interpret as symbolic that he now had new knowledge and it was a very powerful knowledge, which enabled him to kill the Blue Man who was causing unnatural and chaotic suffering and destruction. Is it the Natural Knowledge from his vision that is really the spear which can save the world environmentally and give it a more peaceful perspective, free from war-fomenting greed and wasteful detraction which is not working? By learning to be peaceful, two leggeds can devote their energy to the environment.

Everyone is free to their own interpretations. This is merely my perspective and we shall wait and watch how the succession of new political administrations in this land shall deal with the Blue Men that surrounds them daily. I expect little from them and I hope that they prove me wrong. I have more faith in the people rising up with a renewed spiritual imagery and consequently destroying the Blue Man, along with the corrupt politicians and their supporters.

The colors to be remembered as representing the four directions are; black (west) and following clockwise, white (north), red (east), and yellow (south). Blue, for the life giving rains, often represented the west also.

Black Elk's vision continued after he had killed the Blue Man. He went through four ascents to make the center of the nation's hoop live. He came to a village of sick and starving people and was instructed by a voice to give the people the flowering stick so that they could flourish, to give the pipe so that they would know the power of peace, and the wing of the white north so that the people would have endurance and face all winds with courage.

When Black Elk placed the bright red stick into the earth it became a tall cottonwood tree with singing birds. After the pipe of peace came flying from the east on eagle's wings a Voice spoke: "It shall be a relative to them; and who shall see it, shall see much more, for thence comes wisdom; and those who do not see it shall be dark."

This is an extremely important passage for me, for it tells me to be very aware of wisdom, for those who seek to avoid wisdom—"shall be dark."

The great Voice then said: "Behold the circle of the nation's hoop, for it is holy, being endless, and thus all powers shall be one power in the people without end. Now they shall break camp and go forth upon the good red road, and your Grandfathers shall walk with them."

As the people walked forth on the good red road, Black Elk followed. Behind him all of the ancestors, the ghosts of the past, followed. The Voice spoke: "Behold a good nation walking in a sacred manner in a good land!"

The Four Ascents:

When Black Elk looked up, there were four ascents before him. He recognized these ascents before his road as generations in his life that he would know.

After the first ascent the people camped in a sacred circle and still the land was green. I believe that this was the generation that Black Elk knew as a boy. It was a time when the Great Plains remained in their natural state and the people followed the sacred Natural Way.

After the second ascent, the people camped in a sacred circle and land still remained green but there was a nervousness in the air and the leaves started to drop from the holy tree. Even the animals grew restless. I believe that this generation was when the people first knew of, and many had even seen, the Washichu—the white man.

The Voice spoke and warned of great difficulties for the nation.

At the beginning of the third ascent the people had no choice but to follow the black road which now stretched before them. It was the beginning of the time when the people began to be scattered, each following their own small visions and establishing their own rules. "All over the world, I could hear the winds at war like wild beasts fighting," Black Elk said. He added that he believed that he was presently in that time span as he related his story. At the top of the third ascent the nation's hoop was broken and the holy tree withered and was dying. I believe that this generation existed when the people had been placed on the reservations, a black road of no choice. This time span was just before the wars within Asia and Europe. World War II would see millions die or be displaced and hundreds of thousands, maybe millions of Jews would disappear in the Holocaust.

At the beginning of the fourth ascent Black Elk could see that it would be dark and terrible. Yet, a sacred man with a spear appeared who was painted red all over. The man walked to the center of the people and rolled. When he rose he was a bison of plenty. A sacred herb grew, bearing four blossoms, where the bison stood, each blossom represented one of the sacred colors. This event gave the people spirit and the flowering tree reappeared where the four-rayed herb had blossomed.

Black Elk commented: "I was still the spotted eagle floating, and I could see that I was already in the fourth ascent and the people were camping yonder at the top of the third long rise. It was dark and terrible about me, for all the winds of the world were fighting. It was like rapid gun-fire and like whirling smoke, and like women and children wailing and like horses screaming all over the world." When he was telling this to John Neihardt in the 1930's, the setting for World War II was in its beginning stages. The Korean War, Vietnam and many others would follow with lethal weapons of great destruction when compared to bows and spears.

Black Elk intended that the world should know of his vision. Several writers had earlier attempted to secure Black Elk's story but he was not satisfied with them. When John Neihardt came to his cabin, he told Neihardt that he was the one he was waiting for. It was in the fall. Black Elk said that it was too late that year to relate his vision. "You come back when the grass is so high," the holy man held out his hand to indicate the height of spring grass, "and I will tell you my story."

As previously mentioned, Ben Black Elk interpreted between Neihardt and the holy man, Black Elk. Ben was well satisfied with the finished writing, *Black Elk Speaks*. It was published in 1932 but at that time there existed so much prejudice and ignorance that it went into remainder and copies were sold for 45 cents apiece. It wasn't until thirty years later that the importance of such a profound vision would be rediscovered, thanks to the interest of Carl Jung and Dick Cavett. The book has now sold well over a million copies and has been printed in many languages, including Japanese.

Ben Black Elk

The reservation missionaries made a strong attempt to dislodge Black Elk's vision and were almost successful. Many Sioux know little about it, or they believe the detracting dogma perpetuated against it. However, there are many from all walks who are taking a serious look at this vision. Joseph Campbell's remark that this vision is the best example of spiritual imagery is very appropriate. There are many people who have discovered the visible Six Powers of this earth and who are now relating these daily entities in balance, acknowledgement and kinship to their everyday lifestyle.

What does this "religion" teach about the end of time? An old woman doing her quill work, sits with a dog in the spirit world. She has a kettle boiling herbs upon a fire. She makes her patterns and goes to the fire to stir the pot every so often. When she does so, the dog unravels her quill work. When she returns she begins anew, but the dog always unravels her work. If she ever finishes, the end of the world will happen. Ben Black Elk told this Sioux myth to me. It is generally known among tribal members familiar with the old cosmology myths.

I do not know of any Sioux myths that focus on the end of time. As far as the end of the world is concerned, Black Elk's vision holds an environmental warning of ominous destruction by the Blue Man of greed and corruption. I believe that this time is upon us now.

The Hopi prophecy says the world as we know it will end if the White Brother does not heed the Sacred Way of the Red Brother and share his mission to develop technology in that spirit; yet, it also says, the destruction of Purification will be stalled as long as one Hopi still holds to the right path with his simple digging stick.

The present environmental dilemma makes me believe that the planet could become uninhabitable if present values, lifestyles and even certain religious beliefs are not seriously introspected and altered. The idea that human is the unlimited inheritor of this earth and that the planet must be subdued to satisfy his materialistic appetite is proving to be a totally false assumption.

The finned ones are the first to signal future tragedy. Anne Swardson, a journalist for the Washington Post, tells us that the world's supply of fish cannot meet demand.

"The bluefin (tuna) is considered a treasured resource—one whose abundance is suddenly threatened. In 1975, the breeding population of bluefin in the western Atlantic was 250,000. Today there are 22,000. So great is the decline that the bluefin tuna has been proposed for listing as an internationally endangered species, its decimation due not to disease or to natural predators, but to man: Too many fishing boats have caught too many tuna.

"The bluefin tuna embodies everything that has gone wrong in fisheries around the world," said Carl Safina of the National Audubon Society. "It symbolizes everything that is wrong, negligent, criminal and bad.

"To the tuna, add cod off the coast of New England and Newfoundland, red snapper in the Gulf of Mexico, pollock in Russia's Sea of Okhotsk, Peru's anchovies, New Zealand's orange ruffy, Caribbean redfish, Pacific perch, Atlantic herring, mackerel, flounder, haddock, hake, swordfish and shrimp.

"The oceans, long thought to hold unlimited bounty, are emptying. From Iceland to India, from Namibia to Norway, fish catches are decreasing every year. The global marine catch has been declining since 1989."[8]

The unchecked multiplication rate of the human population explosion is the most serious of man's acts to bring forth a planetary apocalypse and now the oceans are obvious proof. World Population Balance, an organization dedicated to raising awareness about the benefits of population stabilization, submitted the following data.

"Our massive social and environmental problems—garbage, urban crowding, food and water shortages, traffic jams, toxic waste, vanishing species, oil spills, rain forest destruction, air and noise pollution, increasing violence, desertification—continue to worsen as our numbers increase by almost 100 million more people every year. Over 250,000 people are born per day!!!! World population is 5.5 Billion. It has doubled in the past 40 years."[9]

We are not only crowding in on ourselves but we are also sending dangerous substances into the atmosphere. Due to an exploding population increase coupled with excessive materialism, the protective ozone layer has been steadily decreasing over North America. Materialism supports industries that leak out gasses which damage the ozone layer. Dangerous radiation that causes skin cancer is not being shielded by this once protective layer. F. Sherwood Rowland, a chemist at the University of California in Irvine, was one of the first scientists to sound an alarm on ozone depletion.

"As a result of his work and others', chlorofluorocarbon compounds, CFC's, were banned by the Montreal Protocol of 1987 and a new one in 1990 ended CFC production by year 2000. Such a serious deterioration of the ozone layer has been ongoing and this pact was revised in 1992 to end CFC production totally by 1996. The cooling agents in refrigerators, air-conditioners and the manufacture of styrofoam results in the production of CFC's which escape into the atmosphere. CFC's last as long as 100 yrs in the atmosphere and take years to work their way up into the higher strata. They destroy vast numbers of ozone molecules. Rowland expects depletion of these destructive entities to peak in about ten years."[10]

Think of the thousands of years that indigenous people lived in this hemisphere. Century upon century they lived upon this land and did not overpopulate, did not cause endangered species, did not drain the wetlands and did not pollute the topsoil or the waters. They did not take more than they needed and they lived in harmony with their environment.

They did not endanger this planet because they were strongly influenced by their spirituality. They could understand that they were related to all that was around them. Their life was lived in accordance with these beliefs.

A close friend, Janice Lynn, wrote the following newspaper article excerpted from The Santa Fe Sun, a monthly paper.

The Renegade Family of Light.

Long predicted by Hopi spiritual elders and in the prophecies of other indigenous people is the time of the Purification—in Hopi, Powateoni. That time is now, according to spiritual seers, when as a result of ecological, social, and spiritual imbalances in all cycles of life, the forces of nature, which have already been set in motion, will take over to bring about a necessary balance of Earth's life forms. Will we and Earth survive? This was one of the questions on my mind as I drove to Hopiland over the spring equinox to escape the deadline driven publication world I too often inhabit, and to offer prayers for the Kachinas—for surely prayers are needed at this time—and to receive, as I did, in return, an abundance of blessings from the Hopi gods.

"It's too late!" Martin Gashweseoma vehemently struck the kitchen table the following morning after the Kachinas had danced for the welfare of the people of the villages and for all living beings. "The purification cannot be reversed," he said, predicting the time of the purification to continue for the next five to seven years. To fulfill his spiritual instructions, Gashweseoma, the keeper of the Hopi Fire Clan tablets that bear the prophecies, had brought the sacred tablets to Santa Fe, the oldest European capitol in North America, in December 1990, to plant within modern culture the seed of the secret by which wisdom can be placed in power. He followed in the steps of his uncle, Yukiuma, who, in 1911, carrying the tablets in a sash around his waist, had visited President Taft to warn of the vast destruction that would result because of forced schooling of Hopi children and usurpation of Hopi land title by the US and other foreign governments.

Other Hopi leaders, including Thomas Banyaca, now the last living of four elders and messengers instructed to carry the Hopi warning and peace to the world, have attempted to prepare the way to deliver the Hopi prophecy to the "Great House of Mica," the United Nations since 1948. The Hopi prophecy is depicted on rock drawings that describe two paths open to humanity. The first path is one of materialism, separate from natural and spiritual laws, and leads to confusion and chaos. The lower path is characterized by the original instructions of prayer in harmony with natural law. A line that bridges the paths represents a choice between destruction or living in harmony with creation through honest labor and spiritual understanding.

"Only a few will survive the purification," says Martin Gashweseoma, who believes that the Fourth World—Earth as we know it—is finished. Earthquakes, volcano eruptions, drought, and famine follow centuries of abuse of the land through oil and gas drilling and nuclear weapons testing, unlike the ways of Indigenous People who, before European usurpation of their life ways, kept the cycles of nature in balance through ritual and ceremony.[11]

Janice told me that Thomas Banyaca stated, "The choice is the people's to purify their lives while there is still time." Martin Gashweseoma said, "Only the pure of heart will pass through the evolutionary net of the Purification."

What is the purpose of humans on Earth? The Great Spirit created us. It would seem therefore that we have a purpose. Does Nature have a purpose? That would be the first question to myself. Here, again, I look to Nature to provide an answer, a supposition or an opinion.

I am influenced by Bill Eagle Feather in the manner of response to questions. I used to travel with him and heard him answer many questions after he would give a talk or do a ceremony. Our audiences were mostly Indians in those days, but the questions were not much different than those that I hear now. In those times, many Indian people were just starting to see the light behind the Natural Way; especially after they had taken part in one of Bill's ceremonies. When they saw and experienced the depth of his sweat lodges or yuwipi ceremonies and the nature revealing power within, they would be quite moved. I remember a strong male figure named Sky who came out of his first sweat lodge. He looked me straight in the eye and stated rather frankly, "That's for me. That's my religion from now on." The way he said it, I knew that he definitely meant his statement. All that this person needed, it seemed, was a ceremony that allowed him to reach back into Nature and the natural harmony that is found within. The ceremony was a strong catalyst to make Mr. Sky issue his statement.

Aside from the obvious purpose that is immediately before us, to save the planet, I think that we have a purpose as humans to learn to bring our lives into the harmony that Nature demonstrates for us. Do not the flora and the fauna of an island eventually attain a harmony of existence wherein all of the island's inhabitants live in mutual cooperation? I use an island as an example, because it is easier to fathom. For a continental land mass, the same interweaving of coexistence would hold true.

Mitakuye Oyasin, "We are all relatives, we are all relations, we are related to each other." This Sioux statement sums up what our harmonic purpose is while we are on this planet. It can bring the most joy and contentment and can actually diminish misery, strife, agitation and even war which opposite thinking will bring upon two leggeds. We all have memories. If I were one of those people who have not seriously contemplated and, worse, one who is taking way more than he needs, I would be very conscious of memory. It is the one entity of this body that we take with us into the spirit world. Everything else is left behind. Why not apply your life now and begin to create good memories of your actions and inactions? Why not prepare yourself now? You are ignorant if you cannot see what is happening right before your eyes.

There is a myth of an old woman who waits on the south trail after you leave this planet. You will be judged by your deeds when you come before the old woman at the crossroads. Even in Sioux mythology, there is a judgement.

Introspection should be a word adopted by all tribes and all societies. It allows us to learn from our mistakes and this is where knowledge and communication will be our helpers to correct past imbalance. It is mostly humans who bring imbalance to Nature. When he or she brings a new species of plant or animal like a Norwegian rat or a Scottish thistle to the shores of an island, this introduction can cause an imbalance and a disharmony upon the whole island. When human establishes questionable agricultural practices, especially those that are formulated by greed instead of mutual existence, then disaster can result. We are now seeing the results of greed-inspired agricultural practices and of course the devastation of Nature due to human overpopulation. A good purpose is to introspect, especially once we gain knowledge from all of the communication that allows us to become so much more aware. Indirectly it is happening, even to the Archie Bunkers and the soap opera Sarahs, every time they watch the evening news or watch 60 Minutes or accidentally stumble across a good documentary. Introspection can bring tremendous knowledge toward a sensible worldview because it removes what is blocking our ability to reach for more truth.

Human has ignored self-introspection and many have become the Blue Man. Where one species gets out of hand, chaos occurs, but always Nature corrects the imbalance. These days are upon us as Nature is beginning to demonstrate her correction power. Some of it will be extremely harsh. The more correction that we employ now, the less severe will Nature's retaliation be upon us; the less that the Generations Unborn will suffer and be exposed to. We will have to co-exist in the spirit world with those Generations Unborn for they shall enter the spirit world as well. We were Generations Unborn at one time. They will ask us in the spirit world what did we do or not do while we were here. Just as certainly, we will ask the same questions to those that were here before us, especially those who greedily used up the resources that could have been shared. We will ask them for an eternity. I doubt if truth gets erased. All of this is part of the purpose behind Mitakuye Oyasin, "We are all relatives upon this planet." It is a big statement.

After hearing a presentation I made in Sydney, Australia, Dr. Jaroslav Boublik wrote an article in the Banksia News. I believe that his interpretation relates precisely to our purpose while we are here on Planet Earth.

"Eagle Man conveyed through stories and song the Native American view of the universe as an expression of the Great Spirit. Spirit appears to us through the four elements, which manifest themselves in the four directions of the compass, the dawn, the dusk and the two winds of change and the four colors of mankind. This is orchestrated by Father Sky and Mother Earth and finally expressed in each of us, the children of the planet. We are thus inextricably linked to the planet on which we live. This may sound obvious but if one looks at the ways in which we violated that link it clearly needs to be reaffirmed. A reaffirmation of that link is the environmental movement.

To quote from *Mother Earth Spirituality*, "The plight of the non-Indian world is that it has lost respect for Mother Earth from whom and where we all come." We need to open our hearts to Spirit. It is too easy to overlook the mystery that surrounds us in the natural world. Technology is as much a part of that natural world and as much an expression of that mystery as a flower or a buffalo. Technology may also be one of the paths back to balance, provided that it is applied with heart, with a reverence for the power it represents.

"We must consider the Generations Unborn. Our children and their children will be left to contend with whatever legacy we provide for them. It could be a world where our ignorance of the Natural Way means that the world we bequeath is hardly a worthwhile place in which to live. Or it could be that we leave them with a planet where the healing has begun and needs only their continued support. The choice seems obvious and it is only when some decry the financial cost of making the repairs that there is decension. The cost should not be measured in dollars but in the days of the lives that follow. And Spirit will look after those that walk the Path of the Natural Way and reward them regardless."[12]

Indeed, our lives are inextricably linked to the planet, Spirit does reward and look after those who walk the Natural Way and our purpose is to live for the Generations Unborn. It is an absolute worldview.

* * * *

4

Good, Evil and Afterlife. Reward, Punishment and Retribution.

I love and don't fear mankind where God has made and left them, for there they are children.

* * * *

Is your God totally good? Does a totally bad God also exist?
Is your God all forgiving?
Do you believe in sin?
Does your religion have the concept of ultimate good and evil?
Is humankind inherently good or evil?
What does your religion teach about an afterlife?
Do people of other religious persuasions go to "heaven," or do they all go to "hell"?
What does the religion believe about reincarnation?
What is your view of occultism and astrology?
How do the attributes of your Supreme Being relate to those of humankind?

* * * *

My God is totally good. It gave me life. That is where I would have to start. Is it a bad God? How could God be bad when it allows us so much freedom? And look at all it gave us. I live, I breathe, I think, I have flown through the sky at twice the speed of sound, I have seen many lands and I am allowed to be here. I just think that I should be thankful for my life. There is a beautiful song that I heard a woman sing. It is simply;

Wakan Tanka
Wakan Tanka
Pilamaya
Wichoni heh

Great Spirit
Great Spirit
Thank you
For my life

I live. I am here. I should not complain. If I enter the spirit world today or tomorrow, at least I have lived. I must be thankful for all that I have been allowed to see, to hear and the continuance of my adventures.

It is difficult for me to think of this Great Mystery as bad. Maybe I will know more when I enter the spirit world. If there is bad in Nature then it is possible there could be a bad God. I do not see such evidence, however. A snake or a spider could be considered bad because they can deliver a poisonous bite. Yet, it appears that snakes catch rodents whose population could run amuck if they were not kept in check. Then the grains that we rely upon would be consumed. The spider catches bothersome insects, especially mosquitoes that come in the night.

I watched a spider build his web while I stayed in a jungle hut in Hawaii. What an architect! There were not that many mosquitoes to make you too uncomfortable and after a certain time every evening, they seemed to disappear as though Nature had programmed them to let everyone get some sleep. The spider had his web right up underneath the lone light for the hut which was solar battery powered. I enjoyed lying there and looking up at the spider with his net catching the mosquitoes and assorted flies. His glistening web and its design had an elegant beauty. Out on the window openings, other spiders were at work. I wished them well and respected them. Was I afraid of this spider? No, even though I knew that he had come down to the table the night before to anchor his web to a vase that was on the table. I slept not far from this table but I did not expect him to crawl further down the table to come over and bother me. Why would he or she have need for that? I was not a part of his own truth, which was to trap other insects, not humans. This bottom anchoring had been consistently interfered with by humans who broke this connection by reaching accidentally across the vase and thus severing his anchoring, causing the web to hang loosely. I took a ball of string the next day and strung it from one wall of the hut to the other and right below his web at about eight feet high out of the way of humans. That evening when we were asleep, the spider anchored firmly to several points along the string. Obviously he knew that the string was there to serve that purpose. I think that he or she was doing its own tiny part in the great circle of life and was made and programmed by the God who is good. The spider learned immediately to adapt also. It did not go back down to the vase to anchor. It is strange how an Indian would take a measly spider and attempt to answer whether or not God was good or bad. A learned and high degree carrying academic would never do such a thing. It would be too simple and certainly would not boost one's ego.

What is bad in Nature? It would have to be against the harmony that has endured. Ever since we humans were allowed to be here, Nature has provided for us. I can not conceive of anything that is "bad" in Nature. Is death bad? I think that this world would be pretty crowded if there was no death. There would not be much room and the Generations Unborn would be cheated out of their space if we did not depart and make room for them. It is getting crowded as it is. Is pain bad? When you sprain or break a limb the pain is there to keep you from using it and it can become healed. Is a blizzard, a hurricane, a tidal wave bad? At the time of the happening one would think so, but new growth returns and more open space is usually accessible for the future generations. As in the case of my hometown, a major flood came through the town down a usually serene mountain stream that was becoming overcrowded by housing. Now quiet bike paths follow the stream bed for miles. Runners jog and Nature is allowed to be enjoyed by all of the residents. Maybe that flood was not so bad after all, at least, for the new generations who enjoy access to that beautiful mountain stream.

Is God all forgiving? Whether or not God is all forgiving is beyond my comprehension. It would be comforting to think so. Hollywood movies always have a happy ending and that is how most people in the dominant society are programmed. Life is not the movies, however. How does Nature handle real life situations? What clues can we gain from Nature, which the Great Spirit has created? How does the Creator resolve life and death which is a constant factor across the planet at every tick of the clock of time?

A lazy son or daughter is influenced by overly doting parents. They might foolishly believe that their parents will care for them on into their adulthood. Tragedy could befall, however. The parents may pass on with little assets to bequeath and the drone offspring will have to fend for themselves and, of course, will have honed few skills for independent survival. Such could be a scenario for our spirit life.

There are extreme differences between the people of organized religion and those people of indigenous beliefs in regard to their actual conduct here on this earth. Historically, these differences were reflected and made visible in the values of truthfulness, generosity and consideration and also the vices of greed and prejudice. I believe that the root cause of much of this difference lies within the concept of ownership and possession. I also believe that the concept of forgiveness should be explored. For many of indigenous belief, there was an actual fear of going into the spirit world with the guilt of having done harmful acts to others, to society or to the animals that provided for you. There was no erasure of deeds done, good or bad. If they occurred, the result and the memory would be taken on into the spirit world. What happened, *happened*, and it could not be obliterated. The record of memory would be a significant portion of your spirit, and those who were affected, for better or for worse, would contribute to that memory. Old time Indians were very cautious about their conduct because they had a definite belief that the hereafter did exist and they would pay dearly in isolation and chastisement in the spirit world for offenses committed against others in this life. This was an effective restraint towards harmful conduct while they walked upon this planet.

I have observed that most Christians are not very fearful about their conduct in this present mortal life. Most Christians believe that they can be forgiven for any offense, even the most heinous. When brought to trial, they usually declare their innocence. Rarely do they admit, "I am guilty, or I did it." They have indicated to me little fear or worry about their perceived spirit life that lies beyond, in comparison to how many indigenous people contemplate this presumption. This attitude is a very key difference. (Forgiveness is a major consideration when I wonder why there is such a displayed difference in the track record between the dominant society and that of indigenous people.)

If I wanted to "sell" a particular religion, or make one appealing in order to increase its membership, then I would offer some promises of forgiveness or attainment to the hereafter. I would promise that happy ending just like the movies. Such a promise would state that a person will come face to face with God after death if only they have exhibited a "faith" while they were yet upon the earth. It is also appealing to throw in a sudden retention of vast knowledge and of course be able to sit "at the right hand of God" for joining a particular church or belief system. This salesmanship has such an appeal, it is why the television evangelists are so popular, especially with the aging.

Where does Nature convince us that such bliss may be attained and with so little effort expended? Go out and live in Nature for a few days or a week. Discover how non-forgiving Nature is. Harsh reality is quickly observed. I cannot find any clues that even hint that the Creator is all forgiving. I might want to wish it was so, and I suspect that this is what has happened for those who fervently believe that we can so easily attain a spiritual nirvana.

Too much marketing has fallen into religion. Just turn on a television set on Sunday morning. By "marketing" I mean that a religion is tailored to become appealable to an audience. The people are hearing what they want to hear and of course are encouraged to join with their pocket books. The religious leaders wind up living in lavish style. The depth and wisdom of spirituality becomes totally ignored. The followers of this charade are left with an exuberant promise and most bask for awhile with benevolent feelings, but the actual result is the society that we see now. It has become very greedy, selfish, distant and even dangerous. A spirituality or a religion should be able to encompass the entire society with its values as it actually did for the indigenous peoples of the past.

What was it that actually helped indigenous people fulfill and direct their life style toward a higher state of harmony? What power, what knowledge, what discovery or what mystery was it that could actually bring forth fruitful results from a people who had no jails, no poor houses, no orphans, no rich and no poor and yet, had an elected leadership?

Native peoples took responsibility for their own actions. They lived this life as if it had a high degree of significance for their life in the spirit world. They knew of the spirit world through their ceremonies. They were quite convinced that a spirit world did exist and that they would some day become a very integral part of that mystery.

We used to have many old time Indians visit us and stay overnight or several days with us when I was a child. These people still retained their old values and knowledge. I do not believe that they integrated forgiveness into their spirituality, at least to the degree that Christians have integrated it.

Native peoples were so truthful that I believe it would be difficult for them to contemplate that a truth, a happening could be erased as though nothing happened, especially a harm that left serious suffering. How could that be erased if the one whom it was inflicted upon bore some very painful and denigrating memories throughout their lifetime as a result? Surely incest victims would bear miserable scars for their entire lives. And this could be forgiven? Old time indigenous people did not believe that all sins are forgiven or that their conduct would all be forgiven if they asked for forgiveness in a ceremony. Such an act would run counter to real truth. Humans would be assuming that what happened did not happen in essence. This is a serious difference between dominant thought and indigenous thought. It is why the native people could live without locks and keys and needed no written laws, and why the dominant society is otherwise.

As will be stated many times, the evidence of such a promise of easy bliss in the spirit world that lies beyond does not hold much water when we observe how Nature will not promise easy bliss and comfort. We usually have a frigid winter and often experience searing heat in the summer in most parts of the world. Even the equator is not that comfortable. Nature is harsh, exacting, even deadly when we get right down to close observation. Nature is above all, truthful and does not erase its truths.

The more intelligent, the more aware, the more balanced a species; the higher their chance of survival. Where species did not adapt then that species became extinct. Such was the harshness of God-designed nature down through eons. Humans who did not adapt or provide for themselves rarely survived. When humans lie to themselves over resources, land management or population control, we see their calamities unfold. Where human habitually lied throughout its society and great inequality and control by an elite became the rule, these societies eventually decayed and fell from within.

Where is forgiveness exhibited in God made nature? It does not exist. In real life, the human created movie ending does not exist either!

I have also witnessed a history of lies upon lies told to us as Indian people by the dominant society and now in this age of communication many good and honest people from the dominant society hold similar viewpoints—that we were lied to. Much suffering was caused by those who perpetuated those lies. Do you think that the victims are going to erase their memory of such suffering when they enter the spirit world? Have the Jewish people forgotten the Holocaust? I do not believe that this was the intention or purpose of the powerful movie, *Schindler's List*.

Does a poor victim of incest or sexual abuse ever forget those grievous and heinous acts perpetrated upon them? The psychologists that I have asked have told me that they do not forget. I was so fortunate that I escaped that horrible crime. As innocent children we knew very little about such conduct and as we grew older we thought there were only a few people who perpetrated such things and they had to be crazy in the first place to do such a thing. Eventually, we thought, they would all be discovered and placed in insane asylums. And all that time, church authorities were shuffling their own child molesting leaders around and were even protecting these clergymen. They lied. They were so intent on covering up that they ignored the degradation and violations committed upon the children of their very own followers. They did not care about the consequences. Period.

As an Indian in a white town, I was not good enough to be an altar boy, thankfully, even though I tried unsuccessfully several times to be one. I back that statement up with what happened to my aunt who wanted to be a nun. She was rejected from two orders because she was an Indian. Times have changed, I know, but that was the thinking when I was young. After I grew older and knew more about it, I asked my mom what happened in the old Indian way about this incest. She said that the Indians would kill anyone who did such a thing. My mom was no historical authority but when I read a book by Ohiyesa, a credible Sioux writer; he said that an Indian could be put to death for lying. If that was so, I believe that the old time Indians must have done the same to the child molester. There is very little record of this in our society. How can I back up this statement? Come to the reservations—at least to the Sioux reservations. I do not know that much about the other tribes. Come out and count all of the deformed, Mongoloids, midgets, dwarfs and other people who are not of the average two legged. All of these categories or classifications are not a result of incest, I will admit, but it is worth noting especially when a group of people do not display such reflections or very little in their descendants. Then set up a graph and a chart like most academics do. I think that you will discover that maybe there was not much incest among those who had the least contact with the dominant society. (Unfortunately, there is alcoholic and drug syndrome that has come into our reservations. Those offspring are not the result of incest, however.)

I have received hundreds of letters that bear a definite respect for so many of the concepts that indigenous people followed. The majority of these letters are from non-Indian people. I do not want to take a chance with the words of the "other" white man, this dominant society minister, priest or bishop or television evangelist, when it comes to my spiritual life beyond. What you do and how you wish to follow their guidance is your choice. I have my choice also as long as this is still a free country. Those who do not see Nature as reverently as the tribal people did, they have not exhibited enough of a positive track record to convince me to believe them. I think that the dominant culture's forgiveness concept has taken a lot of discipline and exemplary conduct out of present day society when I compare the two religious/spiritual ideologies.

Because of my belief that nothing is erased, I am going to try to be very truthful in my conduct. If I lie or do wrong then I believe I will be so charged in the spirit world. If I lie in my writings the spirit world will know. You will know when you enter because observing spirits will tell you so. Nothing will be erased. That is an effective deterrent toward harmful conduct that worked well upon this continent for a long time. What happened did in fact occur. If it caused a painful memory, the victim retains that memory. If good deeds were performed or risk was taken to save a life then the person saved or helped will always remember the good deed. We can meet a person and we either have a good memory or a disappointed or even a fearful memory of that person. We often burst out in admiration when we meet a certain person from our past. Obviously, that person has treated us with dignity and respect and beyond. Are there different degrees of lies? Are there different degrees of harm that you can do to a person with a lie or a series of lies? I think there are but you can answer that from your own experience. If I had to lie to save a person who was being terribly oppressed or was in a concentration camp of inhuman suffering and I could help them escape, I would have no problem telling a lie, but that does not justify one bit lying and harming an innocent person, especially for my own gain.

It is almost a lie, in my perception, to think that mere human can erase what was. In a sense, you are stating that something that happened did not happen. If we did not have memory and if we did not retain the harms that were done to us, then I could possibly believe in this forgiveness aspect that the white man is so adamant about, but yet when I compare track records, I do not think that I would care to embrace the white man's concept of forgiveness.

Do I believe in sin and does my belief system have the concept of ultimate good and evil? I have never seen "sin." What does it look like? I do not think the Sioux had this concept and yet, they set a high example of being without it in more ways than one. Sin was not a word in their language prior to their exposure to the missionaries.

Is this another conjuration of dominant society? This "sin." Where is it evidenced in Nature? Is it something like this devil, which also I can not see or comprehend? I know that the television evangelists make a big "to do" over it. I think it must be pretty useful to draw money out of people and it probably keeps them scared. If I can address some questions in this area, then maybe I can project some related viewpoints.

A few native medicine people possibly did dwell on "evil spirits" and yet the majority, at least in my tribe, were more intent on discovering or applying the healing medicine which they were familiar with. My teachers did not spend time on man designed entities such as "evil" but this does not rule out that some other medicine people might have tried to connect in this area. No one to my knowledge was ever successful at bringing in anything "evil" or had any power to bring such a superstition into a spirit calling ceremony. Because of the nature of our spirituality, such thoughts are usually beyond even speculating. There is no need for it and I believe that most northern tribal practitioners of spiritual healing and communication would believe that an attempt to communicate with what is not harmonic would not be possible in the Creator's harmonic spirit world.

Medicine people and holy men had reputations for their curative or connecting power throughout the reservations. When you have been to a genuine spirit calling ceremony and have experienced the spirit helpers that come in to aid the holy man in prediction or healing, you just do not think of nor do you associate your tribal ceremonies with any type of "evil" connection. It is like looking at a mountain stream or a clear lake that is jumping with trout after evening flies. How could such a happening be evil? How could calling upon the Great Mystery, or through spirit helpers wherein this Great Mystery is always recognized, have any "evil" association? Any other way which does not perceive spiritual calling as good will not work.

My views on good and evil are not held by the dominant society from what I have observed. I do not know if there is evil. I tend to think that good is knowledge and bad is lack of knowledge. Bad is being loaded with ignorance and good is avoiding ignorance by striving to increase one's knowledge. Good is also what the Creator has created. Everything created, then, would be perceived as good, in some way or some design.

It seems that when some people attain knowledge, especially in the area of human relations or the humanities, they have less of a tendency to be prejudiced and hateful. Nature is not hateful, therefore I think that knowledge must move us closer to the higher good, closer to this all providing Nature. Knowledge about a society can certainly remove false fears, stereotypes, misconceptions and even harmful prejudice. That is proof alone that knowledge can cure so-called "evil" which is really ignorance in all appearances. It seems that those who are kept in a closed society, and also choose not to learn about other societies or the natural world around them, they are much easier led down a path of hatred, contempt and disrespect for differing cultures, religions or races. A broader person will couple his or her world knowledge with nature knowledge. One can then attain a higher degree of harmony and will function on a higher plane within society.

I can see where this "sin" spoken about previously is identified with "evil." But I am more concerned with the prevention of it than I am its religious connotation. We are aware that ignorance can cause much suffering. Knowledge gives me hope that a wrongdoer can be changed by knowledge. Often, it is the lack of knowledge by society as a whole that can cause a wrong-doer to become so frustrated and angry that he will go out and "sin" or commit "evil." In another society he might have been a better citizen. Yes, society can actually enlighten itself and grow positively with affecting knowledge. I honestly believe that indigenous society had such a high regard for ethical and moral knowledge and spiritual harmony that it did "affect" its participants in a positive way.

I am sure that many of us know of, or have known a person, who was close to Nature and demonstrated to us that they truly had a profound respect for the ways of the natural world. I hear of a person's uncle who chose to spend most of his time in the woods or a person's friend who nursed a flower garden year upon year or watched many species of birds for a hobby. Rarely are these people unkind, cruel or devious. What is it that has them exhibit harmonic characteristics? The answer is simple. Their closeness to Nature has soothed them and empowered them to be harmonic. Nature has given them more variety to sharpen their intellect. Nature is much more dramatic than a city street or a soap opera. Go out into Nature, stay overnight and find a whole new dimension that changes several times during the night and can have added alteration because of the weather.

For some, a mere flower garden is adequate to follow one's bliss. Thoreau seemed to be well satisfied with his area of bliss. You do not have to travel to the ends of the earth to satisfy or find your bliss. But then again, life is allowed to be so diverse that for some, to travel and take in new knowledge may well be a means of satisfying one's bliss. Other forces will have their effect as well but immersion in Nature is strong medicine for the spirit.

What can bring about a positive change for humanitarian sharing and understanding? That is simply answered. Knowledge. Knowledge leads to wisdom, wisdom leads to understanding and understanding can bring peace. When you blend all of this with nature knowledge, it becomes a spiritual grace. I do not mean this statement to be merely poetic or flowery. It is a fact. People who are deeply knowledgeable and also immersed within Nature, actually do exhibit a spiritual grace. It is a pleasure to be around them.

The depth of these questions which young students have submitted are optimistic indicators of the availability of knowledge and its resultant influence. Modern students now have ready access to worldview knowledge and information, therefore they are asking probing questions which my age group would never have pondered when we were young.

I have observed that the more knowledgeable a people are, the happier they are. The more hateful and ignorant a people choose to be then the more despondent and pessimistic they show themselves. So-called "evil" and unhappiness seem to go together. In the later years of life, few people want to be around a person who has been notoriously "evil" or ignorant. These people lead lonely lives, nobody wants to have anything to do with them and their disks are so blank that they cannot entertain themselves. In but a few decades past, it was "in" to be a spiteful and racist "good old boy" in many parts of the country. Celebrities could even hint that they espoused a racist and prejudiced way of thinking and that leaning did not endanger their social status. That is not the case at present and I hope that such conduct will never be tolerated again. What has brought about this change? It has been the tremendous increase in communication throughout the globe. A Bull Connor from Birmingham, Alabama or a Shelton Grand Wizard of the KKK can no longer command a significant following. Even George Wallace had to change his campaign practices.

Is humankind inherently good or evil? My friend, Manitonquat (Medicine Story), a Wampanoag tribal member, tells us, "The Creator made no evil. Every baby born is good, lovable, loving, intelligent, beautiful special and wonderful. That's who you really are."[1]

"Evil is an illusion. The illusion that there is really something fundamentally wrong in Creation. That sense of evil, of wrongness at the very heart of Creation, strikes terror in our souls."[2]

Could there be entities...Good and Evil? I would have to link them with humans and not with the spiritual. Yes, humans could be good and evil if the concept of knowledge and ignorance is too difficult to reason with. Whenever so-called "evil" is done by humans, I believe it is of their own choosing, their own manipulation and/or creation. I do not ascribe to the excuse, "The devil made me do it."

The system or the tribe can prevent a human from doing "evil" acts. Why is it that indigenous people were not inclined to do the "evil" or ignorant acts that the dominant society did when they came to these shores? Why could early explorers and trappers simply leave their belongings in a pile in Indian territory and identify them with a marking stick? This stick would bear a carved symbol to denote ownership. Indigenous people would leave these possessions alone and secure. Only among indigenous people could this happen. Back in the trapper's own society, his pile of goods would have been stolen. The dominant society allowed some very "evil" acts, such as not keeping one's word, making false treaties, capturing and selling slaves, coveting other people's lands and eventually the entire continent.

What practical reasoning could support such an intelligent power to have a need to create evil? Why would it have any need for creating a devil. I was told by missionaries that this entity actually projected evil? This devil seems to be a strong force in Christianity and among Islamic thought. Most of these followers believe that it exists, yet I have never met a person that could tell me truthfully that they have actually seen a so-called devil as we see forces in Nature such as a storm, lightning, a waterfall, the waves of the ocean, etc.

I once heard and watched a television preacher state that the Devil had appeared to him in his hotel room. I do not make it a practice of listening to television preachers but this happened by accident. I was in a television store when I was exposed to Reverend Robert Tilton. He was investigated by the Attorney General of Texas soon afterwards. He said that the Devil spoke to him stating that he, the Devil, was very unhappy and his demons were unhappy because of all the work for good which the television preacher was doing. Then Reverend Tilton made a pitch for more donations to keep the Devil unhappy.

I did not believe the preacher's statements regarding the Devil appearing in his hotel room. I strongly believe that this man was lying and worse, he was lying over spiritual matters. He was using this devil conjuration simply to bring in more money for his practice. If he is not lying then he should be able to make this devil appear again. I would gladly go with him to see if he was telling the truth. I would like to interview this devil if it really exists. But all of this is moot. I do not believe one bit that the preacher is telling the truth. His story is all made up and for obvious reasons. When a man or a woman has to lie when they are discussing spirituality, then they lose their credibility in my view. I find it difficult to believe what they are saying after that. These people's society does not chastise them to any preventive degree. They obviously are not fearful that in the spirit world they will pay dearly for their lies. Their society has not taught them to be seriously concerned about lying in this life.

If the Devil exists, then why is it no one, absolutely no one can ever come up with one? Possibly, when one is into hallucinogens or drugs they may experience such an entity but this example I would not consider as a credible experience. If people state that they have seen a devil or talked to a devil then why is it that they can not reproduce it when called upon? If an eagle comes to an Indian ceremony and hovers over it, usually that phenomenon will happen again. If a prediction is made by a sincere and devout holy man and from a powerful ceremony, usually that holy man will go on and do another ceremony or many just as powerful and with similar strong predictions. When Bill Eagle Feather's ceremony found the six bodies under snow and ice within a few days after his yuwipi was held at the University of South Dakota, that was spiritual connection. The ceremony was in the interest of good or harmony—to find the missing bodies for the bereaved parents. Bill Eagle Feather performed other ceremonies that called on the spirit world to help people. He was able to be repetitive, like Nature can be repetitive.

To believe in a devil or a so called "bad force," indicates to me that this Great Creator is not harmonic or has some kind of "bad" tendencies. Simply hold and observe a bouquet of flowers and you should be able to understand. Yes, a bouquet of intricately designed, refreshing and pleasant flowers! This creation is a positive indicator that the Creator does not create "bad forces."

What of men like Hitler, General Sheridan or Hussein? Were these men evil? I think that they were allowed into power by other men similar to them. The Nazi party brought Hitler into power and the German people cheered and condoned his inflammatory and nationalistic speeches. He appealed to their egos, their false sense of Aryan superiority, to their fear of unemployment while stirring prejudice against the Jews.

Had Hitler had a childhood with kind and loving parents, had his peerage with other children been blessed with play and acceptance and had he been exposed to a kinder and more humanistic spirituality, he might not have been such an incendiary for World War II. Was he inherently evil? I do not think so. I think that he was extremely ignorant and yet he was allowed to spread his hate and destruction because of the weakness of a society that had nowhere near the communication that we are so fortunate to have in this era. There are ignorant people, unfortunately, as hateful and ignorant as Hitler in this day and age regardless of communication but, thankfully, the age of communication prevents them from coming into power.

What does my belief system teach about an afterlife? What about this heaven and hell that the dominant society taught most of us since we were children? Is there a heaven and a hell? Again, my respect for truth. I don't know! I can't be like Billy Graham who advertised in the Minneapolis Tribune for his speaking tour, How to Get to Heaven. I could never begin to tell people that I could get them to this place.

Did indigenous people contemplate an afterlife that held punishment or reward? They were extremely conscious of the Generations Unborn. They knew of a spirit world, if we are to recognize visual proof from the power of the spirit calling ceremony. The Sioux have the Yuwipi ceremony. The Navajo have the Kiva, the Iroquois have the Long House and the Objibway have the Shaking Lodge ceremony. I have attended some powerful Sioux Yuwipi ceremonies that convinced me of an afterlife. I believe that the other tribes had just as powerful connections into the beyond, such was the commonality of the native North American spiritual approach through ceremony. Of course, their values and environmentalism were also in common. They were not carbon copies but they were certainly more akin than they were to European values, ceremony and philosophy.

Because of this visualization in the spirit calling, where one or more spirits come in, I remain quite convinced that a spirit world does exist. It is not only the visualization but the predictions as well that can readily convert a skeptic. We will go into a spirit ceremony from an experiencing point of observation in an ensuing chapter but for now, I think that we have established that native peoples who had access to such a ceremony had little doubt that a spirit world waited for them beyond the great veil or shroud that all will pass through some day. What are spirits? What else can they be but former human beings who are now in the spirit world? I would have to qualify that those who enter our ceremonies appear to be former humans who applied themselves toward a higher plane while they were here. These "spirit helpers" that have entered ceremony have exhibited a definite familiarity or a special knowledge with what we are doing or seeking.

When I was a sun dancer, we were told to sit down under a shade bowery. Peter Catches, a very devout sun dancer, took the microphone and spoke of his vision into the spirit world. It left a powerful message for me.

He said that he traveled down into the spirit world. There, he saw those who had caused others to suffer while they were here on this earth. He said that drunks who had left their children for the bottle always had a bottle out in front of them, but they could not drink. Instead, wails and cries of loneliness came from their children. He said that these drunks were mostly men and they told him to go back and tell of their loneliness and that they always have to hear the screams of their children when they were not fed and were made to be lonely. He did not leave out the women

Peter Catches

in his vision either. He said that he went on in this terrible place where only unhappy people were. He came upon the women who had left their children for the bottle. They too were haunted by the cries of lonely children crying out forlornly for their mothers. This despair haunted these spirits forever. The vision of Catches does not project forgiveness.

Well, I have heard the white man speak over and over about their concepts of the spirit world beyond but the spiritual experience of Peter Catches has left a deeper impression on me. I always strived to be especially good to my children and be there when they needed me. Talk is cheap and the best proof of someone's character or reputation is to ask their offspring how they feel about their parents. I am not worried about my children's responses but it is more truthful to hear from them on such a matter. I hope that the reader will not forget my father's story about the Battle of the Little Big Horn veteran who wanted to be so truthful that he told the writer to ask the man downstream to get closer to the truth. Ask my children, if you want to get closer to the truth as to my input as a parent. I am close to my children and still do many things with them even as they become older and their interests become more independent. We still take trips together and play many sports. I am fortunate that three of my favorite sports are somewhat skillful. At this writing I can still beat all of them in tennis but that is steadily drawing to a close. Tennis is a good father-daughter sport. I have placed thousands of balls to them since they were small and just learning. Pheasant hunting and fly fishing are happy times in our lives. My last son plays hockey and is a strong defenseman. I am not much of an ice-skater but I enjoy driving him to his many games and practice.

Somewhere along my path I concluded that this realm beyond played a great influence upon the native peoples to bring them to a highly developed state, allowing harmony to flow within their environment. Consequently they developed a high state of sociability and humanitarian performance. Did they have a heaven and hell? I do not think that they perceived the beyond in that manner but they most certainly believed in an afterlife.

Heaven and hell do not make that much sense to me when I fall back upon the hypothesis of observation in Nature. Where is it exhibited, suggested or hinted upon? Is there fire and brimstone? I have not seen it in created nature other than associated with a volcano. When a volcano cools in the ocean, great islands can be formed. The Hawaiian Islands are places of beauty and a virtual paradise in my opinion. The spirits that enter our spirit ceremonies never seem to be in any state of fear of this made up place. Where has this Great Spirit revealed an association with the afterlife of fire and brimstone? The Great Mystery certainly has revealed, allowed and unfolded millions and billions, actually endless revelations to us down through time. Thankfully, it is an ongoing process that usually makes our lives so much fuller and even more comfortable so that we now have the time and the security to have the luxury of probing and contemplating more and more. Yes, unlike medieval times, most of us do not have to worry about the next famine or the next war or raid that would prevent us from being able to contemplate, gather together or travel freely to exchange new wisdom and knowledge. Maybe the fear of heaven and hell worked to control the ignorant masses. The priesthood in league with a nobility could keep control and keep themselves in power. I suspect strongly that "Heaven and Hell" is a concoction of those who want to control.

To bring our created mind with us into the spirit world, I believe, is much more practical than a concept of heaven and a hell. It can be explained quite simply. Those who enter the spirit world with a basically blank disk will probably remain that way because they may be relegated with the rest of the blank disks—the Archie Bunkers and soap opera Sarahs of the spirit world. It seems reasonable that this Ultimate Creator who allows us to be here is undescribable knowledge. Would this creator not place a high regard for knowledge, quest, curiosity, motivation, searching, truthful accumulation and the sincere attempt to discover what it has created? If there is to be a reward, this would certainly seem far more practical. The Creator indicates to me that it gives forth a reward before we even enter the spirit world! The more that you put into your Disk of Life, the more of a reward you will enjoy right here let alone waiting to enter the "pearly gates" of the beyond. The higher the plane of knowledge, the more of your own kind you seem to be able to associate with here, and no doubt more so in the beyond. The mind is limitless in its capacity to receive and glean information. This is a God-given gift. It is a fact. It does exist and there is certainly endless proof that such a statement is so. Therefore I am going to try and put as much knowledge upon my Disk of Life as I can and believe that THAT is what I will take with me into the spirit world. I would hate to go into the spirit world with a blank disk and a weak assurance that all will be fine. A blank disk would not be a happy ending.

Let us consider the simple workings of a computer or of a word processor that has memory. If you have never sat in front of one then go to a store and turn one on. One brand, in particular, is relatively simple to operate.

A basic computer has a disk upon which you can place your information. You can type and type. All day you can type information that you have read, stories you have been told or you can put down your own personal experiences. All this time that you are typing away, this disk inside of this computer is gradually accumulating every key stroke. When you write a book, you separate your chapters into files so that you will have some organization and be able to relate your accumulating material into specific subject areas. Most computers have a permanent disk that is a part of the machine. It is called a "hard" disk and can store a considerable amount of typed material. Many books can be placed upon a hard disk and the disk will still have room to receive more book-sized reams of information. Some hard disks are so voluminous with capacity that a single human could type the rest of his life and never fill the hard disk.

At any time, you can take the material you have accumulated and transfer that material to another computer for safe storage or place it upon a travel computer so that you can work on your project while you are away from your main computer. A smaller disk, called a "floppy" disk is often used to transfer material from the hard disk to the traveling computer. Older model transferable disks were pliant, therefore the name "floppy" was used. Now, modern transfer disks are rigid. The entire contents of an average sized book, such as *Indian Givers* by Jack Weatherford or my book, *Mother Earth Spirituality* fits on one of these floppy disks. To transfer your typed works onto a disk, you place your smaller disk inside of the computer and press an instruction. Within seconds, the entire book that you have worked on for a considerable period of time, that information, is transferred immediately to the confines of the small thin transfer disk that is three and a half inches wide and not much thicker than a nickel coin. Presto! Every period, indentation, sentence, paragraph, heading, quotation mark, etc., will be accurately copied. The entire book will be held by the disk and transferred onto your travel computer or if finished, sent to your publisher for final processing. Now that is what I call a miracle working right before your eyes.

This episode or happening has a powerful teaching behind it and should not be taken lightly. Actually many teachings. Bill Eagle Feather would consider it a powerful teaching. I see this happening as the Great

Spirit actually demonstrating through the technology which it has allowed for us modern two leggeds to grasp. It is revealing how vast a mind can be. This happening also teaches me that as babies we all have basically blank disks just like the brand new disk that comes out of the store. Some of these new disks will be little used, others will reach beyond their capacity and more disks will be needed.

What allows such a marvel to be able to so function? This copying facet is a small accomplishment compared to the feats it performs for engineers and scientists. The graphic arts capability is another fascinating feature. Behind this great marvel is a much higher power than mere humans who egotistically think that they have invented all of this.

Over and over I will make the simple statement: something must have created all of this. Not just natural nature is created nor the physiological phenomena of living organisms, but all of the inner workings and forces that we use through technology are creations by some higher mind. My spirituality is based on what I observe directly; what I perceive from the Creation that is all around me. I cannot ignore technology when it is all around me. It is put here by some higher force, some Supreme Being that I contemplate as Wakan Tanka—the Great Mystery, the Great Spirit. I interpret this as a new communication which is being put here before us. We can use it wisely and already it is bringing profound results; much better results than what was before medieval man. This pitiful, unwashed creature was too easily fooled or rallied to go off to war by an unelected king and he was too afraid to question religious dogma which wanted to restrict his thinking.

If I was going to sell a religion and wanted followers, I could easily say, "Well, you really don't have to do much thinking, just join up with us and all knowledge will come to you when you die. You'll even be sitting in God's hands and <u>He</u> will be whispering in your ear. Now those others who do not join us and disregard what I am teaching, well they will burn forever in hell and also will be tormented by these devils that God has created just for this purpose. This place of fire is called hell and our place in the soft clouds will be heaven."

This widely accepted concept just does not seem to make any reasonable sense, at least for me. It sounds too much like that phony TV preacher. There just is not enough substance.

What of a person who has committed molestation or incest to a child? What of a person who has performed such an act over and over to their own offspring? What of a person who has caused extreme hardship to another and done it through untruth and outright deception? We have all experienced this deception it seems, where we have lost a job, were cheated out of a livelihood, or suffered wrongful ridicule because another told some "hellacious" lies.

In this life, most of those who have offended us seem to go free. Those who stole millions in the savings and loans scandals served little or no incarceration time and when they were confined they had luxury quarters. We will be paying taxes on their deception and greed for a lifetime, yet they have had to make little retribution.

In the spirit world it would seem that these people will become fair victims for our memories. I doubt if an incest victim ever forgets what was done to them. I believe that such a victim will be able to chastise the offender for an eternity. I believe that I will be able to point out several persons who have told some very degrading lies about myself. I certainly intend to settle the score with them since this society pretty well prevents me from having an equal retaliation. This society is controlled by dominant society man but in the spirit world I believe it will be a far different matter. The memories of those offended will not forget when they enter the spirit world. Consequently, the mind will not forget those who have been kind, considerate, brave and helpful. They will be honored. It seems to make so much more sense to consider that the memories of the people will be the heaven, the fire or the brimstone.

And what of those who just accept the status quo? Could it be that the Archie Bunkers will have to associate with each other because the more contemplative minds will have a greater intellect? What would a person who observed have in common with the unobservant? Martin Luther King, Ghandhi or Einstein will have little in intellectual commonality with the Archie Bunkers that must abound in the spirit world. I do not believe that I will want to associate with those who are locked into prejudice, hate and ethnic purity. I certainly will not want anything to do with jealous detractors other than to expose them and demand truth where they have outright lied. Can you imagine what an eternity would be like if you would have to associate totally with those who seldom used or exercised their minds? It seems quite reasonable that this will not be the case.

Do not athletes who have constantly developed and trained prefer to associate with their own kind? Why? Because they have common experiences, similar goals and a quest for an attainment which they can relate to. Others outside of this circle are incapable of reaching into that realm and are less interesting to the athlete. And here is another teaching; the Great Spirit lets us advance to a higher degree of perfection when we constantly pursue that which does not come all that easily. The athlete who trains and trains supports this concept. Does not a motor skill, dexterity and perception improve by diligent application? Even the cells of the body form a new coordination. And the mind, the Disk of Life, probing into the realm of the spiritual develops and improves through truthful quest.

Will the vacant Disks of Life have more in common with each other? It certainly appears that way to me. I could be wrong. Maybe we all just sit down in this great hand of a male figured God and become suddenly enlightened. Maybe some of us intellectual "smart alecks" who contemplated too much and did not buy into all of this controlling fear will all be sent off to this Great Hell. Could be. All human thought is mere supposition, including my own. I have to be truthful. I could just as well be as wrong as the next person. But you know what? I'm just not going to accept what does not make common sense or has not been illustrated for me from created nature and all of its revelations. I am certainly not going to believe in a system that has a very poor track record in relation to true humanistic relationship and proven care for our planet. On the contrary, such a poor record especially when we are at the brink of losing our planet, is enough indication to me that the dominant belief system is not in harmony with what the Great Spirit exhibits. Therefore, a considerable amount of indigenous thought and practice is well worth exploring. They have a track record. They preserved their portion of the planet, in particular, the western hemisphere, for thousands and thousands of years. The dominant society has been here for a short span of time and already we are overcrowded, our resources are almost gone. Now, homeless and orphans abound, especially in South America.

What proof do I have that there could be a conscious separation in the beyond? I have no proof other than to relate to what happens here in this realm, this world that we live in today. Do people tend to associate with each other based on an economic, trade, class, job-related, special interest, age, hobby, sport preference, recreational preference, religious preference, background, educational level, etc? In other words, those of like interests, and to some degree, similar thought, have a social interest in common with each other. They generally apply their social exchange more so toward each other. One could say that, "They prefer to be with their own kind."

Sheer quest or application of intellect alone, is not the discerning ingredient toward spiritual advancement, however. An intellectual person could still conceivably be lost if their intellect was unconcerned, cold and tied too materialistically to the dominant system's values—whereas, for example, a poor, uneducated Taro farmer who was concerned about the environmental well being of the planet could be highly developed in the Natural Way.

Let us take another grouping. Those who are atheists. This group even has its own national association. Thankfully in America, they are allowed to have an association. If there happens to be a spirit world, this group would probably have much more in common with each other. Quite possibly, they would still have their association but in somewhat differing form. I do not have any idea if spirits can scratch their heads. I doubt it. Maybe these folks will try if there happens to be a spirit world. They could be right, however. If they are right, then what I surmise about a spirit life, is moot. At least we won't be placed in the predicament that we will have to scratch our heads if there is no spirit world. I have a higher degree of respect, however, for an atheist who will allow me my suppositions over a detractor who sees his own dogma as the ultimate truth to such a degree that he will try to keep me from professing my suppositions.

What does the "religion" believe about reincarnation? In my lecturing experience, the possibility of reincarnation is an often asked question. My understanding is that to be reincarnated you will come back in some other form or some other life. Romantically thinking, I would not mind going on to the spirit world and then coming back as an eagle or some other winged one that is allowed the freedom of flight. But this is just a romantic musing and from what I observe in Nature, there is little evidence that such a phenomenon is allowed. I probably will not put much energy regarding reincarnation into my musings.

I think that we are all distinct entities and we create ourselves anew, every day and every time we bring in new knowledge or happenings that cause or implant memory into our Disk of Life.

When you write a book you can add to it daily. You start out with nothing on your beginning disk within your word processor. Usually you give your work a name but often you even change this title during the course of your writing. At the end of your daily input you look back on the growth of your disk and if you are wise in the way of computers and human nature you will make a copy upon the hard disk and another copy that you may carry with you in case your computer or word processor should be stolen or if it crashes. Daily you add to your production, you change it and rearrange what you are creating. New information is discovered, your chapter issue might alter and you may even remove outdated material or less relevant material you have labored upon. You might store this material in another part of your hard disk expecting to use it in another chapter. If you kept a copy at the end of every day, each would be different and yet share a commonality, especially from their beginning. The book grows toward completion and at some point you decide that it is finished. If you wouldn't publish, however and adjusted your writings over a period of time, the completed works would also change because you would change with your new experiences.

Most authors can understand intrinsically what I am attempting to communicate in regard to ongoing change within all individuals. Writers are very aware of this phenomenon because we see it revealed to us when we write, especially books, since it takes a period of time. At the end of this book I have become a "much newer" individual. I have added much more to my Disk of Life as I went about gathering and compiling all of this information.

What does all of this have to do with reincarnation? It is difficult for me to believe that we are not distinct entities. I think that we are such special entities from our own creation that we keep our own identity on into the spirit world. Many Indian people believe in spirit helpers, however, and this belief might help one understand a new concept for one's self pertaining to reincarnation.

Fools Crow and Eagle Feather relied on spirit helpers when they conducted a Yuwipi ceremony or a sweat lodge. These were distinct spirits that would come into the ceremony to help predict, acknowledge or heal. Many people believe that they are in close contact with an entity that lived in another time yet seems to be expressing an interest in them or their efforts. I think that they are experiencing a spirit helper but on a lesser level of contact than what Fools Crow and Eagle Feather were able to maintain. People identify with their spirit helper and often with the time span that the spirit was upon this earth when it was in its human or earth dwelling identity. Consequently, many people think that they are reincarnated from another time span.

I think that it is a possibility that they are confusing a spirit helper with that time span. We are all so very intricate and diverse. This fact makes it difficult for me to believe in reincarnation but this is just my point of view, my supposition. I could be wrong. You might be right. What do I know?

What is my view of occultism and astrology? A reply to this question would depend upon what is meant by "occultism." So many of our definitions are based on Christian-influenced explanation. We native people have had to endure a considerable amount of false imagery about ourselves from the same source—dominant society's definition.

The description from a 1972 Webster's Collegiate dictionary.
Occult:

1 : not revealed: SECRET

2 : ABSTRUSE, MYSTERIOUS

3 : not able to be seen or detected: CONCEALED

4 : of or relating to supernatural agencies, their effects and knowledge of them.

Occultism: A belief in or study of supernatural powers and the possibility of subjecting them to human control.

I think of the spirit world as a place that we all go after we die. Most religions hold that view. The many books on near death and the dying experience are accounts of people who briefly entered into that realm and returned with the positive affirmation that it is not a bad place after all. To seek contact with that other world is precisely what a spirit ceremony attempts to do.

It is common knowledge that those of Bible Belt-thinking associate occultism with satanism. I am glad that I do not have this belief of this Satan thing. It is comforting to think that the Great Spirit is all powerful. I am not naive, however. Humans can create all kinds of deceptive thinking and as a result many people suffer and get hurt. Humans create and perform wrongs, harms and wanton deeds. The Great Spirit allows us our free will to do so. It also lets us see and do good. Thankfully there were peoples, tribes upon tribes, that minimized their faults and did live in much greater harmony. They knew nothing of this Satan contrivance.

Do we (Indians) attempt to control a spirit guide? I do not think that this is possible. We have nothing to offer it to entice or control it. Many Indians do not believe in a devil or evil forces unless they have been exposed or converted to Christian thought. A spirit calling ceremony might be mysterious, as is much of religion and spirituality. It is all a mystery. Fortunately when you have a belief system that sees the Ultimate Authority as all good, there is not worry or fear when you attempt to seek guidance or help from the realm of mystery. I guess it all boils down to which direction you are coming from.

As far as my view of astrology, which I understand is the study of the arrangement of the stars from our planet, this is just another area where humans are curious. It could possibly have some influence if the Creator has so intended it to be that way. Many North American Indians look into stones and read images from them. You are welcome to study the many images that are in my stone. More than likely you will discover an image that I have never seen. Many people have pointed out newly discovered images for me in this harmless little creation. The stars and their arrangement is a mystery as well. Possibly, the Creator may have arranged a teaching or many teachings by such arrangement. If my little stone can have so many images, and they were put there by you-know-who, then it is not difficult for me to believe that the Great Spirit can place a myriad of discoveries before us in various ways, shapes and forms. It is certainly foolish to downplay what people are studying. More than likely, the astrology people are finding great enjoyment from their study of outer space.

At least they are not couch potatoes in front of a TV set or barflies on a bar stool. They are not sacrosanctly huddled and patriarchally accusing others who do not practice astrology as being evil and satanic.

I would have to consider first, if the subject being scrutinized is a creation of the Creator? Anything that is a creation merits study. Does not the moon govern the tides? The sun spots, the great solar storms on the sun surface, do they not affect our planetary weather from the point of view of scientists? The Big Dipper influences me when I vision quest. It has been arranged by the Creator. The seven stars tell me there are Six Powers to watch over us and the initial star is the beginning star—the Creator. The four stars that form the bowl of the dipper are the Four Directions. That is a concept formed while I sat under the immense galaxies up on the peak of Spirit Mountain in the Black Hills. Meteors streaked across the skies, or were they satellites? In another time I saw Pleiades dance, yes the stars actually danced. I have not been alone in witnessing this apparition, either. Others saw what I saw. The snow behind me took on a mottled "dancing" appearance the last time Pleiades appeared to me when I took an evening climb to the top of Spirit Mountain with a friend who also saw this happening. Observation or study within or beneath the Natural Way definitely has a teaching. Maybe I am an astrologer in a small way.

How do the attributes of the Supreme Being relate to those of humankind? All creations, all functions of the Creator are attributes. Everything that we observe or come into association with or become dependent upon can relate to us. We can learn to be closer to the Great Spirit by attempting to perceive or understand these relationships and their functions. The Great Spirit gave us this power to perceive, wonder, rationalize and seek. The animal world does not have these distinctions and yet it functions harmonically. It has been functioning for quite some time. By observing animals, we can conclude what attributes they do not have in comparison to ourselves. Let us look at the Ultimate and attempt to discern some commonality and what differences we have with it.

A major attribute of the Supreme Being is the absence of "evil." This great power is all knowledge and it is not ignorant of what it has created. Nothing could exist if this Creator did not know about it in the first place. For me, the following statements simply have no credence and sound so out of place: the Great Spirit does not know what It has created; the Great Spirit is ignorant of certain of Its creations or does not have control of a certain "evil" entity somehow coming from its creation. This ignorance of Its creation or any kind of "evil entity" within, I cannot link or connect with the Great Spirit. Ignorance can be explained as lack of knowledge. Knowledge is an attribute of what God is or what It represents. Truth is the way this divine knowledge always functions. How can we define evil other than in human terms? Human, however, has this so-called "evil" which I defer to as ignorance instead of the term "evil." Some humans have successfully injected/promulgated/marketed this "evil" devil conjuration into mainstream thought, and yet, no one can prove that they have come into contact with it or can solidly verify such a presence.

I think we can move closer to the Great Spirit by shedding our ignorance. Human is, however, considerably ignorant in regard to the Creator's creations. Only recently has European based human made some inroads into the mysteries of creation. Before that time, in European feudal society, most humans existed in dirty villages and the masses seldom went much farther than the horizon. Boundaries were established by non-elected rulers and the common people were merely subjects. It was a dangerous time to travel because of the acquisitive values of society. It was also dangerous to speculate or question religion which was controlled by a harsh priesthood in league with a nobility. They both had a common cause and that was to stay in power. The most efficient method to stay in power was to keep the people ignorant. The Inquisition was created and used for over five centuries against those who questioned church dogma. In times of war, and there were many, medieval man was easily led to battle. He had no say as to his views because democracy did not exist. In traveling off to war, however, soldiers were exposed to more of the world around them and consequently, some gained new knowledge. Ironically, wars had a positive role for some of the people in this materialistic and landowner based society. Indirectly, they were able to broaden and expand their knowledge of the world around them.

In nonmaterialistic society, individuals had more freedom to roam and since the concept of boundaries was unknown, these people had much more freedom to travel and trade with other villages and other tribes. A hierarchy of holy men did not exist nor was there a controlling nobility down through the centuries wherein this society was allowed to flourish. Observation was a key element in the advancement of these people toward an honorable value system. Their connection to Nature was quite possibly their source of such a rewarding development in terms of freedom, laughter, humor, contentment and an ability to preserve their surroundings. Their lives contrasted sharply with the opposite-valued people an ocean away. Indians were not restricted to hunt in their own immediate areas. Like wolves, they had flowing boundaries and could endanger themselves by wandering into another tribe's territory, but nevertheless they wandered and brought back information from their new experiences. If they stayed within these unmarked boundaries they were allowed to provide abundantly. An indication of their abundance was a ceremony in which they would give away possessions. It was also an honorable custom to deliver your meat from the hunt to a widow, or an aged one to take the first cut for themselves. Indians ranged considerably, swam in the streams and lakes and enjoyed all of Nature's resources around them. Their abundant food supply allowed them more time to contemplate, contrary to the endless famines that the Europeans were experiencing. Religion or spirituality was not organized to restrict them from wonderment or observation and among the northern tribes of the Americas, religious wonderment, discussion and adaptation was not banned or deemed "inquisitional".

Because of this freedom, I can understand how indigenous people (tribes) would arrive at seeing the attributes of the Great Spirit as reflective of itself. Consequently, their religious or spiritual focus was the connection to the Natural. That you can learn and advance your knowledge through observing created nature was a natural perspective based upon their free, yet respectful way of life.

Is the Great Spirit kind and loving? Is it an artistic creator? Does it specialize? Is it extremely intricate? Is it amazing? Does it duplicate? Can it be soft, delicate and extremely pleasing in its creation? Does it pattern some of its creations? Is there a relationship concept which can be discerned within its design? This list of informative questions could go on and on. It all goes back to the supposition that everything made or every function could have a teaching for a perceptive human because all of these visible attributes are reflections of supernatural knowledge which we are allowed to contact and observe.

* * * *

5

Beseechment

I love a people who love their neighbors as they love themselves.

* * * *

What ceremonies are carried out in this religion?
Describe a worship service.
How do you get in touch with your God?
Is prayer personal or relatively structured?
Where do you worship?
What do you worship?
Does this religion have an initiation procedure or ceremony?
Does this religion have a language used in worship?
Does your religion have sacrifices?
Is there a holy place for the religion?
What religious holidays are recognized?
How has your religion shaped art, literature or music?

* * * *

What is ceremony? It could be described as a gathering of people to beseech, respect, acknowledge, thank or recognize their concept of the Great Spirit or their Higher Power. Down through time, people of all tribes held ceremony. Ceremony was not performed only by Native Americans. Tribal peoples world wide beseeched or recognized extensions of their Higher Power. Celtic people beseeched to the Higher Force through the Four Directions long before the age of Columbus.

Those Sioux who respect and are aware of Black Elk's vision recognize the Six Powers as integral to life for all living entities upon this planet. In ceremony, these entities are called upon or recognized. In all of the ceremonies that I observed Chief Fools Crow and Chief Eagle Feather conduct, these entities were always recognized, yet the main indication to me was that both renowned holy men were beseeching to the Great Spirit, Wakan Tanka.

The Sioux, the Lakota/Dakota people, were the last of the big tribes to come in from their natural freedom on the plains. Consequently, they retained more of their culture, more of their religious ways than those tribes that have spent several centuries under the rule of the dominant culture. Other tribes do not like to hear this or admit this fact but if ego can be shed, it allows us to understand why the Sioux have retained so much of their culture in relation to most other tribes. The Navajo, Apache, Hopi and the Pueblo tribes have also retained their language, culture and religion. The geography of their lands allowed them a high degree of privacy and less intrusion from the dominant society. For centuries, however, the patriarchal Spanish Church has exerted a strong influence among the Pueblo and the Navajo. The Pueblo suffered severely under the close scrutiny of the Spanish church for a period of time and even recently, many of their ceremonies were opened in conjunction with Catholic priests. I saw this with my own eyes. The Mormon Church has made deep inroads among the Navajo.

In Sioux history, and from the perspective of Black Elk, a holy woman appeared to one of the Sioux bands. Many believed this episode happened when the Sioux were entering the Great Plains and leaving what is presently Minnesota. It may have happened when they were close to the pipe stone quarries which are still worked in southwestern Minnesota. The woman was called the Buffalo Calf Woman and taught the people the use of the pipe in seven sacred ceremonies.

These ceremonies were:
1. The Sweat Lodge
2. The Vision Quest
3. The Sun Dance
4. The Making of Relatives
5. The Keeping of the Soul
6. The Womanhood Ceremony
7. The Throwing of the Ball

These ceremonies are explored in detail through Black Elk's words as told to Joseph Epes Brown who later wrote *The Sacred Pipe*. Several of these seven ceremonies were actually banned by the Federal Government, among them were the Sun Dance and the Keeping of the Soul ceremony. Times change, however, and at present, two ceremonies, the Peace Pipe ceremony and the Spirit Calling ceremony, are practiced more frequently than two of the original ceremonies listed above. Not that they were superseded by the seven ceremonies of the Buffalo Calf Woman, as mentioned earlier, I have a supposition that it was the Yuwipi or the Spirit Calling ceremony that led the tribe to make their initial exodus to avoid the early white man many centuries ago.

Some ceremonies have changed very little and their essence or meaning remain the same. The Pipe ceremony is probably the most popular of the Sioux ceremonies in this day and the Sweat Lodge could well be the second most popular ceremony or a ceremony that more people have become familiar with. Often a pipe ceremony or a ceremony beseeching to the four directions will be within a major ceremony such as a Sweat Lodge, the Sun Dance or a Yuwipi (spirit calling) ceremony. I call the newer category, listed below in terms of popularity or participation, the Seven Mother Earth ceremonies. If practiced, they can convey a meaningful connection in establishing a spiritual relationship with Mother Earth and all of the rest of the Great Spirit's creation. I use my own personal terminology simply to emphasize a later time and the higher frequency of ceremonial practice or usage that these ceremonies have proven to exhibit. Tribal people are free to apply their own terminology.

These Mother Earth ceremonies are:
1. The Pipe Ceremony
2. The Sweat Lodge
3. The Vision Quest
4. The Sun Dance
5. The Making of Relatives
6. The Giveaway
7. The Yuwipi Spirit Calling.

Ceremonies have a wide range. The Vision Quest is for a lone individual and takes place in an isolated area. The lone vision quester usually beseeches up on a mountain, a hill or on a badland butte. The participant is attempting to commune with the Great Spirit and often receives communication through the lesser entities that are created by the Great Spirit. The vision quester seeks direction, guidance and spiritual advice for his or her earth journey. Maybe a bear or another animal will appear in their dreams while they are on the mountain and maybe the bear will have words. Maybe a real bear will come by, or an eagle or another winged, or four legged will appear close by or maybe the winged will hover right over the vision quester in a most unusual manner. These acts would be considered symbolic and also convey acknowledgement from the natural world.

The Sun Dance is opposite from Vision Quest in that in this ceremony the whole tribe is gathered out in a wide place to camp and be together. The tribe will offer their annual thanksgiving to the Creator for all that it has provided. So there we have two ceremonies that are considerably different, sharing a common belief in the Great Spirit that controls all things except for two leggeds who get to make their own decisions. Other tribes had Vision Quest and they also had their own way of expressing an annual thanksgiving to their concept of the Great Spirit.

In between, there are the ceremonies where people come together in lesser numbers than they would at a Sun Dance. The Sweat Lodge and the Yuwipi spirit calling have a similarity and are ceremonies where a smaller group of people will pray, beseech or acknowledge together.

In a sweat lodge, a group gathers together in a small igloo shaped lodge usually large enough for five, ten or twenty people to sit in a circle and beseech or pray. The lodge is covered and hot stones are brought into the lodge so that the people will sweat and actually become clean. Steam will be generated by pouring water over the heated stones from a ladle. A bucket of water is placed beside the one who will be conducting the lodge ceremony. The steam and one's sweat make an individual very clean. Usually, there are four parts to the sweat lodge. The lodge that I conduct is in four parts. The first door or endurance is to the West Power and acknowledges greetings and welcome to the spirit world. The second endurance is to the North Power and acknowledges truth, cleanliness and meditation. The third endurance is to the East Power and acknowledges knowledge, wisdom, understanding and peace. The individual prayers are often said during this endurance. The fourth endurance is to the South Power and acknowledges healing, honoring yourself, family members, special friends and the commitment to protect Mother Earth.

The most important part for me, is when the people each say an individual prayer to the Great Spirit. I think that a lodge should be held wherein people are allowed, without fear, to pray individually and from the heart with a minimum amount of distraction or discomfort. A more detailed account of this ceremony and other related ceremonial descriptions are found in *Mother Earth Spirituality* and *Rainbow Tribe*. John Fire offers his sharing of the sweat lodge ceremony in the chapter, Inipi— Grandfather's Breath, *Lame Deer, Seeker of Visions*.[1]

I will describe a worship service and then tell how some Indians attempt to pray to their concept of the higher power. To me, Indian ceremony is more of a calling out to the spirit world than a worship service.

Before a ceremony is to begin, the people participating usually gather together in a circle or stand facing the leader of the ceremony. If sage or sweet grass is available, this offering is lit and the participants are smudged or incensed. Certain items such as a drum or a peace pipe, if present, are also incensed with the pleasant smelling grass or sage.

A welcome is extended to the spirits to enter the ceremony. Who are these spirits? It appears that they are simply former humans who were once here and understand what our ceremony is about. We do not address a specific spirit but assume that they are indeed attending our calling. Hopefully, we will become observing spirits once we pass on to the spirit world. The leader will then beseech to each cardinal direction, west, north, east and south. Most often, the people will also face each direction as it is called upon. I usually hold up my personal wotai stone to use as my portable altar when I beseech to each direction. I hold it outward to the direction I am calling upon and recognizing. I always turn to my right in a clockwise manner as I go from one direction to the other. In this northern hemisphere, water spirals in this manner when it drains through an orifice. Therefore, I want to reach into an encompassing harmony or at least recognize this. In New Zealand and Australia, indigenous people turn ceremonially from right to left to be in their harmony. A medicine wheel ceremony or a power of the hoop ceremony recognizes the meanings of each of the four directions and often a recognition and connection with Father Sky and Mother Earth is included. Bear in mind, these entities are considered as extensions of the Great Spirit because they are created by the Great Spirit. At the conclusion of the beseechment to the Six Powers, the Great Spirit is often formally invoked. I usually make a statement thanking the Great Spirit for giving us the Six Powers which allows us our life.

When a peace pipe is used in connection with this ceremony, tobacco is placed in the pipe after some has been placed back to Mother Earth from where it came. We place only tobacco or a substitute for tobacco, such as kinnic kinnick (red willow bark), in the peace pipe. We do not place any form of hallucinogens in the tobacco. This is absolutely contrary to natural harmony and extremely disrespectful. It is also, no doubt, very displeasing to the spirit world to which the beseechment is being directed. The pipe is then the portable altar and pointed to each direction as its (the direction's) power, teaching and meaning is recognized.

Before a sweat lodge, Chief Eagle Feather would open with a pipe ceremony. When he was teaching me this lodge ceremony, he would often have a woman formally open the Sweat Lodge. One of his reasons was that we all come from a woman, another reason was that the Buffalo Woman was a powerful figure in our history. He also recognized that Mother Earth is very powerful and that we are all made from Mother Earth. Bill was a practical holy man. It seemed that just about everything that he taught me or spoke to people about made a lot of common sense. He was a "no-frills" holy man and did not take long to make his point. He also had a strong sense of humor which he was not afraid to employ, even in ceremony. He definitely was not an angry man. He was a great teacher from my perspective. When Bill would conduct a sweat lodge, he would address each of the four directions at separate times within the Sweat Lodge ceremony. Everyone within the lodge would have their special time to pray out loud and individually. This procedure, he pointed out to me, was highly important.

You, yourself can beseech, acknowledge, respect or seek to the spirit world beyond. Most people now use a simple stone which they carry. If you want to pray but are uncomfortable with something this new, then go to your church and sit and pray or to the place in your home where you pray.

How do I use my stone? I hold it outward at arms' length or hold it up in an offering posture as though I am presenting. I face a direction and call upon what I contend is the power or the representation of that direction. "Oh, West Power, Oh Wiyopeyata," I call out. "I thank you for the life giving rains. I thank you for the fluid, the motion you allow me while I am on my journey across this planet." I have thanked and recognized a gift from God through one of its creations. "Oh spirit world that I associate with the west; Oh spirit world look on and be with us in our small ceremony tonight. We will beseech and acknowledge to the Great Spirit through that which it has created and you are welcome." I have extended a pleasant welcome and in this scenario I would be in an evening ceremony. If I was alone in my home, I would probably say, "I thank you, Great Spirit, for letting me enjoy this day." I might point out something in particular that I learned or experienced that day.

Because the West is where the sun goes down, darkness comes and there is much less distraction. In the daytime, most of us are busy making a living. Our focus then is in another area of life. The night is not something to be fearful of or "spooky" of. Darkness and night are created by the Great Mystery. It allows one to concentrate more and be less distracted, especially in a group. In a dark sweat lodge, you are not distracted by what someone is wearing. You are able to concentrate on the prayer you will be speaking out loud. Don't you like to have someone's attention and focus when you make a special effort to go and visit them? Many of us believe that the spirit beings listening in want our attention without distraction.

By praying to or including spirits in a ceremony, am I praying to another entity and not God? Considering where these spirits are at, I believe that they are much closer to the Great Mystery than I am. I also think that it is the "higher planed" ones, those who are becoming very highly evolved are able to have the "spiritual intellect" to observe our ceremony or beseechment. Their conduct while they were here as humans probably allows them to understand what we are doing. Like the spirit guides that enter the foretelling ceremonies to help the holy men make accurate predictions, they are familiar with what we are doing. Those with "blank disks" have no knowledge of what we are doing, therefore, they are not present and we are spared their ignorance.

I get in touch with my concept of the Higher Power mainly through my everyday thoughts. Maybe this could be called an informal basis. The Native American, no doubt, had this very same informal basis. They were such a spiritual people before their exposure to the dominant society. I believe that this informal reaction of thinking about and relating to Great Spirit was almost automatic. They believed that the Great Spirit was always around them and was constantly revealing itself through its creations which were so highly visible to these people. Consequently, most of them were very reverent and harmonic people. Go out into Nature. A butterfly suddenly floating before you or a tiny waterfall made by a fallen tree across a stream can make you think about God.

Do not leave out the animals, the finned, winged or four footed in your beseechment. The Wamakaskan are already in their own communion with Wakan Tanka. I would say that they have some "direct connections." Even if you live in a city put out bird food or water. The winged will soon stop by and become your friends. Talk to them.

Prayers are usually personal but some songs are structured and for those who are familiar with Black Elk's vision, there is a clockwise structure within the beseechment. In a group ceremony such as Sweat Lodge or a Yuwipi ceremony or the tribal Sun Dance there exists a definite structure, however an "official" or a fearful atmosphere does not (seem to) emanate. Respect is very apparent but it is not cast in a demanding or fearsome tone.

I often perform a semi-formal ceremony which I call a Power of the Hoop ceremony when I want to get in touch with the higher power, or whatever mysterious spirit forces there are around us, that seem to be concerned about our earth journey. I also use this means when I want to center toward or focus on a particular area or need. Often when I rest or sit in a place to contemplate, I draw a circle in the air with my hand and draw two intersecting lines in the circle. This act signifies the four directions and the circle of life. It also can be called the Power of the Hoop and can stand for the Six Powers of the World. I am simply emphasizing at that moment that the Six Powers are all around me and that I am an extension of these powers which were put here by the Creator. I believe that these Six Powers are extensions of the Great Spirit and so in a more remote sense, we two leggeds are extensions of the Great Spirit through these powers.

Earlier, I pointed out that we are physically made up of three of these six powers; the Sun Power, which is within Father Sky, provides our energy; the Earth Spirit, which gives the material for our bodies, and the West Power, which takes up approximately 80% of our bodies in the form of water and henceforth gives us motion and fluid for our physiology. This information is repetitive as is other aspects within this writing. It is intentional because I believe that it is that important and establishes a strong base for you to become established within the Natural Way. You do not learn a song, how to hunt, fly fish or become good at a sport if you do not follow some repetition.

The other three powers that I see, sense and feel, they are within my spirit. They are not as physical as the first three (West Power, Mother Earth and Father Sky) that I have mentioned; they are more from the mental aspect or are a part of our decision making.

From a standpoint of personal prayer; the North Power helps us to recognize endurance, cleanliness, truthfulness, honesty, removal, independence, provision, preparation and politeness. Once learned and recognized, this power is within us. Native peoples often wintered over in the cold, north climes. Their survival depended upon their ability to endure and prepare for the long winter. Polite manners, quietness, respect for space and truthful conduct were virtues to live congenially within confining space limited by restricting snows and cold. The sweat lodge was used to keep clean during the winter. Little water was needed and snow was often used to make cleansing steam. When the snows melted in the springtime Mother Earth was washed clean. The virtue of cleanliness comes through very strong if I think and identify in this manner.

The East Power reminds me to always appreciate a new day. When the red dawn appears in the east, new experiences, new happenings will accumulate more knowledge upon my Disk of Life. I will strive to be cognizant of what is unfolding before me. After the sun has coursed across the sky, I will contemplate what I have learned. In time I will discourse with others and weigh their opinions where this new information might be relevant. When we share new knowledge, wisdom can come into being. Wisdom leads to understanding, and peace can follow. Understanding, wisdom and peace were strong words which Black Elk identified in his vision. These were the gifts from the East Power. I believe the thoughts, memories and deeds related to these virtues carry over into the spirit world.

Growth, medicine, healing and bounty are from the South Power. We all have to make a living. We have to provide, especially if we have dependent children or relatives. If you wish to hone your ability to provide, then beseech to the South Power. Ability, determination, interest, skill, improvising and perseverance are traits that I associate with this direction because they are needed to provide food, shelter and clothing. Itokaga was created by the Creator specifically for provision. It is an extension of the Creator. Why shouldn't we beseech in a specific manner to it? Medicine is made from the plants; their stems, roots and fruits. The South Power causes these plants to grow and all of our foods as well. Even the buffalo was a result of the gift of Itokaga, because it fattened and lived from the grasses that grew tall as a result of the summer sun causing all things to grow. If I was unemployed or was unhappy with my occupation or situation, I would beseech to the South Power. If I was physically sick, I would beseech to Itokaga. If I did a ceremony for a person who was physically sick, I would face that person to the South Power.

For those who are very compassionate and seek to help and to heal; they will be helped greatly if they explore the medicines and herbs and also seek spirit helpers that have gone on with their knowledge of medicine and healing. Naturally, they should seek knowledge from those who are yet living. These kind and loving people will be very pleasant to be around in the spirit world, like butterflies and flowers.

So, these three powers, North, East and South, are of the mind when they are ascribed to humans. The characteristics, the traits and virtues of the North, East and South Power; we can implant these upon our Disks of Life. They will then become a part of us. The application of endurance, truthfulness, seeking of knowledge, ability to share wisdom and understanding, along with our own example of bravery or courage, all help us to harmonize and fit in with our surroundings.

The benevolent Creator has even given us free choice as to how we shall use what is symbolized and made obvious by these powers. If we want to avoid and ignore them, then we have that choice to do so. If we want to sit and detract, make fun of or be jealous and contribute nothing, we have that power also. It will be a long, cold time for these kind in the spirit world. Who will want to associate with them? What is upon their mind except empty, useless detraction? They have avoided the harmony that is so evident in Nature. I believe that jealous detractors are paid back severely in the spirit world, especially those detractors who tell vile lies within their detraction. They will be in a foreign place when they enter the spirit world. I believe strongly that the spiritual realm is so close to the Great Spirit that disharmony is absolutely not condoned, tolerated or allowed. Yet, their distractive habits and character will be with them as will be their former addictions. They will truly be miserable and have to look back with many regrets. Good, harmonic spirits will avoid them because they will have nothing in common to share.

Spiritual Imagery. Joseph Campbell said it right. The description of the Six Powers is a strong part of my spiritual imagery of this Great Spirit while I walk my Earth Journey. It certainly helps me identify and feel related to what I pray to. If it works for me, then what is it hurting? I have no intention of forcing others to believe this way yet there will be many zealous ones who will take offense that an indigenous backgrounded person has decided to put his spiritual suppositions, thoughts and experiences down in response to innocent questions asked by a humanities class; a class that is a reflection of the Generations Unborn. I do not want anyone to haul children off to boarding schools and separate them from their parents and certainly want no one placed in gas chambers if they do not believe in the Six Powers as a form of spiritual imagery to help recognize the Creator's creation. It is all Mystery. Even the zealous religious detractors do not have the ultimate answer which they proclaim. They cannot be truthful and say, "I do not know for sure. You might be right or maybe there exists some truth in what you are expressing."

In the case of a nomadic tribe, there was no specific place to worship although certain geographical areas were deemed as or regarded as significant holy places. Often a tribe, a band or a religious group would return on an annual basis to conduct ceremony in a particular area. Bear Butte in the Black Hills has been a vision quest area for many Sioux. In these modern times other tribal members, especially those from the surrounding plains tribes, come to this promontory at the eastern edge of the Black Hills to vision quest and hold sweat lodges.

I am probably a bit unusual. I do not place much emphasize on worship. In fact, I am not too fond of the word, worship. If I do worship, then naturally I worship the Great Spirit.

Does this Almighty Creator that has created unfathomable space and time, does it have any need for my mere worship? I respect and am thankful to this vast entity but when I visualize the concept of worship, I view an ant or a tiny insignificant bug crawling by and saying to me, "Praise you, Eagle Man. Praise you, Eagle Man."

What is that statement going to actually do for me or what significance does it amount to?

I occasionally sit through a church service and hear the people exhibiting their worship. Once in a while I am asked to speak in churches. Obviously, these are the more liberal churches whose numbers are growing. To be polite, I will attend their services when I am asked. In my opinion, it is good if churchgoers are receiving sincere enjoyment or a wholesome, spiritually enhancing feeling from their worship. Occasionally, there will be a good service and I have heard some extremely good messages from ministers or priests. Some of these words, some of this knowledge, I believe was meant for me to hear or be exposed to. I do not rule out these services entirely. I am not better than these people nor do I consider myself beneath them. I just come from a different area of religious or spiritual exposure and of course, I have my own thoughts on the subject.

I have to be true to myself and do not want to lie to this question even though my answer is probably highly unusual. In the old days I would have surely been burned at the stake if I would have made the statement that I am not exceptionally supportive of the word "worship."

I have a past that has left a bad taste regarding church services. My sister and I had to go to church every Sunday under the fear of going to hell if we missed mass. A mortal sin and you would burn in hell if you died before going to confession. The white man was so smart that he could even categorize sin in different degrees. It was no question, we were not wanted in the redneck neighborhood church where the congregation looked down at us, so we would go across town to a big cathedral and sit in the back. We would get there late and leave early. Two dark little Indian kids sneaking in back. I don't think many people knew we were even there yet God knew and we were free of this mortal sin and could relax for another week. In church, people would worship God yet they could be very prejudiced during the week. My sister and I did not have much of a social life while we were growing up. While we were small, kids did not seem to care if we were Indians. We had a lot of fun playing, but once puberty came about my friends changed. My poor sister even dropped out of school because she did not have much of a social life. Thankfully, I had sports and some new friends who just wanted to play ball. I also danced Indian. That was fun. I stayed in school.

Once I sneaked off with a white friend from sports who was good to me, so I went to his church. They seemed to worship more than ever. There was a lot of praising of God in songs and in their words. They seemed to be a happier group of people. Their songs were easy to sing and I enjoyed trying to sing with them from a hymn book. There was a girl there too and she was good to me. We had cookies and Kool-Aid afterwards so I went back the next week. Where I went to church there was very little socializing, at least not on a weekly basis like this Protestant church. But then the priest found out about it and scared me into staying away from that church. When you have a young forming mind, you can easily be manipulated. Those fears can become entrenched but thankfully we are allowed our maturity if we choose to take it and can cast inhibiting fears aside.

At Christian funerals, often there are more worship phrases of Jesus than talk of the deceased, and what the deceased did and stood for. I went to a relative's funeral recently and the minister said very little about the deceased. It was disappointing because I wanted to hear more about the person we were having a funeral for.

There are exceptions, however. At my brother's funeral, the priest told us that we could conduct the ceremony since this was the desire of my brother before he died. His two sons wanted the service to be held that way also. The Catholic priest was very understanding so we went ahead and had an Indian service with substantial mention of my brother's military background and artwork. The many Indians in attendance voiced their approval of the ceremony. We all thanked the priest who said some words also. There was a considerable amount of harmony at that service.

Naturally, indigenous people prayed or beseeched in their own language. After the dominant society placed the various tribes on the reservations, and the majority were converted to Christianity, the people learned to pray in English. The Sioux language was forbidden at both the missionary school and the federal government boarding school. Despite this harsh but effective procedure to eradicate culture, language and religion, the native language managed to persist and survive. Many Sioux still speak their language fluently as do the Navajo and other southwestern tribes.

Many other Native Americans are not fluent in their tribal language, however, and these people make up the majority of native descended people. When they pray and beseech, they do so in the English language. I recently watched a very full blooded appearing California Indian lead a sweat lodge ceremony in Hawaii. He used the Sioux phrase, Mitakuye Oyasin—For all our relations, throughout his ceremony but it was the only native language that I heard during the course of the ceremony. I think that this phrase was all the native language he knew. The music within the lodge was chanting instead of songs.

I am not fluent in Lakota although I do understand and make use of many of the subjective names and phrases. I have discovered that the Sioux language is exceptionally beautiful for singing. It is so much easier to sing a song or compose a spiritual song with it in contrast to attempting to sing spiritually in the English language. Wakan Tanka, Wakan Tanka, is much prettier and has a deeper and fuller resonance when sung in Sioux rather than singing one of the English translations, such as Great Spirit, Great Spirit. It seems that the Lakota/Dakota language was honed to a very spiritual degree down through time because of the people's closeness to ceremony. Singing and beseechment must have been a major ingredient within the development and evolvement of the language. Their values and lifestyle were a part of this development as well.

Consequently, as the Natural Way becomes more and more a part of this land, I believe that Sioux language could become the spiritual language of the future, at least, in song and beseechment phrases. Sioux Songs are being sung in all parts of the world. As time goes by and people continue to communicate and travel, the richness of Sioux language in ceremony, especially the singing of beseechment songs, will continue to spread because the songs add so much to a ceremony. On a recent trip to Australia, I was pleasantly surprised to discover people who sang Sioux songs rather fluently. There are many tapes out now of Sioux dance songs and even some beseechment songs. Cinte Gleska (Spotted Tail) College at Mission, South Dakota offers a set of good tapes on Lakota (Sioux) language. A few songs are offered in the Appendix of this book.

Aside from individual tribal languages which are coming back, in North America we all do speak and understand a common language. The English language does provide for our communication among all tribes and of course with the dominant society.

Does this religion have an initiation procedure or ceremony? I am not aware of an initiation ceremony into Native American spirituality, at least from the Sioux perspective. An initiation ceremony was not one of the seven ceremonies referred to by Black Elk.

There is an avoidance of ownership in spiritual values. One cannot own the Four Winds, the eagles, the streams and certainly not the spirit world. Conversely, one should not be owned spiritually. Our spirit is the most free entity that we have. I do not intend for anyone to own mine. In old tribal warrior societies there were initiations but these were more in line with acceptance according to your reputation rather than an initiation. One had to prove oneself worthy to be a part of a particular society. These societies represented social structures more so than existing for religious interest. The Silent Eaters were older warriors who had paid their dues upon the field of combat and generosity from the hunt. They would meet to discuss the welfare of the tribe. The Dog Soldiers were a society, considerably younger and still building upon and establishing their reputations. They served as the front line of defense. This society lived among themselves and were placed strategically in the camp where they could defend and react suddenly to attack. In peacetime they were the hunters and the scouts. At a certain age, young men would enter the realm of the Dog Soldiers. They would be required to perform certain tests of skill or prowess, often learned from an older teacher.

An initiation ceremony such as baptism, first communion or confirmation was not within the scope of Sioux religious ceremony, to my knowledge.

What about sacrifices? North American spirituality never had the human sacrifices which are attributed to the Christian Inquisition or the Central and South American Aztec and Inca sacrifices. Within the same time span, the medieval Christian and the major Central and South American tribes similarly had an organized religion, a priesthood and a class system controlled by a nobility that co-existed in league with the supporting priesthood. Like the Inquisition, the Aztec and Inca priesthood originated human sacrifices which utilized fear and superstition to enhance or perpetuate their power.

Charles Van Doren's book, *A History of Knowledge*, tells us: "Sacrifice, one of the most fundamental and ubiquitous of religious rituals, was or is practiced in almost all of the religions that have ever existed. Great latitude is found in the types of living beings or other things that are or have been sacrificed, as well as in the ritual itself.

"Human sacrifice seems to have originated among the first agricultural peoples. Apparently rarely practiced by the hunter-gatherers who preceded them, it existed in all of the most ancient religions. The early Greeks and Romans, the earliest Jews, the Chinese and Japanese, the Indians, and many other ancient peoples sacrificed human beings to their gods. The victim was often dressed in magnificent garments and adorned with jewels so that he or she might go in glory to the god. The victims, often chosen for their youth and beauty (the god wanted the best), were drowned or buried alive, or their throats were cut so that their blood might bedew the ground, fructifying it, or be spattered upon the altar. The throats of bulls, rams, and goats were also ritually cut, their blood spilled upon the ground in the effort to please the god or produce a communion between the god and those who sought his help."[2]

Van Doren chose the example of the Aztecs and the Incas to illustrate, in gruesome, but believable detail, the practice of human sacrifice within a religion. "Why were the Spaniards able to destroy two flourishing civilizations so quickly and easily, so that today little is known of them and hardly anything survives except the monumental buildings, a few gold ornaments out of the millions that were made, and the foods that they grew? (The last is far from insignificant.) The answer may lie in the principles by which both empires were organized.

"Fear and force ruled both empires. Both the Aztec and the Inca were relative *arrivistes*. In each case a ruthless, semibarbarian minority had taken over a previous, probably decadent civilization. These new rulers, having conquered by the merciless use of military power, saw no reason not to rule by it, too. They did not bother to try to acquire the love and loyalty of those they ruled. They had nothing they wished to give their subjects, except a measure of security against want and external enemies. But the enemy within—the rulers themselves—were more fearsome than any foreign foe. And the price exacted for freedom from want, turned out to be very high.

"It was paid in the blood of children and young people. Human sacrifice was practiced by both these unregretted civilizations of the recent past. Among the Aztec, the toll of sacrifice stuns the mind. In the last years before the Spanish conquest, a thousand of the finest children and young people were offered up each week. Dressed in splendid robes, they were drugged and then helped up the steps of the high pyramids and held down upon the altars. A priest, bloody knife in hand, parted the robes, made a quick incision, reached in his other hand and drew forth the heart, still beating, which he held high before the people assembled in the plaza below. A thousand a week, many of them captured in raids among the neighboring tribes in the Valley of Mexico. A thousand a week of the finest among the children and youth, who huddled in prisons before their turn came. It is no wonder that all the enemies of the Aztecs rushed to become the allies of the conquering Spaniards and helped overthrow that brutal regime. Not that doing so helped these fervent allies. They were also enslaved by the victorious conquistadores.

"The Inca did not regularly sacrifice large numbers of human beings, but whenever an Inca emperor died, the toll was terrible. Hundreds of maidens would be drugged, beheaded, and buried with the dead ruler. Hundreds of others would die whenever the state faced a difficult problem or decision. Stolid priests proclaimed that only thus would the gods be pleased to help, and so the beautiful boys and girls died on the reeking altars."[3]

Van Doren goes on to state that following the example of Abraham and his son, the Jews were the first to decide that human sacrifice was wrong, that God did not desire it. And oddly, he states that the Christians, following the traditions of the Jews, never practiced human sacrifice.[4] No details of the Great Inquisition nor of the thousands (or possibly, millions) of victims who were sacrificed in Europe is to be found in his book subtitled: *The Pivotal Events, People, and Achievements of World History.*

Very little has been written in fact about the truth of the Holy Inquisition, which was an extremely important part of European history. Such is the power of organized religion to suppress the truth. If you do not believe me then go to your local library and see how much you can find regarding informative resources. Why should this information be swept under a rug? It most certainly did have an effect upon history. We in these modern times should allow this knowledge to fortify our intellect so that these happenings will never occur again. The Jewish people are so very right to reveal the Holocaust in all its intensity. Down through time they have suffered repeated holocausts. They do not want its reoccurrence and most certainly believe in the value of knowledge and portrayal.

James Haught, author of the unusual book, *Holy Horrors*, describes in detail the human sacrifice within the Great Inquisition which existed over 500 years and even reached into the New World to punish Indians who adhered to their native beliefs. "Efforts to establish heresy led to the establishment of the Holy Inquisition, one of mankind's supreme horrors. In the early 1200s, local bishops were empowered to identify, try, and punish heretics. When the bishops proved ineffective, traveling papal inquisitors, usually Dominican priests, were sent from Rome to conduct the purge.

"Pope Innocent IV authorized torture in 1252, and the Inquisition chambers became places of terror. Accused heretics were seized and locked in cells, unable to see their families, unable to know the names of their accusers. If they didn't confess quickly, unspeakable cruelties began...

"Swiss historian Walter Nigg recounted... "So that the torturers would not be disturbed by the shrieking of the victim, his mouth was stuffed with cloth. Three-and four hour sessions of torture were nothing unusual. During the procedure the instruments were frequently sprinkled with holy water.

"The victim was required not only to confess that he was a heretic, but also to accuse his children, wife, friends, and others as fellow heretics, so that they might be subjected to the same process. Minor offenders and those who confessed immediately received lighter sentences. Serious heretics who repented were given life imprisonment and their possessions confiscated. Others were led to the stake in a procession and church ceremony called the "auto-da-fé" (act of the faith). A papal statute of 1231 decreed burning as the standard penalty. The actual executions were performed by civil officers, not priests, as a way of preserving the church's sanctity.

"Some inquisitors cut terrible swaths. Robert le Bourge sent 183 to the stake in a single week. Bernard Gui convicted 930—confiscating the property of all 930, sending 307 to prison and burning forty-two. Conrad of Marburg burned every suspect who claimed innocence."[5]

Haught includes numerous paintings and drawings from medieval artists which portray torture scenes to add further proof that these agonizing horrors did happen. Some illustrations exhibit a pope or a bishop looking on with their cortege and often wearing a halo. Examples of the descriptions are as follows:

"Albigenses, Christians, also called Cathari and Publicani, were burned by Catholic bishops in the late 1100s, before the pope declared a military crusade against them."[6] This painting was a courtesy from the Lancaster Mennonite Historical Society.

"About 2,000 Waldensian Protestants in Calabria, southern Italy, were massacred in 1560 by Catholic troops under Grand Inquisitor Michele Ghislieri, who later became Pope Pius V and was sainted.[7]

"St. Dominic wears a halo in this church painting as he presides over an Inquisition session deciding the fate of two accused heretics stripped and bound to posts at lower right.[8]

"Pope Pius V and his cardinals (background) watch the Roman Inquisition burn a nonconforming religious scholar, about 1570.[9]

"Ceremonious burning of convicted heretics at a religious "auto-da-fé" (act of faith) climaxed the Inquisition process. Engraved in 1723 by Bernhard Picart.[10]

"Accused "witches" first were stripped and searched for "devil marks"—then the torture began.The process usually ended in execution."[11] This painting depicts an attractive woman in terror bound and nude before two male torturers, one who is reading a manual on torture.

"Burning at the stake was the chief fate of accused witches, but others were hanged, drowned, or crushed."[12] This portrait portrays an accused woman repentedly holding a crucifix as she looks to the heavens while tied to a burning stake. It is no wonder that so many Christians have a fear of their religion or their concept of God. The DNA blueprint which all beings have would surely carry over some of that fear implant-

ed in such a horrible age of ignorance that lasted down through generations.

* * * *

The Inquisition was divided into three phases: the medieval extermi-
nation of heretics; the Spanish Inquisition in the 1400s; and the Roman
Inquisition, which began after the Reformation.

"In Spain, thousands of Jews had converted to Christianity to escape
death in recurring Christian massacres. So, too, had some Muslims. They
were, however, suspected of being insincere converts clandestinely practicing their old religion. In 1478 the pope authorized King Ferdinand and
Queen Isabella to revive the Inquisition to hunt "secret Jews" and their
Muslim counterparts. Dominican friar Tomas de Torquemada was
appointed inquisitor general, and he became a symbol of religious cruelty. Thousands upon thousands of screaming victims were tortured, and
at least 2,000 were burned.

"The Roman period began in 1542 when Pope Paul III sought to eradicate Protestant influences in Italy. Under Pope Paul IV, this inquisition
was a reign of terror, killing many "heretics" on mere suspicion. Its victims included scientist-philosopher Giordano Bruno, who espoused
Copernicus's theory that planets orbit the sun. He was burned at the
stake in 1600 in Rome.

"The Inquisition blighted many lands for centuries. In Portugal,
records recount that 184 were burned alive and auto-da-fé processions
contained as many as 1,500 "penitents" at a time. The Inquisition was
brought by Spaniards to the American colonies, to punish Indians who
reverted to native religions. A total of 879 heresy trials were recorded in
Mexico in the late 1500s.

"The horror persisted until modern times. The Spanish Inquisition
was suppressed by Joseph Bonaparte in 1808, restored by Ferdinand VII
in 1814, suppressed again in 1823, and finally eradicated in 1834.

"Lord Acton, himself a Catholic, wrote in the late 1800s, "The principle of the Inquisition was murderous... The popes were not only murder-
ers in the great style, but they also made murder a legal basis of the
Christian Church and a condition of salvation."[13]

Women were special targets of the Inquisition: "During the 1400s, the
Holy Inquisition shifted its focus toward witchcraft, and the next three
centuries witnessed a bizarre orgy of religious delusion. Agents of the

church tortured untold thousands of women, and some men into con-
fessing that they flew through the sky on demonic missions, engaged in
sex with Satan, turned themselves into animals, made themselves invisi-
ble, and performed other supernatural evils. Virtually all the accused
were put to death. The number of victims is estimated widely from
100,000 to 2 million.

"Pope Gregory IX originally authorized the killing of witches in the
1200s, and random witch trials were held, but the craze didn't catch fire
until the 15th century. In 1484 Pope Innocent VIII issued a bull declaring
the absolute reality of witches—thus it became heresy to doubt their existence. Prosecutions soared. The inquisitor Cumanus burned forty-one
women the following year, and a colleague in the Piedmont of Italy exe-
cuted 100.

"Soon afterward, two Dominican inquisitors, Jakob Sprenger and
Heinrich Kramer, published their infamous *Malleus Maleficarum* (Witches
Hammer) outlining a lurid litany of magical acts performed by witches
and their imps, familiars, phantoms, demons, succubi, and incubi. It
described how the evil women blighted crops, devoured children, caused
disease, and wrought spells. The book was filled with witches sexual acts
and portrayed women as treacherous and contemptible. "All witchcraft
comes from carnal lust, which is in women insatiable," they wrote.
Modern psychology easily perceives the sexual neurosis of these
priests—yet for centuries their book was the official manual used by
inquisitors sending women to horrible deaths.

"Witch-hunts flared in France, Germany, Hungary, Spain, Italy,
Switzerland, Sweden, and nearly every corner of Europe—finally reaching England, Scotland, and the Massachusetts Bay Colony. Most of the
victims were old women who roused suspicion of neighbors. Others
were young, pretty women. Some were men. Many in continental Europe
were simply citizens whose names were shrieked out by torture victims
when commanded to identify fellow witches.

The standard Inquisition procedure of isolating and grilling suspects
was followed—plus an added step: the victims were stripped naked,
shaved of all body hair, and "pricked." The *Malleus Maleficarum* specified
that every witch bore a numb "devils mark," which could be detected by
jabbing with a sharp object. Inquisitors also looked for "witches' tits,"
blemishes that might be secret nipples whereby the women suckled their
demons."[14]

"A profound irony of the witch-hunts is that they were directed, not by superstitious savages, but by learned bishops, judges, professors, and other leaders of society. The centuries of witch obsession demonstrated the terrible power of supernatural beliefs."[15]

As I have said over and over, an elevated priesthood that does not recognize the balance of woman and her leadership can prove to be a very dangerous thing. Human sacrifice is a horrendous example of extreme zealousness. People get too carried away with "knowing" that they are right and the others, the outsiders, "are definitely wrong." This idea—that God does not care if the zealous exterminate the victims of their choosing—has been a tragic part of human history. Pretending that this past did not exist or blaming it all on the Incas and Aztecs is not beneficial knowledge if we are desiring to seek balanced harmony amongst all creeds. Such history assures me that my mere perspective—"I do not know" and "It is all a mystery,"—seems like a harmless butterfly flitting through the woods, in comparison. I believe there is a spirit world. Those poor medieval victims are quite possibly in that spirit world and they just might be reminding their tormentors for an eternity how wrong they were.

The Sioux had a personal sacrifice which was freely originated or initiated by a pledger of the tribe. A desperate hunter might take a vow to be pierced in the forthcoming Sun Dance if he would see a deer to bring back to hungry people. I personally took a vow to pierce in the Sun Dance if I would come back from the war in Vietnam. No one forced me to take this vow and the pain that I endured was of my own choosing much like a woman who gives birth to a baby. She chooses her own pain so that the people might live.

The Sun Dance is a time when the people thank the Great Spirit. It is also a time, in Sioux culture, that certain men can and will fulfill their sun dance vows, usually for a favor or a request that was made in time of need. When the need or request was fulfilled, the pledger honored his promise.

Around the sun dance tree, which was a cottonwood tree placed earlier in the center of the tribal arena in Sioux custom, the sun dancer would dance. Singers gathered around a large drum to sing old tribal songs. For me, these songs are hauntingly beautiful. I can hear them as I write this description. A bed of sage would be placed beneath this "tree of life" and the dancer would be taken to this spot and be pierced in the chest by the Sun Dance Chief, the intercessor for the ceremony. A pair of small slits would be made in the man's skin and a wooden peg would be skewered through; in and under the skin. The end of a rope would be brought down from the tree, and it would be attached to the wooden peg by a buckskin thong. The other end of the long rope would be attached toward the top of the tree. The dancer would rise after he was attached and would slowly dance backward, away from the tree's base to the end of his rope. Other dancers would be pierced and after all were pierced the piercing song would be sung and the dancers would dance inward toward the base of the tree to beseech strongly to the Great Spirit who was believed to be looking on. After the dancers touched the tree, they would go back, away from the center to the end of their ropes. Four times, this beseechment would take place. The onlooking tribe would be in very serious prayer, with very little distraction. The tribe praying together in a concerted effort was considered to be far more powerful and beneficial than the drama of the sun dancers. This was the main focus of the Sun Dance—the tribe praying as a unit, praying together. The drama of the piercing assures an unbroken, undistracted spiritual focus. After the fourth time, the fourth beseechment, the dancers would be free to lean back and break themselves free by putting their weight upon their tether to the tree of life embedded into Mother Earth. The rope was their spiritual umbilical. When the peg would break through, their sun dance vow would be fulfilled.

In the sun dances that I was in with Chief Fools Crow as the Intercessor, we were only pierced under the skin and never down through the chest muscles. No one was pierced in two places as the illustration displays within this chapter. This is the artist's concept to convey spiritual meaning moreso than actual depiction.

Such is a description of the Sun Dance, **which is a personal and a freely chosen sacrifice.** No one is required to Sun Dance and the majority of tribal members do not actually become pledgers or sun dancers. The Sun Dance is a minor sacrifice and also honorable when compared to the fearful ordeal of human sacrifice. Our concept of God is one where we see and appreciate that It makes a simple thing such as flowers, beautiful waterfalls, eagles and wondrous life. We realize that we would be going way beyond our ego to take other two leggeds and kill them just because they do not share our beliefs. It is all mystery—a great realm of unknown. Woman can also sun dance, **but she does not pierce because she has given her pain so that the people may live every time she gives birth.** Such also is the depth and recognition of Sioux ceremony. To this day, among many Indian traditionals, it is believed that one's medicine can have added power or a ceremony of healing can often end with favorable results if a pledge to do something honorable or a related personal commitment (personal sacrifice) is made. But it is always an honorable and a reasonable request.

A more detailed description of Sun Dance is found in *Mother Earth Spirituality* and *Lame Deer, Seeker of Visions*.

Chief Fools Crow and Sun Dance procession.

Is there a holy place for the religion and what religious holidays are recognized? Certain areas for many tribes were considered as special holy places. The Sioux were a nomadic tribe yet certain places in the Black Hills had significant meaning. Bear Butte was regarded as a powerful vision quest location. I call this place Spirit Mountain.

Years ago, I used to vision quest on this mountain and occasionally I would accompany a group of sincere friends who would go out to beseech. We would hold a sweat lodge down below and then change into dry clothes and go up on the mountain to vision quest in separate areas. We would often go out in the fall when there were but few people around. This was a time when the Rainbow Tribe was insignificant and no one even knew that they existed or cared what they did, maybe like my sister and I, two little, innocent, dark specks from the summer sun, sneaking into the back of that great white cathedral unnoticed, to pray. No one paid a bit of attention to us, which was what we wanted. Followers of the Natural Path are people who simply want to pray also.

Much change has taken place since those days and now I no longer take sincere friends out to Spirit Mountain. A tremendous resurgence of Native American spirituality has swept back to native peoples and now Spirit Mountain has become a popular place. This is good. It is much better than when Chief Fools Crow used to be the only person up on the mountain. Because of space, I ask all non-Indians to allow the traditional returning native people their space on Spirit Mountain. It is more important that these traditionals be there, in my opinion. They have suffered at the hands of the dominant society that tried zealously to take this very spirituality away from them. It is only fair that they should have the mountain. There are many mountains and hills and buttes in this land. I am sure that the Great Spirit does not have a requirement that you can only vision quest on Spirit Mountain or Mt. Sinai. I suggest strongly that non-Indians now find their own mountains, buttes, hills and valleys. America and the planet have many places from which to beseech.

The dominant society still refuses to give back the Black Hills, at least in accordance with the treaty of 1868, a treaty that Chief Red Cloud's warriors won, fairly and squarely. Can we not even have some of our Black Hills back? Why not a goodly portion of the federal lands in the Black Hills? I was raised in the Black Hills. I know the thrill, the blessing of swimming almost daily in her summer mountain streams. Maybe my bathing in Rapid Creek almost everyday was the reason I regained my health from a serious case of pneumonia. Maybe this clear stream helped me to become spiritual. You can help the tribal people regain their lands in accordance to treaty agreement signed by the U.S. government through urging and educating the elected federal representatives of your respective states.

No specific holiday related to the Natural Way is recognized or perpetuated. In the future, possibly, Earth Day or Earth Week could become an identifiable holiday for those who embark upon this path that is so closely associated with saving the Earth.

How has this religion (spirituality) shaped art, literature or music? The life style of the indigenous people brought great gifts to the people of planet earth. Their past environmental conduct down through time resulted in the western hemisphere retaining its resources intact for centuries upon centuries, generations upon generations. Indigenous Spirituality was the main reason why they had such an excellent track record in regard to their high state of agricultural development and ability to live in harmony with their environment. When South American and North American foods went to Europe, the cyclical famines were severely curtailed. People had more leisure and fuller stomachs to pursue their own arts, literature and music. Indirectly, indigenous religion/spirituality allowed these arts to flourish from a healthier and better fed populace. Population increased as did the versatility and variety of the arts.

In early European dominated America, Native American art, music and literature was little recognized or appreciated. Initially, as the tribes were being subdued and conquered, indigenous art, literature and music were not allowed to influence the dominant society. Within native circles, however, cultural arts, oral retention and music sung to the language were maintained. Early twentieth century appreciated native oral history from an academic viewpoint only, through paternalistic archaeologists and anthropologists caught up with their false sense of academic superiority. A few recorders of the oral tradition, such as Neihardt and Joseph E. Brown, were scoffed at as poetic romanticists because they came too close to indigenous truth; an area beyond the intellect of the scientifically bent academics. Only in the twentieth century did a beginning interest take place in native arts. Since World War II, as nations opened through communication and civil rights became an issue, cultural art has slowly but steadily been appreciated by the dominant society. Indigenous art now commands high prices in the art markets.

Indigenous music is just beginning to be appreciated. Spiritual song within ceremony is far more powerful than what I have experienced from the religious songs of dominant society. Once you become involved in singing Native spiritual songs, you will discover a fulfillment and enjoyment that will be difficult to equal. Sioux language has been honed down through time toward spirituality. This is why the language fits so well in spiritual beseechment.

Native literature is beginning to be published and consumed but Native American authorship is still lacking. The prevailing mode is still the white writer compiling photo albums with selected Indians in short biographies, a select gathering of interviews or a white author focussing on a notable Indian. One merely needs to look at the current bookstore bookshelfs for verification. Obviously, book publishers are still favoring Anglo authors in Native American subjects but gradually Native writers are becoming published. Native American writers are beginning to write oral traditions and cultural experiences from their own perspective and no longer through the "imprimatur" of reservation missionaries or the structured and paternalistic hoops required by academia and some publishers.

* * * *

6

Miracles

I love a people who have always made me welcome to the best they had.

* * * *

Have miracles occurred in the religion?
Have you ever had a revelation, or intensely spiritual experience occur?
What objects are sacred in your religion?

* * * *

Have miracles occurred in the Natural Way? So-called "miracles" occur every time a genuine spirit calling ceremony takes place. I think these "miracles" could be termed *communications* because they are phenomena wherein holy persons or spiritual leaders have the ability to communicate into the spirit world. A miracle is a visualized or experienced happening that is occasioned or effected by the spirit world and/or ultimately by the Creator's power.

Holy people conduct ceremonies wherein "miracles" happen frequently. What gives an indigenous holy person that power whereas learned and scholarly degreed white men do not have that power; not even great church leaders who speak from elevated pulpits or travel the world to command massive audiences? It is quite simple. Those indigenous leaders who can reach into the spirit world and receive prediction, knowledge or healing have one common trait: they are extremely truthful. I also think that the materialism and maintenance of patriarchal power connected with world renowned church leaders diverts or detracts from their purpose. All must maintain some degree of attention or focus toward this attraction whereas Fools Crow and Eagle Feather did not have to sustain power over people or become distracted by financial and property interests.

There are many ceremonies in which the spirit world and the Great Spirit are called upon by two leggeds. A sweat lodge is simply a gathering of humans calling on the harmonic forces that are in the world beyond and the Ultimate Force allows acknowledgement to happen. You also make yourself clean in such a ceremony, through the bath of steam and your own cleansing sweat. You feel more clean than after taking/indulging in the warmest bath or shower. Mainly, your mind feels clean after a sweat lodge ceremony where you have recognized and beseeched to the spirit world. How odd that some Christian churches view this form of beseechment as somehow connected with a bad force.

How this happens is not for me to analyze and dissect. The dominant society seems to analyze everything, even themselves. Indians just accept but in so doing they move much farther into the beyond with their beseechments and therefore experience "miracles" more frequently in their ceremonies. We do not burden ourselves down with regimental analysis when it comes to mystery. Our minds are much more free to accept and partake with mystery when we remove such barriers.

John Fire was often an assistant to Fools Crow at the Oglala Sun Dance. The last time I was pierced in the Sun Dance, it was Fire who pierced me because we had many dancers that year and Chief Fools Crow needed some help in piercing. John Fire relates in his book, *Lame Deer Seeker of Visions,* the following information concerning the Yuwipi spirit calling ceremony:

"Imagine darkness so intense and so complete that it is almost solid, flowing around you like ink, covering you like a velvet blanket. A blackness which cuts you off from the everyday world, which forces you to withdraw into yourself, which makes you see with your heart instead of with your eyes. You can't see, but your eyes are opened. You are isolated, but you know that you are part of the Great Spirit, united with all living things.

"And out of this utter blackness comes the roaring of drums, the sound of prayers, the high-pitched songs. And among all these sounds your ear catches the voices of the spirits—tiny voices, ghostlike, whispering to you from unseen lips. Lights are flitting through the room, almost touching you, little flashes of lightning coming at you from the darkness. Rattles are flying through the air, knocking against your head and shoulders. You feel the wings of birds brushing your face, feel the light touch of a feather on your skin. And always you hear the throbbing drums filling the darkness with their beating, filling the empty spaces inside yourself, making you forget the things that clutter up your mind, making your body sway to their rhythm.

"And across the black nothingness you feel the presence of the man lying down in the center of the room, his fingers laced together with rawhide, his body tied and wrapped in a blanket, a living mummy, through whom the spirits are talking to you. This is what you experience during a yuwipi ceremony."[1]

I have chosen the following, told in storytelling form, to convey the power of a convincing communication that takes place in a yuwipi ceremony.

Bill Eagle Feather conducted this particular ceremony in the basement of an old abandoned church on a Sioux reservation. It is a communication that world religious leaders do not have. Billy Graham, the Pope, Oral Roberts or the Archbishop of Canterbury, they have never been able to exhibit this form of communication. Instead of recognizing that such communication is an allowance by the Ultimate Power, I am sure that they would downplay it.

A note on storytelling: In the past, indigenous culture was preserved through storytelling. Down through generations, stories were told and retold about the unfolding drama of cultural life. Young boys could vicariously be warriors as they sat listening to real warriors. The Great Spirit has allowed all minds this ability. Hunters could hunt long after the buffalo were gone and long after they could no longer hunt. Confining winters became shorter. In story form, description could entwine with drama as actual events were brought forth. The surrounding domain, environment, characters and viewpoint, along with a myriad of finer points can flow like a mountain stream, cascading, soothing, rapidly falling and yet stilling in soft pools of reflection. Retention, focus of the issue and meaning within a story: story telling has its own special power. To honor the art of story telling, I offer the following. Rest assured, the form will convey an expressive message. Stories preserved our spirituality.

* * * *

Wakpala Yuwipi

That evening a stream of battered cars from the surrounding communities gathered at the abandoned mission grounds. Eagle Feather studied the growing crowd from the porch of the community hall for a few moments then nodded his agreement to Irma Three Stars. It was decided that the Yuwipi ceremony would be held in the basement of the abandoned church.

As the people filled the old structure, Irma's husband overheard a conversation disputing the decision to have the ceremony in the bottom of a church. After the crowd had settled in their places the Hunkpapa strode to the center of the room. "The missionaries have brainwashed the people. Everything is bad unless it has their approval. The spirits will enter this ceremony if we ask for their presence and not because of a piece of brick or concrete or whatever use this dwelling has had. We are praying to the same God. We call for power in a different way." He eyed the participants reprovingly. "We do not accuse the Washichus (white people) of having evil present when they appeal to the Almighty. Why should they tell us that our way is evil?" A murmur of assenting "haus" swept the room.

Bill sat in a corner holding a conversation with a tall Hunkpapa, Isaac Ghosthawk, who was the father of a young girl who had been killed while walking with another Indian girl along a highway. The girl had been run down by a carload of white teenage boys who had been drinking. The two girls fled from the car into the ditch, but the Ghosthawk girl stumbled in a badger hole and was killed. The driver was held in an off-reservation jail awaiting trial, while his attorney contended that the girl had tried to commit suicide. Rarely were white men convicted for killing Indians. The Yuwipi would be held to reveal the true cause of the girl's death.

Bill emptied a pail of earth onto the floor of the basement. He formed a small mound and patted one side smooth. He then drew a figure on the flattened surface. It was the same face of the man inscribed on his pipe, and who appeared in the water the night before.

Charging Shield held a bundle of sage, passing out a piece to each of the participants. The closely packed bodies sitting on the basement floor caused the cement walls to sweat. No windows or ventilation circulated the air. He wondered how Bill's heart would take the conditions as he

Chief Eagle Feather

passed out the fragrant plant. "Put a piece over your ear or in your hair," he said as the Hunkpapas took the sage.

Bill placed a small red flag in an earthen container and set it on the eastern side of the altar area. The yellow flag, in its container, was placed facing south. The black flag was placed next to the altar and faced west. The white flag faced north.

The wife of Isaac Ghosthawk, Alvina Ghosthawk, unwound a long string of black tobacco pouches around the outside of the four flags forming a large square enclosing the dirt altar and the area where the holy man would lay after he was tied. Eagle Feather stood up from the altar with his pipe and removed his shirt. His Sun Dance scars covered his chest.

"Cousins, for many of you this is your first spirit ceremony. Do not be afraid of what you see here. It is only the old way that we are using to communicate to the powers that are beyond. Nothing will harm you as long as you show respect. If you are here only for curiosity or some kind of show I hope that you will leave now before the ceremony starts. It will get hot, worse than it is now. Take a piece of sage and chew on it if you have trouble breathing." Eagle Feather reached down into his medicine bag for his wotai stone. He held the rainbow rimmed agate briefly before returning it to the fringed deerskin bag that also contained his peace pipe within a smaller, narrow red cloth sack. Eagle Feather withdrew the pipe sack and connected the green jade bowl to the sumac pipe stem. The pipe was offered to the four directions, loaded with a mixture of red willow bark, fall sumac leaves and Prince Albert tobacco, before being handed to Alvina Ghosthawk, who sat on the opposite side of the dirt altar, the place of honor position for holding the pipe.

"I'm ready to be tied," the holy man said to his assistant while pointing to a rawhide tying rope.

Charging Shield tied the holy man's hands behind his back with the rawhide cord, then picked up the special quilt made for yuwipi and placed it over his head. A moon, stars and special designs had been quilted upon it. The attached eagle feather draped backward at the top of Bill's head. "Say a prayer for me, cousins," Bill spoke in a muffled tone through the thin blanket.

Charging Shield then took a longer rawhide rope, made a noose and dropped it over the holy man's covered head and drew it tight. He wrapped it around Eagle Feather's body once and made a tie, then looped it again around the holy man and made a tie. He continued the procedure until there were seven loops around the holy man ending at his ankles with the final tying.

Isaac Ghosthawk stood to help lay the massive body of the holy man face forward towards the west, and directly in front of the dirt altar.

Eagle Feather had received his powers through Fools Crow and the similarity between the two men's ceremony preparation was noted by the holy man's attendant. Charging Shield observed that the buckskin rattles, placement of the flags, and Yuwipi blanket were almost identical to Fools Crows. Only the peace pipe bowl and the designs on the stem lacked conformity. Eagle Feather's pipe, which had a green jade bowl, was different from everyone's and no doubt reflective, to some degree, of his personality and manner. The stem bore four strange designs. No one had a pipe like Eagle Feather.

The two kerosene lanterns that lit the room were blown out. Charging Shield groped in the dark and sat down. Two Hunkpapa men sang the calling song to the beat of a cowhide drum. The song was concluded and Eagle Feather called out for them to sing it again. At the end of the second song, Bill spoke out from under the Yuwipi blanket.

"Ho, there are some here that do not believe this way is for them. The spirit people will not enter until those persons leave. I will help those persons identify themselves. One is sitting with her back against the north wall and is resting her left arm against her knee which is bent. One leg is straight out. There is a piece of sage lying on the floor beside her and she is sitting close to someone that I have traveled with."

"Ho, Charging Shield, reach behind you on your right side. There is a woman behind you. Tell her she must leave so we can get on with the ceremony."

Charging Shield turned to place his hand behind him. He felt a rough textured boot. He then reached up and placed his hand on the woman's arm resting on her knee. He felt the broad turquoise bracelet that he noticed she wore when they had hauled the wood and rocks for the sweat lodge.

"Rosalie, you'll have to leave. I guess this isn't for you," he said.

"I'm sorry, I guess I've got too many doubts," Rosalie Christianson whispered as she rose to leave.

"There is a couple, a man and a woman near the doorway," Eagle Feather murmured from the blanket. "You do not believe either. You have planned to move away from here soon where a job is waiting for you that a church group has promised to get you to join them. You have come here

for curiosity and to spy for them. You think this is the work of a bad spirit, this devil that they have invented."

The door opened and Rosalie and the couple left. Charging Shield
thought about their conversation at the sweat lodge site; how it had
caused him to cast a reproving glance at her acrid remarks about the
return of native religion. Worse, she had chastised him for his participation in the Sun Dance and traveling with the holy man. It was obvious
that Rosalie wanted him to be successful in the white man's world, where
she was the most comfortable. His initial attraction to the half-breed
Indian girl whose blood line was similar to his had suddenly evaporated
because of her remarks.

The drumstick hit the rawhide drum and the calling song began.
Midway through the song the spirit beings manifested themselves, entering as blue lights dancing in a frenzy across the ceiling, bouncing off the
walls as if in a whirling ball, yet keeping steady timing with the rapid
beat of the drum.

The buckskin rattles were equally active, dashing back and forth
within the square enclosure formed by the tobacco offerings. The room
was stifling hot and nearly suffocating, causing Charging Shield to reach
for the sage. He chewed several leaves and worried about Eagle Feather.
Suddenly a cool breeze flowed through the room. A flapping sound came
from the center, as if a large bird were actually flying before them. The
cool blowing breeze caused a stir among the descendants of Gall and
Sitting Bull. The singers burst into Gall's war song, joined by the
Hunkpapas, proudly aware of the power of the Yuwipi.

The fanning breeze blew strong as the singing drew to a close. The
room was almost cold as the drum ceased beating and the song ended.
"Ho, Tankashilah. Ho Tankashilah. Thank you. Thank you for allowing
us all to be here tonight," Eagle Feather's muffled voice called through
the blackness.

"Grandfather, we are here to ask for the return of the old ways of Gall
and Sitting Bull. Bless a family here with the strength and wisdom that
Sitting Bull had through his medicine.

"We also are gathered to call on Thelma Ghosthawk who was killed
before the Sun Dance. We hope that some word or sign may be sent concerning the daughter of the parents who sit here mourning the loss of
their loved one. Ho, Hupo, Hupo." Bill called for the middle song.

The bluish lights returned and paraded around the room in a circle at
a marching pace. The breeze again returned and Charging Shield felt the

floor shake as if horses abreast were marching in the center of the room. He could hear the clopping of hooves through the loud drumbeat and chanting of the singers.

Isaac Ghosthawk cried out, "My daughter is here! My daughter is here! She's talking to me." The singers ended the song but Bill urged them to continue. All joined in a loud chorus leaving Isaac Ghosthawk to converse with his daughter in the way of the Yuwipi. The song ended; Isaac and his wife could be heard crying to themselves.

Bill called on each participant to pray, commencing with the first person at the left of the place of honor.

The Hunkpapas expressed appreciation for the ceremonies, beseeching special blessings on behalf of the holy man's health. A measure of comfort was sought for the Ghosthawks. It took more than an hour to hear each petition, sending the temperature rising. Finally the bearer of the pipe prayed and the circle was complete.

Bill called for the untying song. A cooling breeze accompanied the spirit people's final entry. A buckskin rattle danced before Charging Shield, shaking itself furiously, emitting sparks at its base. The dim glow tempted a closer observation. When he bent forward, a cold sponge-like finger poked him in the forehead, sinking itself with a numbing projection. He jerked back in fear, his heart thumping against his ribs. Suddenly an eagle screamed. The breeze grew stronger, then stopped abruptly. The blue lights whirled over the holy man, hovered, then disappeared into the ceiling at the song's end.

Eagle Feather's strong voice instructed the crowd to light the kerosene lamps. Matches were struck.

Bill was sitting up untied and without his blanket when the soft glow from the glass chimney lamps illuminated the room. The long rawhide tying rope was wound in a tight ball beside the buckskin rattles.

After the pipe was summoned from Alvina Ghosthawk, it was lit. Awed whispers accompanied the passing of the green stone pipe to each participant.

Bill was the last to smoke, when he finished he asked if Isaac Ghosthawk had any comments.

"My daughter appeared to me tonight. She said that she was run down by the car. It was like we all knew." The tall man began sobbing.

Bill broke in. "You have seen the power of the Indian way. Treat this ceremony with respect and it can become a great blessing. Your hearts prayed for power and we experienced a lot of it. It is an honor to be with you, my Hunkpapa cousins. Gall and Sitting Bull are proud of their grandchildren gathered here tonight."

Sandwiches were served with gallons of Kool-Aid and coffee at the community hall. The Hunkpapas clustered around the holy man discussing yuwipis and powers of holy men, most of whom had long since been deceased. Charging Shield noted Rosalie's absence from the hall.

Later, he walked with Bill back to the bunkhouse. The kerosene lamp was lit and soon they were sitting on the edge of their beds, ready for a welcome night's sleep.

"Bill, don't you ever worry about your heart in a situation like tonight?" Charging Shield asked. He looked in the direction of the church. "It was hard to breathe in there."

"Oh, I must admit I worry a little. At first I am what you say—apprehension."

"Apprehensive," Charging Shield volunteered.

"Yeah, that's a good college word," Bill laughed. "You're going to have to teach me some of those smart college words." The holy man's humor brought a smile from his pupil.

"I worry a little, Nephew...it's plenty hot under that blanket all tied up, but once that drum starts and the spirits come in, I don't feel a thing," the older man explained.

Charging Shield knew he was hearing a privileged explanation.

Eagle Feather went on. "All I can say is that I am simply a man out there like anyone else. The Great Spirit is using me to bring in the spirit people. It is his power, not mine. I don't worry about my heart, though. If I did, I wouldn't have much faith, would I?"

* * * *

Bill Eagle Feather conducted a yuwipi ceremony at the the University of South Dakota to find six bodies that had crashed in an airplane during a blizzard. His spirit helper, Grey Weasel came into that ceremony and made seven very accurate predictions that led to the finding of the airplane which was covered with snow and ice. In my opinion, the power of a yuwipi man is in his spirit helper. Bill had the ability to contact his helper and bring him forth to help. Bill's life of harmony and shedding of distraction allowed him this contact. I think that harmonic people also have spirit helpers if they seek them. These associates may not come forth in ceremony as a holy man or holy woman can bring them yet they help us in our everyday life in other mysterious ways. I do not believe any are "bad spirits" because the Creator's Nature is total harmony and this is what controls the spirit world. I would say that these spirits have reached a high plane primarily by their conduct and perception while they were here as humans upon this planet. It is an interesting supposition.

John Fire tells us: "Yuwipi is one of our most ancient rites. Some people say that it is not so old, but they are wrong. Their belief stems from the fact that Yuwipi is never mentioned by name in the old books about Indian religion and because it has remained hidden from outsiders. I am an old man now, but my grandmother told me about this yuwipi when I was still a young boy, just as she had been told during her childhood. In this way the knowledge of it goes back through the generations, and nobody knows its beginnings.

"I believe yuwipi to be as old as our people, because its symbolism, the whole thinking about it, goes back to our earliest times. The sacred things used in this ceremony are ties that bind us to the dim past, to a time before the first white man set foot on this continent. Even though it is not mentioned by name, one book describes yuwipi as it was practiced long ago, before we had houses to live in. This book was written by a woman who lived for a number of years among us when I was a small boy, before the First World War. She got her stories from the white haired holy men who still remembered the days before the reservations. Here is a page from this book. *2

When a man skillful in the use of the sacred stones was called to attend a sick person he was expected to give a demonstration of his supernatural power. Many were invited to witness this exhibition, and it is said that harm would come to those who did not "believe in the sacred stones." The sick person filled a pipe, which he gave to the medicine man. After smoking it the man was tightly bound with thongs, even his fingers and toes being interlaced with sinews like those of which bowstrings are made, after which he was firmly tied in a hide. The tent was dark, and the medicine man sang songs addressed to the sacred stones; he sang also his own dream songs. Strange sounds were heard in the darkness, and objects were felt to be flying through the air. Voices of animals were speaking. One said, "My grandchild, you are very sick, but I will cure you." Frequently a buffalo came, and those who did not believe in the sacred stones were kicked by the buffalo or struck by flying stone or bundle of clothing. At last the medicine man called, "Hasten, make a light!" Dry grass, which was ready, was placed on the fire. In its light the man was seen wedged between the poles near the top of the tipi, with all the restraining cords cast from him.

*Frances Densmore, *Teton Sioux Music*.[3]

I mentioned earlier that I believed the Yuwipi, the foretelling power, reaches back way beyond into our generations preceding the Sioux migration out onto the Great Plains. It is a good feeling to learn that John Fire also feels this way. The Yuwipi—could it be the power that told us to leave our lands in the east? If we would not have done so, our tribe would have been swallowed up and may have even disappeared. Had we survived, we would have had several extra centuries of contact with the European immigrants who would have wiped out thousands of us and thoroughly Christianized the rest. In less than a hundred years of contact, they almost destroyed our culture. We would have lost our language and our spirituality as surely as what has happened to those Siouan people who remained in the Carolinas. We owe much to the Yuwipi and the people who believed in its message.

Have I ever had a revelation, or intensely spiritual experience occur? Yes, when I found my special wotai stone in the Black Hills and of course when I was fortunate to be present at Fools Crow's or Bill's ceremonies.

I had a strong indication of Neihardt's presence when I slept in his bed after a rainbow appeared at the edge of the bed. Earlier that evening an intense ceremony was held. Hilda Neihardt, his daughter, was present at this ceremony and she too felt a strong presence of her father.

I have been fortunate that a medicine which Fools Crow showed me seemed to be a major ingredient in several recoveries of people who had been sick.

In one Sun Dance on the last day, I was dancing beside Bill. He said, "Nephew, look up there." I had seen this lone cloud earlier, slowly drifting toward us. You are so tired on the fourth day, the piercing day— some things just do not register, at least for me, when I get tired. "Nephew, watch that cloud. It is coming right at us." Bill's words seemed to animate the cloud because it floated faster and came right over us and then it rained ever so lightly, just a fine mist. "That's power, Nephew. That's power." I can still hear Bill Eagle Feather's words and can feel the mystical rain that fell. I guess this happening affirms my thoughts that the Great Spirit may, indeed be watching.

In other sun dances we had eagles hover over us.

Vision Quest has occasioned some happenings—one could consider them so highly unusual that they would fall into the category of "spiritual affiliation," if I were to be academic about my response. Several happenings were so mystical that I would lose too much credibility if I attempted to state what I saw. It was too impossible. I would be accused of hallucination or "squirrel-dom" (no insult intended to the squirrels).

I do not conduct many ceremonies as I get older, but almost always, there seems to be considerable presence and indication of spiritual form, especially lately. The black interior of the sweat lodge no longer is black is the best way that I can explain it. A shroud of changing color seems to occupy the lodge. When we sing, it seems to intensify. Faint red, grey, olive green and a grey blue seem to be the dominant colors that fill the lodge. Little lights come in and then shades of blue, dark blue and purple projections begin. At the end of the third endurance, it seems like we are within a galaxy of stars much like what was described by Eileen Nauman in the sweat lodge chapter within *Rainbow Tribe*. This phenomenon has kept on reoccurring since that time. I keep thinking it will all end but actually the intensity seems to be increasing, slowly but surely and at times with new phenomena, but always in some light form while in ceremony.

I only do ceremony with respecting people or I at least try to make that a condition. Like the Indian that told of the Custer battle, I would prefer that those who have been in these particular ceremonies with me, mostly sweat lodge beseechments; let them verify their personal accounts as to certain phenomenon that most all seemed to view. I would be lying, however, if I were to say that this indicating presence did not take place. Usually during the third endurance it seems to be more obvious. The lights are becoming quite obvious and what I am seeing, the other participants are seeing. It is pretty definite that the spirit world is acknowledging what we are doing. Why should I deny what is taking place? It would be dishonoring or an insult to such a gracious presence to deny that which seems to enhance and acknowledge our ceremony. Despite all of this, I am not a medicine man and do not intend to be one. I prefer being an author. I just hate the idea that I would have to live in some glass house and have to follow a bunch of rules for the sake of appearance. I am reclusive enough and certainly do not live fancy, that is for sure.

I believe that most anyone can do certain ceremonies. One can beseech, acknowledge and respect to the beyond and the mystery. That is the attempt, the intention of ceremony. Some inexperienced editor of an Indian newspaper might disagree with me but I won't lose much sleep over his statements especially when he does not have much of a track record in the spiritual realm and was never there to support us when we were in the trenches, trying to bring back The Way. I do not believe that the powerful mystery has a restriction on attempting to talk to it. It is mere man who says that you can or cannot do this or how to go about it.

Old ceremonies such as a yuwipi are a different matter. This ceremony seems to need special tribal songs to precede or begin it. The spirit world also has some stringent qualifications as well that the conductor needs to uphold. You have to prove your harmony before the spirits will respond in the manner that has been described. The Sun Dance has its special songs sung in the old way. I have no desire to, nor would I attempt to conduct a yuwipi ceremony or conduct a Sun Dance. Bill Eagle Feather offered to help me attain the Yuwipi power but I respectfully declined. Maybe I should have moved with his suggestion but then I would not have embarked upon my recent direction. Who knows? I do not lose much sleep over my decision.

What about objects deemed sacred? The peace pipe is considered quite sacred by most Native Americans, especially those who use this portable altar in their ceremonies. I think that the pipe was very essential when the Sioux were placed upon the reservations and the authorities set out to destroy our spiritual ways. Many Indians hid their pipes from the cavalry troops who were sent out to gather up our medicine bundles because of political orders instigated by the Christian missionaries. What bundles were collected were destroyed and the Indians had to stand and watch their symbols go up in smoke. It always puzzles me why so many modern Indians deny or overlook these historical events as though they never happened. It is like a Jew who would deny the events within the movie, *Schindler's List*.

Unlike a sweat lodge or a sun dance area, the pipe was small and concealable. It was even broken down into two pieces, hence the name—canupa (chan oon pah)—part of it is from a tree and it comes in two pieces. At night time, when the cavalry enforcers were gone, it was brought out and assembled for ceremony. Our culture was preserved. Such a sad time those days must have been. Many Indians lost hope and I can not blame them. Even Black Elk gave up for awhile until he saw through the dominant society. The Buffalo Calf Woman must have known those times would come upon us and our spirituality would suffer. She emphasized the use of the pipe within our ceremonies and we survived. Now we must turn to help the Earth survive.

I seldom use my pipe any more. I use my special wotai stone as my portable altar in the few ceremonies that I conduct. But as far as having a sacred object, I am tending to drift more and more away from that concept. Too much controversy has evolved over what is sacred. I like to keep things simple and avoid controversy because we are dealing with mystery. The stone is more simple and it avoids controversy. My stone has its own personal sacredness for me because it has many images that were placed upon it by the Creator. It gives me a close feeling toward the Creator because it was personally made for me, such is my belief. If you find your wotai, that stone is your personal connection. You can go through life without a personal stone but this is just another part of our spirituality that allows us another closer contact with our Creator. Our ceremonies do the same. The whole Natural Way allows one to be so much closer while they walk their Earth Journey. No wonder that those tribal people whom George Catlin came in contact with exemplified all what he said about them.

There are less grounds for argument toward having one's own special stone. The world is full of special stones. They are like sea shells in that they are so abundant. Clearly, people are simply trying to make trouble and spread disharmony if they complain about you or me having our own personal stone. Avoid these kind of people. They will have lonely lives when we reach the spirit world.

The Earth is sacred, that is what we have to focus upon. We are sacred if we sincerely strive to work together in harmony in these perilous times that are finally recognizing that she is in great danger.

* * * *

7

Rules, Restrictions and Conflict

I love a people who are honest without laws, who have no jails and no poorhouses.

* * * *

Does the religion have a set of rules to live by?
What restrictions do members follow?
Are there restrictions on who may participate in the religion or parts of it?
Do members have any special forms of dress?
Can a member marry outside the religion?
Can members practice more than one religion?
Is there conflict in this religion? Over what issues?
Have you encountered any prejudice because of your religion?

* * * *

All religions have rules because all religions are originated by humans. Native religions and the Natural Way had unwritten rules because they employed the oral tradition yet their discipline toward lawbreakers or rule breakers would be considered more extreme than modern day retribution for offenses against society. When you can be put to death for lying, they had stringent rules. Unwritten rules are based on truthfulness and respect for all living things to be regarded as a relative. They are not listed as ten commandments. All of the ten commandments would be respected, however, except that "Lord, thy God" would probably be interpreted as the Creator, or the Great Mystery. Keeping holy the Sabbath would be a moot commandment. All days were considered holy.

They were a closer knit society, therefore their established rules and restrictions were more severe than what we see today in our present society. Contrariwise, they also had customs which avoided harshness or would excuse wrongdoing, especially regarding acts committed by children. In Nature, animal offspring were observed to be playful and at times endangered themselves. Reaction of animal parents is not in the spirit of retaliation or revenge toward their offspring. Toleration and leniency toward children was the general rule for Indian people.

Try disciplining a child that you have had very little to do with. You will have a difficult task. It is easier to discipline a child if you have played many games with that child. If you have helped your young get ready for life's tasks, play or sports, have demonstrated repeatedly your strong interest toward them and conveyed your love and concern for a child, fairly and often, you will not have much of a problem with administration of reasonable discipline. Because you are closely knit, the child does not want to lose your companionship, love and concern.

The same restrictions found in general by most members of human society who truly want to live in harmony would apply to those who seek to walk the Natural Way. In this day and age of communication I do not think a specific blue print of what each restriction would be needs to be put forth. Common sense should be a sufficient guide. Medieval people, tribal people or modern people living in suburbia, on an island or in Greenland, all have common principles in regard to expectations of treatment from others. Down through time, people had unwritten restrictions. Some had a higher harmony than those who wrote most everything down.

Most Natural Way people are against alcohol and drugs. Prior to European contact, American natives were blessed with vast, unfenced, unowned expanse and the absence of alcohol. Drugs or hallucinogens in North American tribes were practically non-existent as well. If they did exist they were used for healing. Maybe intelligent Natural Way followers see the correlation or extreme benefit from that absence, as they are quite adamant against such usage in or around spiritual beseechment or communication.

I received a letter from a youth who chastised me for my view on drug or alcohol usage. He was appreciative of what else he had read in *Mother Earth Spirituality*, however. He quoted my statement that I am against such usage when recognizing traditional plains Indian culture and ways. I think that he wanted me to favor inclusion of drugs in ceremony. I am quite ignorant regarding drugs and intend to stay that way but am not a teetotaler regarding alcohol. I learned how to handle alcohol as a pilot in the Marine Corps. The majority of us loved our flying more than we did any possession by a bottle. We had our good times but we also policed each other. Jets that fly several times the speed of sound do not tolerate unsteady hands or inhibited nerves, especially in combat. I have a glass of wine at times but yet am wary of the danger of alcohol in excess. Hard liquor does not taste that good to me. An old bottle of scotch, a Christmas gift, has been standing in a cabinet for several years but I have no taste for it. I wrote back:

Alcohol and Drugs: My reasoning on drugs and psychedelics is that the old time Plains Indian of which I am partially descended from and have taken most, but not all, of my teachings from; this society was drug free and psychedelic free. They had no peyote either. This did not grow upon the plains and was introduced from the southwest.

I believe that the plains Indian was extremely moral, environmental and very honest. I think that their minds were quite clear and that the absence of drugs and especially the absence of alcohol was a tremendous advantage. I think that the European was very corrupt in comparison and that alcohol usage caused much of this. I could be wrong in my suppositions as I am but a mere human. It is a free country and so far we are allowed our opinions.

On the other hand I have to respect the right of the Native American Church in their usage of Peyote in their ceremonies. This is a religious usage and even like some Catholics and Protestants who use wine (alcohol) in their ceremonies, they too should be allowed to do so. In my own ceremony conduct, I do not want alcohol around as the old time plains Indian did not allow it either. I have to go with the best track record.

I also have seen some tragic results of some who have gone too far in all three of these mind influencing substances. It is pretty scary. When you have been in a yuwipi ceremony, a Vision Quest or a good strong Sweat Lodge, there is no need for anything else, from my experience. This is my opinion. You are free to do what you prefer, however.

In hindsight, I should have been more adamant to this young person who has a long road before him.

Are there restrictions on who may participate in the religion? In the Sun Dance, a pledger was allowed to be in the annual ceremony. A person who simply "walked on" was not allowed to participate other than as a member of the onlooking audience. Even then, I have observed a rare exception to this restriction. I am basing my observation on what I saw at six separate sun dances conducted by Frank Fools Crow.

In a yuwipi ceremony, I have observed Chief Eagle Feather restrict some persons from participating in the ceremony because of their disbelief once it had started. Those who had a sincere, respectful attitude yet knew nothing about the ceremony or the Lakota language used therein; they were allowed to stay and participate.

Women are not to be restricted in any way, from what I have observed among modern people who respect and seek to participate in the Natural Way. Bill Eagle Feather did not place gender restrictions upon anyone when I was his assistant in yuwipi and sweat lodge ceremonies. Fools Crow and Bill were powerful holy men and you did not have a problem with this definition (powerful holy man) once you witnessed their ability to call in the spirits. Yet, they were not loaded down with all of these rules which so many latter day medicine aspirants have come up with. Maybe if you do not have as great an ability to contact into the spirit world or if the spirits do not exhibit much spiritual activity in your ceremony, maybe that shortcoming can spawn a bunch of restrictions so that you will at least look like some kind of holy man or medicine person. I have always said that if I can find someone who has the equivalent spirit communication power as Chief Fools Crow or Chief Eagle Feather, then I will gladly abide by this person's rules.

Rainbow Tribe people usually do not invite to their ceremonies those who are not respectful of their attempts to beseech or acknowledge the higher Power. They will definitely restrict those who have alcohol with them or if they are so influenced, but this is a very rare occasion from what I have experienced.

Once I had an individual who wanted to sneak some beer into a sweat lodge. This was the only time that I have had this kind of an experience and the episode should not be looked at as any form of association with Rainbow Tribe people. People have been shot in churches, churches have been bombed, priests have sodomized little altar boys in churches and recently a fugitive from the law committed suicide in a church. I hope this information does not detour participants from attending the church of their choice. These are rare happenings, as was my incident with this individual in a sweat lodge. Actually, my opinion of this person was that he was deranged mentally. (He was a college psychology professor.) I had observed this person a year before at the same location where I had lectured. He was strange, different and unusual. He certainly exhibited a lack of harmony. It seemed that the spirit world wanted me to detect what he was attempting to do. I was led to the back of the lodge and there on the outside was an unopened can of beer with his belongings. I remembered that this psychology professor had entered under a strange garb enabling him to conceal a small water cooler. Yes, a small water cooler, somewhat like a squat, fat thermos. This person actually resembled that thermos except that he was not overly fat. He was bulky and quite solid in his build like a miniature tank. He was different and odd, possibly this is why I did not pay much attention to him or the weird rug-type covering that he was under. Everyone has a right to go into a lodge and pray if they are sincere in my opinion. I do not want to play God and exclude anyone just because of unusual appearance. My sister and I suffered that chastisement when we were little, therefore I try to be charitable. I am impressed with the depth and dignity of the majority of people who I come in contact with—they respect the Natural Way— but when you are involved with humans on any numerical basis, sooner or later you will meet some odd sorts. Even our nation's presidency, the cabinets and congressional members have displayed this quirk at times.

The end result was, I made this person leave after I called him on what he had in his thermos jug. He was belligerent but I was enthusiastically supported by all of the members of that lodge. There are some restrictions.

Do any special forms of dress exist? In certain ceremonies, specific dress is required. A male sun dancer wears a skirt or a kilt down past the knees and usually his top above the waist is bare. A woman sun dancer wears a very plain dress with little ornamentation. In the sweat lodge, I require all participants to have themselves covered to some degree. Men wear a pair of shorts and the women wear shorts and also a top or a bathing suit. Women can also wear a plain cotton dress if they so choose. I frown on nudity within sweat lodges because I believe it can be distracting and I also wish to honor and respect the modesty of Indian people, especially in ceremony. At social events, a certain decorum should be respected. What decorum? I would say that a dress that promoted lasciviousness or over-materialism would not be welcome at a ceremony or a social function. Why? Because it could be distracting.

Furs are probably frowned on by most espousers of the Natural Way unless one is an indigenous member of a tribe and such articles are customary for a particular tribe or clan and of course would not be from an endangered species. If I were to attend either a Native American function or a gathering of those who believe in the Natural Way or respect indigenous beliefs, I would not be too stylishly dressed, if modern fashion was my dress code. Native Americans are fairly modest with the possible exception of Native jewelry. Most Natural Way people frown on excess materialism yet they can also demonstrate an unlimited admiration for Native jewelry, preferably authentic.

Can a member marry outside the religion and can they practice more than one religion? There are no such restrictions among people who follow the Natural Way. Every person is a distinct individual. Even a spouse has no power to restrict the wonderment of the human mind in this day and age. It is relaxing to have an associate who enhances or adds to your daily infusion of knowledge, but this convenience is no longer a necessity in my opinion. We all come into this world by ourselves and I think that we will all exit the same way. What is upon the Disk of Life in your spouse and what is in yours are two very distinct and separate entities. It may sound unromantic but it is a harsh fact or a pleasant one depending on how you want to interpret.

Often, another religious experience or membership within a household can add insight into one's spiritual concepts. I have had the opportunity to look at many religions or related points of view. If you keep seeking, I believe that you find the path that is the most comfortable in spirit. It seems this is a gift the Great Mystery bestows. Just keep asking the spirit world and keep seeking. You may wish to combine several concepts or many of them. The Natural Way alone might not be the path for you. It could be another road and another journey or a combination of thoughts and insights. In the end, you will know.

What are the major conflicts or issues within the Natural Way? Some Native Americans object to "outsiders" seeking to learn the positive attributes of Natural Way based culture. Other Native Americans do not seem to object. There are differences of opinion regarding this subject.

Sandy Johnson wrote an introduction for Shaman's Drum/Spring Issue 1994. "Not all medicine people are open to whites." One Sioux elder said: "First they took our land, now they want our pipe—all these wannabees, these New Agers, come with their crystals and want to buy a medicine bag to carry them around in. If you want to learn our ways, come walk the red road with us; but be silent and listen."[1]

"Many of the elders included in the book appear in print for the first time, and speak of matters that until now have been considered too sacred to share. They speak out now in the name of Mother Earth, who according to their prophecies and empirical evidence, verges on destruction. They share with us their knowledge of healing: ways to heal ourselves, each other, and the planet."[2]

In the book, over fifty elders were interviewed who did not mind sharing their knowledge.

"Our elders taught us that people would come to this continent in search of the Creator. Just as the Bible was written to tell the true story of world-shaking events of the past, I have asked the public to write down my statement so that when the purification is over, it can be published afterwards. In our prophecies there are two brothers, one dark-skinned younger brother and the light-skinned elder who we call the "White Brother." Together they will decide how the purification will be accomplished.

"The two brothers were with us when we first came to this continent. When their father passed away, the elder brother went out in the direction of the sunrise and the younger brother stayed here. They had agreed the elder brother would go, but would not stay away too long. He would return when people would travel on a road built in the air. At that time we would know that the earth had been corrupted to the point that it must be purified.

"We've come to that point now. Everything has been corrupted. Because we're out of balance, we don't obey the laws. Like right now in California, in spite of our warning, bad things are happening. It's too late now for gradual voluntary corrections. People say that they'll worry about it next year, but next year might be too late. So that's why we warned the people, "Wake up right now! Do something for yourself." So that they might stop all the wrongdoing and get balanced.

"As Hopis, we don't own the land, we're just the caretakers. We use it, but not with electricity and coal mines. We're calling for the purification because it is our obligation. We're ready, we want it to happen. We know we can't get people to change, but we're near. Very near. We pray to the Creator and tell him it's not what we want, but we feel there's no choice. We've already gone over the time limit that was given to us in the prophecy. Even the leaders of our village have put it off because they don't want to see it happen in their lifetimes."[3] —Martin Gashweseoma

There are some who want to keep the Natural Way to themselves but the very powerful holy men and holy women I have known believed that it should be shared.

"The power and ways are given to us to be passed on to others. To think or do anything else is pure selfishness. We only keep them and get more by giving them away, and if we do not give them away we lose them."[4] —Frank Fools Crow

"The survival of the world depends upon our sharing what we have and working together. If we don't, the whole world will die. First the planet, and next the people. **The ones who complain and talk the most about giving away medicine secrets are always those who know the least."[5]** —Frank Fools Crow

A white buffalo calf was born to a white family on a Wisconsin farm. An Oneida medicine man stated that such an event was a sign that the white people and the red people must work together. Harry Brown Bear of the Oneidas was quoted by the Associated Press. "The impact of this and enormity of it to the Red Nation is immense, this was meant to be because the teachings of our people and elders say there would be a time when the Anglo nation and American Indian would come together in goodness." Floyd Hand, an Oglala medicine man made a pilgrimage to the birth site and declared that the arrival of a white buffalo is like the second coming of Christ. "It will bring purity of mind, body and spirit, and unify all nations, black, red, yellow and white."[6]

Black Elk told his vision to John Neihardt to record and pass on. Ten years later Black Elk told the same vision to J. Epes Brown. It is quite obvious Black Elk intended this vision should be shared. My two main mentors, Chief Fools Crow and Chief Eagle Feather, also shared. Their truth was substantiated by their conduct. A very important indicator to me of their truth was their exceptional power and connection into spirit calling ceremony. If a detractor states otherwise I would want to know if they have equivalent power and substance in relationship to these three stalwarts who believed that the only way for the dominant society to truly change was to learn from indigenous philosophy. If dominant society does not change, we lose the planet. It is as simple as that.

The following is an article that I wrote in regard to conflict and the return of the Natural Way. Some of this is repetitive of issues raised in previous and succeeding chapters but overall I believe it conveys my views regarding conflict and the Natural Way.

In the sixties, we who were trying to bring back the Sun Dance had our hands full with the local Pine Ridge Reservation missionaries and most critical were our own Lakota people. The "traditionals" in those days were vastly outnumbered by the non-traditional Christian espousing Indians and they made it difficult for our great holy men, Chief Fools Crow and the Rosebud holy man, Bill Eagle Feather. Now, several decades later, there are very few who will admit honestly that they opposed us. Just about every one claims that they were all avid defenders of the Natural Way Spirituality.

Over a quarter of a century ago, I traveled with a real holy man, Bill Eagle Feather, a Sichangu Sioux. Once, he found six bodies under the snow and ice from seven predictions made in his yuwipi ceremony. I also learned from Chief Fools Crow who was equally in tune with the spirit world. Both men were teachers and shared their knowledge. I also knew Ben Black Elk, the son and interpreter for the great Sioux prophet, Black Elk. All three of these men named me Eagle Man just before we began a Sun Dance that the reservation missionaries were trying to stop. Ben had me carry his father's pipe in that Sun Dance.

There are many now who deeply respect native wisdom and its related prophecies. Some refer to these people as New Agers. Actually they are Old Agers because unlike organized religion, these people respect Old Age philosophy and spirituality. Let us look at the world today. Who is bombing, shooting, torturing and killing humanity? It is not the New Agers. Who killed the thousands of Jews in the Holocaust? Who took the Indians lands and point blank forbade Indian ceremony? Who put up the boarding schools? It was not the New Agers. What church went hand in hand with the Spanish Inquisition and burned the great libraries of knowledge preserved for centuries by the Incas, Mayans and the Aztecs? Who calls Native American ceremonies pagan and heathenish and downgrades them as instruments of their own self-created devil? Why have so many older Native Americans been afraid to attend Sweat Lodge, Spirit Calling, Sun Dance and other traditional ceremonies that did not beseech to the white man's God? Who brainwashed them to ridicule our beautiful ceremonies that beseech to a Great Mystery? It is not the New Age. In Bosnia, we saw three religions killing, raping and fighting. Each believes that they have the sure ticket to God and they don't bat an eye to kill over it. New Agers do not have this philosophy nor this track record to destroy spiritual ways.

Like my mentors, I had hoped most Native Americans who knew their culture, would see the need to educate the white man and this would have been a challenging opportunity for Native and Indigenous teachers to go out and change the dominant ones for the better. There have been a few brave ones who have taught the white man, but not enough. This has been a great disappointment. But, then again, Black Elk never lived to see the Sacred Tree begin to bloom as I believe it is now.

Long ago, the recorded speeches of Native American leaders all called on the dominant society to change. Our leaders were shocked with the disrespect of Nature exhibited by the advancing immigrants. In all the speeches of the old Indian chiefs that I have read, every one of our leaders wanted the white man to change his ways and many warned of serious consequences if this did not happen. When we enter the Spirit World, the old chiefs will no doubt ask, and I would not want to be one of those whom they will chastise eternally, "Why did you try to prevent the changing of the white man? Why didn't you teach the white man the earth stewardship ways especially when Mother Earth was in great danger? Did you detract, squabble and negate what was a sincere attempt to learn?"

Many dominant society people have seen through the fallacy of organized religion and its weak values, and now understand the Blue Man prophecy of Black Elk's Vision—the Blue Man of greed, jealousy, hate and lies; the Blue Man who began by killing off the buffalo and issuing small pox blankets and putting everyone in boarding schools in collusion with organized religion. This Blue Man certainly does not want Native Americans to share proven knowledge that will change the dominant society away from it's present infatuation of Blue Man values that is infesting the Earth and poisoning with hate, crime, jealousy and deception. All sacred sites will be eventually closed and the broken treaties will never be amended if the Blue Man wins. The Earth situation will get so bad that Indigenous People will have to go forth and educate, otherwise Mother Earth, herself, will bring forth destruction. Most, if not all, could perish. Great change upon the planet has happened before and Mother Earth does duplicate and replicate. Down through time she has done so. Modern society is not immune to severe natural change. So be it. I rarely make a prediction but this is my prediction.

I believe that Black Elk's Vision is a true vision and that the Six Powers of the Universe declared that all two leggeds should learn to live in harmony. Black Elk conveyed his vision in order for it to be learned. Why else did he tell his vision? I imagine that he will have much to say to his detractors when they enter the Spirit World for it is an extremely powerful vision and should not be thwarted. I also believe that the Natural Way is such a powerful force that it will sweep the world in its own due time. No one group of people or organization will be able to contain it. Ignorance, jealousy and untruth will be employed by the Blue Man forces, however. If we do not all return to the Natural Way values we will lose the planet and two leggeds will be but a memory.

Some important issues regarding religious conflict are: conduct within certain ceremonies, the use of the peace pipe and sacred sites.

The majority in this nation know little about the Natural Way. There are many who are doing more than just observing, however. There are those who seek to participate in natural beseechment or ceremony. To those people I suggest that maybe you should stay away from specific Indian ceremony if it offends others but that does not mean that you should stop seeking Earth knowledge. If you are invited by Native people to ceremony, respect their customs, their taboos. Be quiet. Be modest. Go slowly. Do not be in a hurry. Do not aggrandize or exaggerate your experiences. These are important advisories. The most important advisory in my opinion is: never stop seeking and learning. The Earth might be lost if you do. No one can take away your religious freedom, at least not unless the religious far right gets back into power. And do not think that they are not trying. They stacked the Supreme Court and when that failed their next move was into the school boards and Congress.

In regard to a peace pipe, what do you need a pipe for to beseech? I use my wotai stone more and more because I am so disgusted with the arguing involving innocent people who are not of Native American blood, wanting to beseech with a peace pipe. Who can keep you from picking up or finding your own special stone that is out there in Mother Earth? There are plenty of them. Pick up your stone which has been waiting for you down through time and lift it toward a direction and identify that which is good with that direction. Beseech to your higher powers in this manner and there will be less occasion for argument.

If you want to pray to your higher power, then go to an isolated place. Why go to Native areas which are becoming crowded? The Four Directions are everywhere; the Great Mystery, the Creator is everywhere. The Spirit World listens to all who are truthful regardless of where you are. You do not have to be on Bear Butte, Mt. Sinai, in Mecca or at the Wailing Wall. To go up on a mountain, or a butte, or into a lodge and beseech one's higher power is not a specific rite that falls under a jurisdiction of any special race, organization or tribe. The Jews were doing the ceremony, Vision Quest, long before the Christians existed. The Celtics beseeched to a Creator in lodges long ago. Across Europe and into Mongolia, spiritual saunas were held to beseech. No one owns beseechment.

What about those who charge for a ceremony? This was not a question asked by the Humanities students but it is an important issue. I believe that medicine men or medicine women should be supported. In *Rainbow Tribe*, I write about a journey I took with Jamie Sams to see Fools Crow about a week before he died. We also visited with another holy man who was very poor. We had the means to bring them good quality meat and food. We also gave freely some financial support. If a holy man is asked to make a journey to help someone and a ceremony is required, he often cannot afford to pay his own expenses. Most are very poor because they are not interested in material gain yet they have to live.

I have a means of support however and cannot charge for a ceremony as long as the spirit world is helping me make a living through my writings and lecturing. If I decide to do a ceremony there will not be a charge. I will not show up if anyone makes a mistake and attempts to advertise that I will conduct one. This is a difficult issue for many of European descent because they are so possession oriented. It is something that they have to learn, however. Unless you are a poor, destitute medicine person like those who are out on a reservation with no means of support, you do not charge, otherwise the spirits will not work with you.

What is customary to charge in dominant society is not a custom in the Natural Way. I have conducted marriage ceremonies and never charged. Recently, a friend had a terrible tragedy, losing his three children and his spouse. He wanted to vision quest to help his mind after hearing me lecture. Several weeks later I met him and we drove in two cars all the way to Northern Minnesota. We built a sweat lodge in the woods and held a ceremony. Afterwards I left him and stayed in his cabin an hour's drive to the south. At the time, I had little money but all that I accepted was a tank of gas for my nine year old car, a candy bar and a bottle of pop when we gassed up. I did sleep in the man's cabin and made some coffee in the morning before returning to my son's modest home where I live. Later, the man gave me a beautiful piece of sculpture which I accepted to keep from hurting his feelings. I soon gave this away because I am attached only to my eagle bone whistle and my wotai stone and if I lose them I have to realize that they are nothing but mere possessions. If you give me something I will eventually give it away. Possessions are too much of a burden to worry about. This way I am free to travel life's journey with little baggage.

Another time I was called to help a man's wife who was dying of cancer. I was reluctant to do a ceremony but since my friend who called was an Assiniboine Indian and knew the man and his wife, I consented to see what I could do. She was pretty far gone and had already had a kidney removed. I still had some of Fools Crow's medicine which I had picked in the summer and used that on her. She was such a young and pretty lady and the saddest part was that she had two sons who were the ages of eleven and nine. For them alone, I wanted her to live in the worst way. I did several ceremonies and even made some severe promises to the spirit world that I would dedicate myself to if she would live. I did not want those two boys to be without their Mom. I had some success earlier on other people with Fools Crow's medicine which is told about in *Rainbow Tribe*. In one of the stories, Loren Hynes was 80 pounds and about six feet two inches. He was definitely dying of cancer and looked like a zombie yet the medicine worked. He is now healthy and very much alive. I knew the medicine was strong and had some hope when she got up the day after the first ceremony and went shopping. She seemed to progress for awhile despite the fact that the cancer had spread considerably. I had to take my son to Colorado where he was going to work and in my absence she passed away. She told her husband that she had, at least, found a beautiful, meaningful spirituality and wanted me to speak first at her funeral. I am usually in command of my emotions because I believe that I have to be, especially in times like these, but that was difficult to do; keeping the composure of a mountain lion while I looked at the two boys in the front row. This was several years ago, and I still see this family every once in awhile. The husband wanted to give me anything I wanted but I could not and did not charge.

I have recently helped Sagebrush Productions make a video presentation about the Pipestone Quarries. It is a good communication to help people understand why we believe the way we do and that the quarries are quite meaningful in our history and culture. It goes along with my theory that the only way you are going to change the white man is to teach him. I do a formal pipe ceremony in the presentation, however. I therefore have decided that **all** royalties due me from this video will go to an Indian school and orphanage close to Chamberlain, South Dakota. I think that I made the right decision in that Indian orphans will receive something for it and I cannot be accused of charging. Any detractor that wants to complain about this, I think the spirit world will not take their detraction lightly. I certainly do not live very fancy and own very little. My books and my lectures are my living. Other authors sell their books and lecture so I believe that I have that right. I still am adamant that poor medicine people with no other means of support should be supported, however and taken care of by those who seek their guidance.

Maybe some of these Indian newspapers that are so busy trying to establish rules should introspect and quit taking in paid advertisements from the missionary churches, especially the Mormons who seek to destroy our traditional beliefs. Maybe if all of the Indian newspapers can find some way not to charge for their newspapers they can teach me and I won't have to sell a book to live.

All in all, religious conflicts are usually based on zealous precepts, arguments, dictates, holdings, proclamations, etc. and all have been brought forth by humans. I doubt if a single spirit has brought forth one issue. Common sense is my suggestion and I certainly would not want to discourage anyone from seeking knowledge, wisdom and understanding from the Natural Way or the Native Wisdom. I would thoroughly check out the background of anyone who does not want you to know more of the Creator's creation. What is their past? Is their home loaded with possessions? What is their lifestyle? How were they to their children? How have they raised their children or do they have some offspring which they never supported? How did they treat their spouses and even their former spouses? Where were they when there were but few who stood up for the Natural Way? Have they always had a history of condemning and negativity? Are they optimistic about any issues? Are they seeking attention? What is their concern or knowledge regarding the environmental and planetary situation? Are they willing to introspect? These are important questions to ask.

Have I encountered any prejudice because of my spiritual beliefs? When members of my tribe attempted to revive the traditional spirituality, prejudice was experienced even from Indian to Indian. Since that time and due to the resurgence of traditionalism on the reservations, religious prejudice surrounding this area has decreased considerably.

A new prejudice has risen, however and that prejudice is pointed at some who have sought to find connection into the Natural Way. Some ethnic groups are discouraging "outsiders" from observing this Natural Way. I have yet to know of any who have profound spirit calling power within these ranks. If I am uninformed, then I hope I am invited to attend such a ceremony and if the spirit world comes in and conveys how wrong I am, then I will be happy to admit my error. Introspection applies to me as well as it does to everyone else. If that should happen, then I will have to wonder about this spirit world if they keep on displaying their acknowledgement in the few ceremonies I have been conducting. Apparently, the spirit world is quite concerned with the direction this world is heading and indicates to me that they see a chance that the dominant society might change and the only way for this to happen is to keep on teaching them. Talk is cheap, however. Any detractors are welcome to attend ceremony with me or share it. Maybe that will be the best approach. This is not an ego thing, it is the planet. Do we share knowledge or do we keep it to ourselves?

Am I wrong about Black Elk's vision and the teachings of Fools Crow and Eagle Feather? I could be wrong. What do I know? Can a detractor ask himself or herself these questions? I think that it is but a matter of time when traditional espousing people discover that they are discouraging staunch allies rather than enemies. The Blue Man is everywhere in control of politics and legislative decision making now. As what is happening in Canada, his next move will be to shut down the reservations. He will disguise this move as cost cutting and balancing the budget yet the wealthy will continue to receive government benefits. We will need every friend we can make when this begins.

Mystery is a pretty powerful entity to be speculating over, let alone arguing about. And then there is the spirit world that lies beyond. The Buffalo Calf Woman let us know immediately that she could be pretty harsh against those who make a move to satisfy themselves alone. She killed the bad warrior who sought to attack her and satisfy his ego and desire with no concern about the planet or the Generations Unborn. High plane thoughts were not within his scope. That bad person even had a good warrior trying to warn him that what he was going to do was not advisable. I do not even want to wonder what his spirit is doing now.

Our existence in the spirit world could be for a long time. How does one's actions, one's condemnations, one's bravery or lack of bravery measure up to what is happening to the planet right before our very eyes? We are in that time span and many of us are aware that these are some extremely serious times. What are you doing to help the dominant society change their destructive values? What will your background exhibit when you enter that world of pure truth? For those who are prejudiced and making conflict to satisfy their own ego, they might wander with that warrior who wasn't thinking very seriously.

* * * *

Hierarchy, Matriarchy and Patriarchy

And oh, how I love a people who don't live for the love of money!

* * * *

Does any hierarchy in the religion oppress the common people in any way?
Is there a human leader in this church?
Where is the leadership based?
Are there priests in this religion?
Is there room for independence of belief and action in your religion?
Is either sex seen as superior to the other in the eyes of the church?
What role do men and women play in this religion?
Are all people equal in this religion?
How is sex viewed in the religion?
Who supposedly wrote the books of authority in the religion?
Is doctrine in your church set in stone or is it changing?
How strongly and carefully is your spoken or written word followed today?

* * * *

A hierarchy of holy men, holy women or medicine persons was not a part of plains culture. Within a band or a village a medicine person or a holy person would serve either as a healer or a spiritualist or both. He or she did not report to a higher medicine man or holy man.

For those who seek to follow the Natural Way, a hierarchy made of spiritual or religious practitioners would be frowned upon and would most likely become suspect as a means to establish personal power.

Furthermore, there are no human leaders who are specifically recognized as the leader or the head of the Natural Way. It is too big for a mere human. You might have a temporary leader of individual groups or a person in charge of an outing but it should not be for too long of a duration. A good teacher does not hold your focus away from the Ultimate Teacher for very long. If they know their subject they should be able to convey their impressions in a reasonable amount of time. You will never match the exact perception which the teacher intends anyway. Religion and spirituality are within the realm of mystery, it may take you a lifetime of study, but this is a path which you alone are upon. Many teachers may be a part of that path. To be placed on a path by a teacher is a good happening but one should expect to course their own journey eventually.

I had leaders or teachers for a period of time. I would not be writing this book if it were not for them. I am thankful that I met these leaders because they allowed me to be exposed to their knowledge. They knew much about Nature and the spirit world. They were good to me and yet they never tried to own me. It puzzles me why so many of my peers did not pay much attention to these teachers, especially when these holy men were in their prime. Only a few young men were among them in later years. Most were wasting their time in the bars. Such a waste when Fools Crow, Bill Eagle Feather, John Fire, Ben Black Elk, Plenty Wolf and others were available. Back when we were struggling to have our Sun Dance return, with few exceptions, I never saw these men who now claim that they were trained by such and such a holy man. Where were they? Many of the young have returned to Native Spirituality, however, and that is what counts. Some of them are becoming spiritual leaders. That I am extremely thankful for. The old holy men are gone now into another dimension but they left their mark upon this return to the Natural Way.

Conversely, the quest for leadership resides in the individual because each person is a unique entity. Many are reaping a myriad of nature experiences and are bringing endless impressions of knowledge upon and into their Disks of Life. We are all followers and we are all leaders; each in our own right. We are extensions of the Great Spirit and we walk with dignity.

The spiritual system, the Natural Way, was so strong, so influential, it was the cohesive force that bonded all the inhabitants of this continent together with a common value system. There was no one leader who was responsible for the pristine forests that stretched unblemished, unfenced, unswathed from the Atlantic to a once blue Mississippi. This preservation, this gift, was the result of individual leaders who knew almost instinctively to lead with the environment in mind. Isn't it strange how history books teach us to remember the names of those leaders who devastated both humanity and the earth and not the leaders who were far more exemplary? We should be taught to remember those who saved great portions of the earth for the ensuing generations.

Our well-being is greatly enhanced when we bring in more and more knowledge, more and more shared wisdom and more and more observation. All of this is what the Great Vastness has made. We approach it intrinsically when we feed our mind these ingredients. In so doing we are fulfilling a need to return to natural harmony. We feel so much better because we are actually coming closer to this Supreme Entity which is all wisdom and all of what we have observed. It's way is the only way that really works.

Blank, non-observant, non-seeking people are not all that happy because they have moved very little toward the Creator. Angry ones are not happy either, but that is obvious. Scheming and cunning people who knew how to focus and manipulate greed became leaders in this land. They are still looked up to and revered. The old land barons, the Blue Man Moguls; most are gone now. Great mausoleums stand over their bones. View where they are buried; their greed is yet reflected because they still take up more space than they need. I have seen these expansive, polished stone markers upon this diminishing earth and often have viewed their monuments in the large cities reaching high into the sky where stately trees should be growing. There was little thought for the Generations Unborn from these Blue Men and their vassals who cut, swathed, blasted and drilled.

We were the Generations Unborn when these past generations cut the trees, sucked the oil and sent much of the steel to the bottom of the ocean or across it, much of it to fight in foreign wars. The resources are becoming few. Yet there was a nation of non-takers that lived before them and so much longer than the recent generations of change and taking. These older indigenous generations needed no monuments and left none. Their legacy is their monument of truth. It was a legacy of living many, many centuries while preserving the great resources and consuming very little. Can you imagine? All of those stately, dignified beings, exemplary leaders in their own right, and not one of them cared to take up six feet of earth or carve a massive boulder above their bones and proclaim to the earth, "This is me. I was here."

Are their priests in this religion? Are they ordained? How?

There are no priests in the Sioux religion. There are holy persons and medicine persons with no relationship to a hierarchy. In the Natural Way, from my experience, there are no established priests or ministers. A heirarchy of priests or ministers is too dangerous. Look at the Inquisition and the priesthoods of the Aztecs and the Inca. So far, I do not know of any gurus either. I may write from my observations but that makes me an author and not a guru driving around in a long car and being followed by devotees. That would be the last thing I would want to be. It implies that one has a special connection to the Mystery and I certainly do not have any more power than anyone else. Everyone has the gift to observe, to seek experiences and adventure.

It is through Nature that a man or woman receives power and often from a spiritual experience. I am not a medicine man and have no desire to be one but I had a strong spiritual experience when I found my special wotai stone. This happened on the same day that I was pierced in the annual Sun Dance. Had I pursued a medicine person's road, I am sure that this event and my stone would have been strong ingredients toward specific medicine duties.

Profound or repeated dreams were also indicators to follow a medicine or holy road. Black Elk had a mystical experience before becoming a healer and a holy man. Chief Fools Crow had a mystical experience and became a powerful holy man. Bill Eagle Feather consulted with Fools Crow to begin his strong power through apprenticeship, vision questing and sun dancing. A holy person with a strong reputation will often be consulted by a younger man or woman and often the holy person will teach an interested follower. The Chips family reaches back, medicine-wise, beyond the time of Chief Crazy Horse. They have always had powerful medicine and have carried this gift down through succeeding generations. Actual ability to cure, heal or predict denoted a holy person's reputation rather than the term "ordination." Ordination is something conferred by humans.

Most all of the powerful Sioux holy men of recent times maintained their strong spiritual connection through prolonged fasts out on lone badland buttes or upon Spirit Mountain (Bear Butte), in the Black Hills. Both Eagle Feather and Fools Crow conducted or danced in the annual Sun Dance for a number of years. I believe that this ceremony also helped them maintain their spiritual connection and ability to help cure, find, protect and foretell.

An established priesthood was not a part of North American tribes. The strength of true Indigenous Spirituality was the absence of a religious organization that could usurp spiritual connection and make it into a power base for self perpetuation. In the Natural Way, an individual is encouraged to beseech directly to their higher power. A holy man or a holy woman is merely a facilitator or a helper. In the Sun Dance, Chief Fools Crow, the Sun Dance Chief, did not stand between us and our personal vision. I danced beside my other mentor, Bill Eagle Feather, several times. He did point out certain phenomena but never tried to get between me and my higher power. In the Vision Quest you are by yourself and beseeching directly to the Great Spirit. Down below at the base of the mountain, a holy man might have prepared you with a sweat lodge and encouragement but you are very alone on that dark mountain. It is not necessary to have anyone below, however. Your Vision Quest is between you and your Higher Power.

In the Sweat Lodge, the facilitator is there only to pour water on the hot stones, maintain decorum and set the endurances so that the participants may have their opportunity to beseech or acknowledge to their higher power. All within become very clean as they do so and the interior will heighten in spiritual acknowledgement as the ceremony continues. The time to pray is the most important endurance in my opinion. The people praying in sincerity, finding their own spiritual confidence, and becoming related to all of creation is more important than the ability or style of the facilitator.

It is good for an experienced sweat lodge facilitator to go into another's lodge occasionally and be a participant with the rest of the people. I recently was a participant at a lodge conducted by two Mohawks on the Mohawk reservation near the Canadian border. At the same time, a woman's lodge was being conducted separately at the opposite end of the lodge site. The men's lodge was a very moving ceremony and gave me new knowledge. I was deeply impressed with the two lodge facilitators and the way they conducted the ceremony.

I will never forget how confident I felt with Sioux religion during and after experiencing my first yuwipi ceremony under Chief Fools Crow. Maybe that is why I use the term, spiritual confidence. At the time of the ceremony, many years go, I used the term religion for all ways. I had yet to infuse the term spirituality into my conceptions.

Is there room for independence of belief and action? We are all distinct entities, especially those of us who live in these modern times and receive various communications, observations and adventures. We are what our minds perceive. These perceptions are different honing experiences, influences and even illusions. We even go so far that we create our own self-religion to some degree. We make ourselves! Our beliefs can be distinctly different from each other. We are all specially unique, yet a spirituality can be a commonality despite differing influences and influencers because of the common dependent relationship we all have. Among the indigenous people there was this commonality yet tribes were distinctly different in many ways; at least tribes were if sedentary, hunter/gatherer, pure nomad or agrarian lifestyle classifications are scrutinized. Freedom was very much a part of their lifestyle. They certainly had their independent freedoms. No wonder that democracy was born from them.

There are four important subjects found in Dr. John Bryde's *Modern Indian Psychology* that in his analysis, led to Sioux values.[1] I call these subjects *respects*.

Respect for the Great Spirit.
Respect for the Earth
Respect for the Tribe
Respect for Individual Freedom.

The Indian thought of God as good. We did not fear our concept of the Higher Power as do many non-Indians.

Indians revered the world and did not use it selfishly to make money or to get ahead. Creation (the earth) was spiritually regarded as the provider, yet Indians were responsible for not taking more than they needed so that future generations could also live as well as they did.

Indians helped and shared with one another to make the tribal group strong. Modern society disdains tribal thought. Modern society uses others to get ahead, seeks ownership and the accumulation of possessions. None of these false symbols of success will go with you into the spirit world.

Indians believed in pride of self and exercised their freedom to do the right thing. They were not forced. The world's experience with communism saw a system where the individual did not count. Respect for individual freedom played a significant role within the tribal social structure. As long as the individual's conduct respected the Great Spirit, the Earth, and the tribe, a tribal member's conduct was allowed a high degree of freedom.

Is either sex seen as superior to the other in the eyes of the church and what role do men and women play in this religion? Officially, no gender is superior, but when the history of organized religion is considered, and how patriarchy led it down its present path, there is a tendency for many within the Natural Way to lean a little more toward giving an extra acknowledgement to the power within woman. She is obviously the most peaceful. There are many women who recognize the Natural Way.

Let us consider balance. Balance is very evident in Nature. To exclude woman's wisdom and leadership within any religious or spiritual movement would be excluding half of what reproductive creation is. A quote from *Rainbow Tribe* :

"Unlike the ceremonies of the dominant society, Sioux ceremonies are very balanced. Woman opens the ceremonies and sits in the place of honor holding the pipe in the spirit calling ceremony. Woman is the first to circle the Sun Dance Tree at the annual Thanksgiving. When woman is present, it is she who will be the first to enter the lodge. Woman is not barred from conducting or leading ceremony. This would be an imbalance against Nature, for it is she from whom we come. It was she (Buffalo Calf Woman) who brought us the red sacred pipe and everyone knows that woman is half of the two legged population. She is our Mother, Ina Maka (Mother Earth) upon whom we are conducting the ceremonies! A great deal of power and harmony never manifests where she is not allowed her equal right in ceremony. Probably, more importantly, a great deal of Wisdom is lost when she is not allowed her rightful voice in spiritual leadership."[2]

A woman's spiritual role in plains society is a bit confusing, however, from what I have observed. The Buffalo Calf Woman was a very powerful figure. She greatly enhanced seven major ceremonies and killed the first man that she came in contact with. He was attracted to her therefore one could conclude that she was in her physical prime. This would also mean that she would be capable of menstruating. Historically, there exist some serious taboos regarding a woman in her menstruation cycle coming close to ritual bundles, peace pipes and ceremonies. Occasionally, tribal people do extend invitations to non-tribal people who are respectful and are friends. My advice is to respect the taboos, or historical restrictions upon reservations or within native led circles. If such compliance does not appeal to you or causes you disharmony, do not attend.

In a college biology class, embryology was a required subject. I learned that the endometrium—the outer lining of the uterine wall—

sloughed off in order for a new egg to implant into a new lining and consequently all humans are thus allowed to be born. This is how the Great Spirit has designed the beginning of each placenta-dependent, warm-blooded organism. This happening occasions the menstrual cycle and such a cycle which occurs monthly lasts until a woman matures into menopause. During this reproductive capability of a woman, she is forbidden among many of tribal thought, to be in ceremony with others and therefore would be seriously handicapped to conduct or assist ceremony and other forms of medicinal and spiritual connection. After menopause, a woman could partake in ceremony or even lead with less restriction. "A woman past menopause could enjoy more ritual obligations inasmuch as menstrual restrictions were no longer applicable. An old woman might assist her husband in sacred rituals to the extent that the death of the wife might be regarded as a partial loss of power by the husband. The potency of the woman was underscored in the sacred myths."[3]

A part of the wisdom from tribal thought could be to keep the mother in close contact with her offspring. If she was off doing medicine duties, then the growing offspring could become neglected, depending upon her degree of involvement. Healing the sick might consume an excessive amount of time. Traditional thought severely frowned on neglect of the young. There would be some solid common sense in this regard, in my opinion. Both sides should be weighed.

Yet I am appalled at what dominant patriarchy has done to organized religion. Man has dominated Christianity and the Moslem faith to such an extent that few women are spiritual leaders and few conduct ceremony. I believe that few women in the Jewish faith conduct ceremony or are allowed to be rabbis. The track record of all of these faiths have trailed through many wars and some wars are still ongoing. The Christian faith, especially, has made deep inroads into many Native American tribes with its patriarchy. Those tribes that have spent the longest time in contact with dominant society have picked up a great deal of this patriarchy. I have a strong supposition that the old tribes, especially those in the northeast, were quite matriarchal or at least balanced between matriarchy and patriarchy. Most North American tribes probably respected matriarchy. If they observed nature, one would think that they must have observed how balanced Nature is. It is very obvious that Nature reveals this balance between male and female. In the long run, I think that the human race will harm itself if they try to stifle and spiritually restrict the gifts and wisdom of woman.

The following article is an example of the deep thought of woman. I do not believe that a man could write with such insight. In an earlier chapter, I am probably perceived as having a harsh view in my regard to forgiveness. I tried to present a view based on my observation as to how Nature exhibits the absence of forgiveness. This is what I have interpreted from my observation and cannot doctor my observation if I want to be truthful. I am sure that many readers do not think in my terms and most certainly have never approached forgiveness in such an austere, practical manner.

Ritt Rousseau gives us another point of view that is softer, kinder and gentler. In my opinion, her approach offers a reasonable, positive application to apply to our life's journey. Her view offers a balance in contrast to my view.

Forgiveness

Is God all forgiving? Who among us has not asked this question, perhaps many times? I have often wondered how many of us live our lives out of a fear of a God that is not all forgiving rather than from a desire to please God and make the world a better place for ourselves and others. And if God is not all forgiving, then what happens to those who die and are not forgiven? Is there truly a heaven and a hell and, if so, what are they like? Or is there no life after death? Do our bodies just stop one day and that's all there is?

Most of us look for an answer to these questions in the spiritual or religious tradition in which we were raised. My response to these questions comes from my religious and spiritual experience, growing up Catholic and gradually moving toward a spirituality with a metaphysical foundation. Metaphysical spirituality is very similar to the Natural Way, differing only in how forgiveness is experienced in this lifetime.

The hometown where I grew up was a small town in Minnesota. The population was about a thousand people. As I look back, I realize that even then I was practicing the Natural Way. We were surrounded by forests, farmlands and lakes. We knew all the best climbing trees, which lakes were best for swimming and which were best for fishing. Our favorite sandy-bottom lake was a mile out of town. If we wanted to take a shortcut we had to go through a pasture where a bull grazed. We never took the shortcut when the bull was out. I remember the time we didn't see the bull and started walking through the pasture. We got about halfway through and spotted the bull and before long he spotted us. We ran for what we suspected were our very lives to reach the fence before he reached us. Even though I was beginning to have mixed feelings about God, I suspect God heard from me while I was running.

The Catholic God I grew up with was not all forgiving. We were taught that if we died with a mortal sin on our soul, we would burn in hell forever. (I remember when it was a mortal sin to eat meat on Fridays. Now it's okay to eat meat on Fridays and I keep wondering what happened to those poor souls who died and supposedly went to hell.) So my experience of God was to fear God. As a child and even as an adult it is difficult to love someone you are afraid of.

We were taught a lot about sins. In the church there were venial sins (disobedience, anger, teasing your siblings, etc.), mortal sins (using the word God when swearing, missing church on Sunday, adultery, drinking too much, etc.) and grievous sin which was called a sacrilege. To my young soul a sacrilege was right up there with incest and murder. The dictionary states a sacrilege is, in part, "The intentional desecration and disrespectful treatment of persons, places, things or ideas held sacred."

Ed wrote about religions that offer forgiveness in a ceremony. The Catholic Church weekly offered a ceremony called confession which I always found to be very intimidating. You go into this little enclosed space and kneel down and wait. There is a door and a veiled partition between the priest and you. The priest slides open the door and you say, "Bless me, Father, for I have sinned. My last confession was... (here you say the day of your last confession). You tell the priest the sins you've committed and make a "firm commitment to sin no more." The priest, acting as God's servant, absolves you of all the sins you confessed. The priest gives you a penance, a prayer, anything from The Lord's Prayer to one or more Rosaries, depending on the gravity of the sins.

Some people may have left confession thinking they could go back out and steal again or be unfaithful to their spouse again or cheat their customers again. However,I was taught that their confession was not valid in the eyes of God because they, in their hearts, did not make a firm commitment to sin no more. The priest may have absolved them but God would be the final judge.

My soul and memory are forever seared with an experience I had as a teenager. Another church rule stated that you could not receive communion on Sunday unless you abstained from food from midnight until you received communion the next day. To violate that rule was a mortal sin. (Since that is no longer a rule I also wonder what happened to those poor souls who ate after midnight and still went to communion.) Well, in our house we had an unspoken rule that everyone had to receive communion every Sunday and on those rare occasions when someone did not, our mother would ask us why, and we knew we had to have a good reason. In fact, though I don't remember anyone telling me this, I always thought it was a sin to not go to communion, and I believed those many people who did not take communion were sinners; I believed they had probably done something horrible the night before. One Saturday night my boyfriend and I went to a movie and he accidentally brushed against my breast. I was convinced I had committed a mortal sin. I didn't dare tell my mother what had happened so I went to communion the next day, certain that this meant I had now committed still another mortal sin. It would be another week before they offered confession again and I was terrified I'd die first and burn in hell forever. The following week when I entered the confessional I confessed one or two venial sins; suddenly I became paralyzed with fear and was too afraid to confess my mortal sins. When I left the confessional I knew I was in big trouble. I was certain I had committed a sacrilege which, in my frightened young mind, meant I was no better than a murderer.

For several weeks I carried around this burden, afraid I might accidentally get killed and go straight to hell. I was too fearful to go back to confession because this was a small town and I suspected that the priest sometimes left his confessional to see who was in the church and then try to guess which person was last in the confessional. (As I look back on it, I assume he probably knew without looking just by hearing our voice and he may have, indeed, needed to visit the bathroom.) Whenever possible I would avoid going to communion. I would lie to my mother, saying I was sick or had accidentally eaten after midnight. I don't think she believed me but, strangely, never questioned me. Finally a friend gave me a ride to a neighboring town about seven miles down the road. I went to confession there, to a priest who did not know me. When I blurted out my sins I half expected police to rush in, arrest me and carry me off to jail. Looking back on this experience and remembering the utter terror I carried around, I believe I lost any notion I might have had of a loving, forgiving God. God became an angry, fearful, punishing God.

I knew there were people in town who hit their wives, got drunk every Saturday night, beat their children and cheated their customers. Yet there they were on Sundays, at church receiving communion. I remember one man who, it was said, molested small girls and boys. One of the girls, my friend, told her parents but because this man was rich and respected, and maybe because he gave a lot of money to the church, nothing was done. This confused me and I began to wonder if God only punished little children and not adults. It made me wonder if adults were always right, no matter what they did.

In our society, it seems to be less about what someone does and more about not getting caught. It seems to be understood and even accepted, that a man may beat his wife but shame on her if she goes out in public with a black eye. People don't want to see evidence of the abuse. Look at the number of people who have committed crimes and become heroes. They are guests on talk shows, write books, go on speaking tours and get rich. A public official in our city was accused of stealing some equipment from the city. He denied it. When he was faced with actual evidence and had no choice but to admit it, the daily newspaper headline said he had "recovered his memory." A lie is no longer a lie, it is a "lapse of memory."

Considering my childhood and the condition of the world and our planet Earth today, is it any wonder I was attracted to a belief system, a spirituality, that embraces a loving, forgiving God? On my refrigerator door is this phrase: "To forgive is to set a prisoner free, and discover the prisoner was me." It is said that Gandhi, falling to the ground after being struck by a bullet that killed him, called out, "I love you." And Jesus, dying on the cross, cried out, "Father, forgive them, for they know not what they do." I believe that the power of one loving person impacts the world to a greater degree than ten thousand angry people. Someone said, "We are not human beings having a spiritual experience, we are spiritual beings having a human experience."

These beliefs tie in with metaphysical doctrine. It has also been referred to as New Age. However, these beliefs have been practiced for thousands of years and encompass many spiritual traditions. The premise is that the spirit of God is within everyone and that God is that spirit. Just as the rays of the sun spread out far and wide to warm and heal and shed their light on everyone and everything, they are still the sun. We are like the sun's rays, each in our human body, seeming to be separate, yet we are still God. We may have never met, yet spiritually, what happens to you happens to me. When you feel hatred, I am affected by your hatred. When you feel love, I am affected by your love. When one person forgives, ten thousand people are forgiven. And here is a beautiful thought, shared by a profoundly spiritual woman, a thought which depicts the impact we have on our planet. "If you pick up a pebble on the beach you have changed the universe." Our acts, thoughts and feelings are not isolated events.

A spiritual young man spent many hours in daily meditation. One day he asked his guru why there are wars. The guru responded that perhaps the disciple caused the wars. "But how is it I cause wars?" he asked. "I have no conflicts. I have not even raised my voice since who knows when." The guru said, "Are you saying you no longer have any anger in you?" Said the disciple, "Well yes, I sometimes have angry thoughts. Who does not?" The guru responded, "Then you cause the wars."

Some will say that this is all well and good but how can we forgive someone who has committed incest, other sexually abusive acts or equally heinous crimes?

How can we forgive someone who has broken our heart or forever changed our life? It is because forgiveness is for you, not the perpetrator. You do not have to go to the perpetrator and say you forgive him or her. Nor do you have to confront them with your anger, grief and rage.

As a psychotherapist, I realize my patients cannot usually move directly to forgiveness. They are angry and sad about being violated and betrayed. They are grieving the loss of a childhood they wanted and deserved. They are resentful that, as adults, they often are not able to sustain loving, nurturing relationships. Many are angry at God. It takes many months to experience the full range of feelings, most of which were blocked. One therapeutic tool is psychodrama. They will choose someone in a group to act as their perpetrator. Once they have expressed all their sadness and anger toward the surrogate perpetrator they are asked, "What did you really want?" Tearfully, they always respond, "I just wanted to be loved." From that point on, their lives begin to open up. Their energy increases, they experience a greater capacity for love, their relationships are healthier and more stable, even their health improves.

It has been scientifically proven that negative thoughts and emotions create toxic energy which, when unreleased, lead to health problems. At a recent Mind/Body Medicine seminar, several physicians stated that hostility is a major factor in the development of cancer and heart disease. One of my patients, in her thirties, had a near fatal heart attack. She was carrying long held anger and resentment toward her mother, who had virtually abandoned her during her childhood. I stressed that it seemed her very life depended on her being able to forgive and that forgiveness was for her, not her mother. We explored other losses and pain in her life and then, in the psychodrama group, she was able to release her pent-up anger, pain and sadness. Additionally, she was shown how to meditate and make friends with her heart, using attention to the heart and soothing words. Several weeks later she saw her doctor and was told her blood pressure was significantly lower than it had been.

During a spirituality workshop, we were told to go out in the forest or by the lake and (1) make a list of those we had not forgiven and what they had done to us; (2) list three benefits to our forgiving that person; (3) list what lessons we had learned from that person regarding the situation; (4) if we were to forgive this person, what is the next action we would have to take? For example, if your spouse was an alcoholic who walked out on you, the next action you might have to take is resolving your fear of getting into a new relationship; (5) how did you contribute to allowing the situation to occur? Another day we made a list of all the things for which we had not forgiven ourselves. It was astonishing how many of our responses paralleled our previous list. For example, one man listed he had not forgiven his mother, father, two ex-wives and an ex-girlfriend for not loving him the way he wanted to be loved. With his second list he came to realize he had never really forgiven himself for not being more self-loving. He smoked, worked 70 hour weeks, ate too much of the wrong kind of foods and did not exercise. Once he became willing to forgive himself for not being more self-loving he quit smoking, worked fewer hours, started an exercise program and lost weight. He began learning how to love himself and, miraculously, people who were more self-loving started coming into his life.

And so it seems we have come almost full circle, from the small town where I grew up, where I learned to fear God, where I learned to climb trees and where I learned to swim and fish and run, to a year ago, when I attended a workshop in the Catskill Mountains. I remember how deep the snow was and how cold was the air. My spirit reminder, the wind, was there, whipping the snow in an upward flow, blending the clouds, the sky, the heavens into vortexes. This is when I finally found an anchor, a "name" to give my own brand of spirituality—the Natural Way. Ed gave me my natural name, Wolf Spirit Woman. The entire setting seemed spiritual, yet I was not prepared for the experience I had during the naming ceremony. It was very dark. Ed was singing and drumming. About halfway through the ceremony I began to feel the resonance of Ed's voice vibrating in my spine. Suddenly I felt as though Ed and I were one and then that the drum and I were one. Within seconds, I experienced that I was Ed and I was the drum, and everyone in the room was one and that we were all one with the universe. It was as though I had no body. This lasted for perhaps ten to twenty seconds. I'm not sure because time no longer existed. I am forever grateful for this wonderful experience and others that have since followed.

And so we return to the original question, "Is God all forgiving?" Using the premise that we are all one in the spirit, it is really up to each of us what the answer is. We are God—we are God's answer. We can condemn the inequity without condemning the person, believing that anyone who does anything unloving is not aware, at the spirit level, of what they are doing; otherwise they wouldn't do it. To commit harmful acts is to deny our spirit self. It is to deny we are all brothers and sisters and children of God. And the pathway to freedom and empowerment is to set the prisoner free, and discover the prisoner was me.

When woman is prevented from being a spiritual leader, this is a loss of a great resource. This taboo poses a dilemma for me. I want to believe that the old time tribal way had most of the answers because of their astonishing track record. They are to be commended, yet no one person or no one way is perfect, in my opinion. I wish I could be wrong. It would be sort of like the movies if one person was perfect or a system was perfect.

Modern Natural Way people do not restrict woman from spiritual leadership. Many who follow this path are women and consider any such restriction as vestiges of macho male domination that led to more wars than it ever led to harmony. Natural Way people encourage woman to take on the mantle of leadership to bring balance back into the human environment and two legged created society. Balance, which is natural, needs to come back to this planet.

Are all people equal in this religion? All people are equal regarding gender, race, heredity and material possession. They begin equal, but I think that they can lose or increase their "equality" as they progress or digress upon their chosen trail of life. I do not want to be misconstrued or not understood because of this statement or opinion. In all ways that do not prepare for our spiritual life, I believe that we must constantly strive to ensure equality. But when it comes to the record that is kept within the Disk of Life, I believe that beings distance themselves from others. It is not a race but there is a difference between those who strive to uphold and live harmonic values and those who just do not care, or worse, those who attempt to circumvent values for their own selfish satisfaction and greed, corruption and possession. In the spirit world I do not believe these types will be equal to those who sought and championed harmony.

How is sex viewed in the religion? The Native people were quite modest. Petroglyphs and winter counts did not exhibit any degree of sexuality as one would find in *Playboy* magazines or related representation from the dominant society. I remember the old timers when they used to dance in pow wows. They were so conscious of even their bare skin and therefore wore long underwear that was dyed orange, light brown or rust colored. The picture of Black Elk praying up on Harney Peak shows him in such fashion. Hilda Neihardt told me that he was very modest and extremely conscious about appearing in bare skin before her and her sister, Enid.

The following is the main portion of a letter that I sent to a group of well meaning and enthusiastic people that espouse the Natural way. They republished this letter in their newsletter.

A comment re nudity in ceremony. Indians were extremely modest and I believe their values worked out quite well. No alcohol, no drugs for centuries and that resulted in a pristine hemisphere. Whites have a tendency to appropriate sexism, porno stores, *Playboy*, movies, art, etc. Contrariwise, indigenous winter counts and petroglyphs were devoid of any such comparable sexuality. When you are in ceremony, the issue is beseechment, acknowledgement, thanksgiving, spiritual contact or a combination thereof. Detraction, which nudity can induce, is not, is not what the spirit world welcomes. In fact, in powerful yuwipi ceremonies, any form of detraction and the spirits hold back. See *Mother Earth Spirituality*, the Yuwipi ceremony. This has been my experience. Also, you must remember that probably at present most of the spirits, if not all, are former two leggeds that once walked this land and were familiar with the particular ceremony you are conducting. Pioneers certainly were not and were hostile toward Native spiritual form: therefore I doubt if these spirits will come in. I haven't experienced any yet.

I don't want to get into a big debate over this but think it is worth passing on. Everything discussed re spirituality is but mere supposition. It is all Mystery but we can certainly piece together practical and positive thought. Many Indians are reluctant to work with the white man and woman in these areas because they believe that the ceremonies will be altered considerably by white values. Nudity and hallucinogens are two areas that are not desired. The Native American church (peyote) is but a small number in comparison to the much larger numbered traditional believers of the various tribes. I have also seen lonely men advocate nudity associated with the lodge and this is not the reason for ceremony. Hugging after and before, especially when scantily clad is not done at traditional ceremonies. We had a lonely volunteer fireman that would always wait for an attractive girl to come out of the lodge and he would walk up and put a big embrace on them. We had to tell him to quit it and he never came back. We all felt better that he was gone.

Native people are quite practical. We obviously reproduced and had a great deal of love in our whole extended families. But we can see a separation when it comes to ceremony. I do not mind mixed ceremony but I want some clothes on when I am so involved. It is much less distraction. Distraction is an important word when it comes to having the spirits come in. In time, as Mockingbirds & Rainbows pass on, they will have the "key" (knowledge) to come into ceremony. I do not believe that we die and then sit at the right hand of God and suddenly receive all knowledge. I think that we take with us only what we have put in. The Great Spirit has shown me a simple computer disk that tells me that. It is blank and you add to it. It can grow considerably or stay quite vacant like many human minds. Knowledge is powerful and I want to take much with me. But you have to work for it. Right now, though, it is a very modest valued group of spirits that we who do ceremony are dealing with so I hope my words have some depth for you.

Who supposedly wrote the books of authority in the religion? As stated earlier, there are no books of authority on Natural Way spirituality. As time moves on there will be an accumulation of material written about experiences, opinions and suppositions. I hope that will happen and expect that it will. I doubt if there will ever be one book of authority, however. I hope that no such book is created and relied upon. I think that much strife, needless dogma, endless interpretations and even wars could result. Maybe it would divert people from studying Nature and that diversion would not be good.

Is doctrine in your church set in stone or is it changing? Nature's functions are always reliable. Nature's truths are "set in stone." How Nature reacts cannot be calculated, however, and she always reveals new truths, new happenings and new observations. Interesting observations will happen as this Natural Way spirituality continues to grow. What new revelations will technology hold for us? Calamities and world changes will certainly have their impact. It will be something when contact from outer space happens. Rationalizing and free choice creations of the Great Spirit will probably be as excited as we will be. A lot of "set in stone" proclamations will no doubt crumble.

We are taught to believe that any contention which believes outer space beings may exist is ludicrous and preposterous. But I believe quite the opposite when I consider the make up of Nature and the formation of our own solar system.

If we ascribe to the "big bang" theory, which most scientists accept, we will first consider the formation or the beginning of our planet. We will also consider the formation of our star, the sun, as well. Astronomers contend that stars have beginnings and they also die. Our sun is predicted to burn out in time and some say that it will first swallow the closest planets including the Earth before this event happens. Let us imagine swirling stardust and gases before this solar system began. These materials gathered into enough intensity that the sun was born and the outer masses became planets. Immediately after the formation, the planets were nothing but molten mass much like the inner core of the Earth today.

Nature demonstrates that repetition occurs in creation. Nature shows that it duplicates and duplicates in pattern. Each species has the same formative process. There is even a pattern within the same genus, class and species. When stars are born, I believe that they have the same beginning process as our sun once experienced. Why would the beginning of other suns (stars) be any different? There are billions of stars out in space. Some are larger, others are smaller than our sun. It is unreasonable for me to believe that our sun had a different formation and is the only one out there with planets rotating around it. The other stars surely have their planets which would be more numerous than there are stars if star formation follows the same formative pattern. Mathematically, it would be impossible for there not to be life on many of those planets when we consider the sheer numbers of planets and each with a life force, its own sun, emanating life-giving energy. Each sun (star) has been designed to sustain life.

Why haven't we been able to see these planets? It is simple, the light from the star we are observing covers up the planets. Our telescopes are not yet that capable but it is only a matter of time before technology will find a way to see through the overpowering light. In time, we will actually have contact with other inhabitants from outer space. Maybe some will be more advanced than we are and will have had other contacts. Yes, a lot of "set in stone" proclamations will no doubt crumble.

How strongly and carefully is your spoken or written word followed today? There exist many beautiful phrases that are spoken. "Mitakuye Oyasin" is an example. "We are all related. We are all relatives. All our relations." This is the meaning of this powerful statement that allows one to visualize harmony and being one with all entities and creation.

In this time span, a new awakening has begun. Technology has become the vehicle for a new visualization, preservation and dissemination of ongoing knowledge. Communication technology is allowing a wide scope of new observation, which was never within reach of past generations who established and maintained society, our laws and religion. People travel. Their communication and interchange with others throughout the world has expanded along with technological enhancement. For many, direct observation is diminishing a dependence on only the so-called spoken or written word of ancient scripture. Where this new thought has been allowed to flourish, harmony is more evident. It has proven healthy for the environment, the world as a tribe and for the Generations Unborn. People gathered worldwide and prayed for peace and communication during the great Harmonic Convergence. Soon, thereafter, the "Wall of Untruth," the Berlin Wall, came crumbling down.

The Communist Empire which repressed Truth, no longer was viable as a world power and the citizens within began to enjoy more freedoms.

Whenever a written word has great strength, its truth will live on. Zealous religious fanatics solely dependent upon the scriptural word should remain calm and not get so "shook up" because some citizens of this free country are aspiring to observe unwritten truths. If the written word has a truth, it should and will endure on that strength alone just like a naturally endowed truth. Quit worrying or agonizing over some of us who seek to broaden and extend ourselves into what the Creator has created. It is still a free country and we have that right unless fanatics change the laws.

A detractor may argue that there is more crime, more homeless, more dejection and immorality, etc., in this time span. I believe that this evidence is a result of an accumulation of the past untruths which were allowed to flourish primarily because the real sources could be hidden, obscured or falsely attributed to other elements. War is a good example. It was always blamed on the other side and never attributed to the grandiose intentions of the war-mongers who have always sought additional power for themselves. They shroud their motives in patriotism and foment prejudice against those whom they want to invade to fool the youth to become the cannon fodder. Another example is within employment. A significant portion of our nation's high crime rate is because of the demoralization of qualified minority people who have strived to comply with what they were promised through education, patriotism and perseverance and yet, over and over they are rejected because of nepotism and the "good-ol'-boy" system rampant in this country. In time, they become demoralized and have to take menial work that their bosses' sons are much more qualified for in comparison. Their young lose faith in the social system. The youth fall into crime when there exists little hope to ever be successful.

Is our present situation of social deterioration a result of minorities, the poor and immigrants? Is all of this unravelling, chaos and mounting suffering the result of people seeking some spiritual answers or satisfaction divergent from established and structured religions? I hardly think so. Except for being within the North American Indian tribes, this philosophy has not returned long enough to make such an impact. The present situation is because of the accumulated maze of interwoven untruths finally surfacing from the old way of thinking that claimed to be dependent on the written word. There is just too much untruth being exposed.

This land is so saturated with untruth that it can no longer be hidden or buried. Knowledge from Creation, along with intercommunication among the increasing numbers who are seeking a truthful society, will eventually bring down the Wall of Untruth within this land! Nature will bring it down in due time with great calamity if human continues to allow it to stand.

* * * *

Government and Society

I love a people who have never raised a hand against me, or stolen my property, where there was no law to punish for either.

I love a people who live and keep what is there own without locks and keys.

I love a people who have never fought a battle with white men, except on their own ground.

* * * *

How does your religion affect government?
Is the religion politically active?
What are the moral standards of the religion?
What wars or conflicts has your religion been involved in?
What stance does your religion take on recent social issues: abortion, euthanasia, the death penalty, pre-marital sex, unwed mothers, gay rights, feminism, birth control, etc.?

* * * *

Some religions have had a positive effect upon government, some have had a negative effect. Actually, most rational people would probably agree that religions have exerted both good and bad influences upon governments, upon society. We do know that indigenous people had much more time to consider the spiritual. Gary Presland of Australia allows us the following:

The Hunter Gatherer Lifestyle

"Like indigenous peoples in all other parts of Australia, the clans in the Port Phillip region were hunters and gatherers, the oldest way of making a living known to the human race. Hunting and gathering remained the *only* economic model from the beginning of the evolution of our species, about three million years ago, until about 7000 or 8000 years ago, when farming first began. Until quite recently it was considered by scholars to be a time- consuming and unproductive way of fulfilling basic needs and one which had led the hunter-gatherer into a nomadic exis- tence, constantly chasing resources. However, recent studies on those few peoples who still practise this way of life (including some Aboriginal groups of North and Central Australia) have shown that in fact most soci- eties can satisfy all their needs easily with the equivalent of a three and a half day working week. The Port Phillip region had plentiful resources and it is likely that Koories in the area were working a thirty hour week. This meant that a good deal of time was available for leisure, for carrying out maintenance of tool kits and for attending to spiritual and clan busi- ness."[1]

Indigenous people, even those who farmed and were more seden- tary, did not seek excess materialism in comparison to modern members of dominant society who rate a man or woman according to how much they own and accumulate. Look around your home and look at what all you have accumulated. None of this will you take into the spirit world. Was it really worth all of the trouble and tribulation? And when you leave your home, you have to lock it all up tightly and then have to worry about it while you are away. The seeking of meaningless material pos- session keeps many people from rewarding, spiritual contemplation.

My friend, Medicine Story has this to say;

"Humankind has created all of the problems which it now faces, and humankind can solve them, if we but will. The same genius that has created weapons of incredible destruction and has probed beyond the earth to the very stars could certainly find a way to bring the peoples of earth together for their own survival.

"....People speak of political problems, economic problems, sociological problems, psychological problems, and everyone has a pet theory of how to solve his or her own pet problems. Those are just bandages on the sores of a diseased body. A deeper remedy must be found for the inner cause of the disease. The disease is caused by oppressive and hurtful social systems. We do not see the fundamentally oppressive nature of these systems because all of society teaches and fosters basic philosophical and spiritual errors.

"At the deepest level the disease is spiritual. Spirituality as I perceive it is simply the relationship of all things in the universe. Instead of thinking only of ourselves, we must consider our families, our children, our unborn generations, our planet and all the beings who share it with us, as well as the star-beings throughout the cosmos, and the connections among all of these.

"Where it must all begin is with trust. Unless we trust that the Creation is good, that it works, that we are good, and that we can learn to live in a good way in this Creation, we give ourselves over to force or despair. When we do not trust, we resort to force for protection, to police and armies, and we set up a counterforce. But once we have this trust, we need only to discover the way that Creation works, find the path and follow it. It is the way of harmony, the way of cooperation with natural law. Fortunately, we have many guides who have followed that path before us and many who are following it now. And we have the guide of the heart within us.

"There is an old native saying that every step we take upon the Earth Mother should be as a prayer. Now, a prayer is just a way of becoming really conscious, really tuning in to all the relationships of everything in existence. To make every step a prayer is simply to be totally conscious in every act we do. Most of us spend our waking hours half asleep, only dimly aware of our feelings, to say nothing of what is going on in the world and of the connections between things.

"Whatever we do has a meaning and an effect. We can ask ourselves, if I am really conscious, what effect will this action have upon Creation? How will it effect me, affect my family and my community? How will it affect the planet? How will it affect the future and the generations yet to come?"[2]

Recently a skull, estimated to be three million years old, was declared to be the ancestor of human. No doubt, this early ancestor, if it was an ancestor, was originally "programmed," so to speak, to adapt and survive within its environment. Maybe this being existed for several million years and did not endanger the environment. In the long run he and she were more intelligent than we are if intellect is to be measured in accord with planetary preservation. If early two legged evolved to our present stage, then somewhere along the way it stopped to ponder or wonder about a higher force. It also started to branch out from its naturally guided pack, flock, herd, pod or colony of congregation into a reasoning or rationalizing form of pack guidance. Eventually the birth of government began. Maybe religion came soon thereafter.

Let us suppose that early two leggeds did evolve into increased rationalization and somewhere disconnected themselves from the natural "programming" that non-rationalizing animals possess. Further along in time, humans spread to other continents. The development of differing governments, religions and values began.

Scientists believe that two leggeds learned to use fire and tools. During this century, scientists have declared classifications of ancient two leggeds according to their degree of intelligence or ability to demonstrate the use of primitive tools. There were two major classifications, Neanderthal and Cro-Magnon. Cro-Magnon appeared later but was believed to exist during the latter stages of Neanderthal. Being presumably more intelligent, Cro-Magnon could have exterminated Neanderthal or maybe carried diseases that Neanderthal had no resistance to. An example would be a disease like smallpox, which wiped out Indian tribes. Remains of this classification (Neanderthal) have been abundant in the regions of Europe. It is interesting to note; Neanderthal evidence has not been found in North or South America. The remains of ancient humans that have been found in the Americas, are closer to Cro-Magnon. Did Cro-Magnon originate in North America or South America and then migrate to displace the Neanderthal? This observation does not set to well with pompous, Euro-centric minded people.

Most archaeologists declare that humans crossed the land bridge from Asia to America via the Bering Strait during the Pleistocene Age or Ice Age. They assume this event would have taken place around 12,000 years ago. This theory is universally accepted among the majority of archaeologists. I believe that Nature duplicates and repeats itself, over and over. 24,000 years ago, the same similar Ice Age circumstances could have happened and before that time and so on. Humans had plenty of opportunities to cross from either direction. Recently, some archaeologists and historians have challenged this initial entry assertion and realistically state that an intelligent human was here long before the last time the Bering Strait was dry enough to be crossed. The author of *American Genesis,* Dr. Jeffrey Goodman, states in his notes, "The test of any new theory is how it stands up to the new data that comes in after it has been proposed. One of the key themes of this book is that modern man was in the Americas at dates, *much, much older* than the traditional 12,000-year-old date associated with the Bering Bridge Entry model."[3]

"American Genesis argues for man being here at least 100,000 years ago ...so it is comforting to note that on April 22, 1981, the Associated Press (Toronto) reported on a new 150,000 year-old dating for mammoth hunting man in the Americas."[4]

When remains of mastodons were found in association with charcoal remains nearby, often the bones were neatly stacked. Did the mastodons have such a "programmed" ritual? Once a mastodon was killed by ancient man, I think it would be quite practical that many hunters would gather to consume and preserve as much of it as possible. A mastodon would be quite a task regarding butchering. If you are at all familiar with killing a large animal and have taken part in the resultant butchering, in my opinion, it would be an ordinary procedure to place aside or stack large bones to economize the butchering site. Time and the resultant spoilage of meat would be an important factor. What is the point? The point is, two leggeds left conclusive evidence beyond their necessary cooking fires to give credence to the theory that they were here in the Americas much longer than most leading scientists give them credit for.

In another section of his notes, Dr. Goodman relates, "Dr. William Irving, an archaeologist with the University of Toronto, told the press that stone tools and broken animal bones found along the Old Crow River in the Yukon were 150,000 years old. ...The 150,000 year dating was confirmed by the bones of an extinct species of lemming common there."[5]

"I have always maintained that *"One-Way Only "* signs were never posted upon the Bering land bridge. Maybe humans crossed from east to west. No doubt, the strait was traveled in both directions during the centuries it was open. There is conclusive proof, however, that homo-sapiens were roaming North America over 12,000 years ago and many other authorities like Dr. Goodman hold that they were here over 100,000 years ago. He also notes Dr. James Bischoff of the U.S. Geological Survey in Menlo Park, California, stated that he used the uranium-thorium dating technique to get an absolute date of 200,000 years on the the late Louis Leakey site at Calico Hills, California."[6] I used to fly a learned professor around while working my way through law school at the University of South Dakota. Dr. John Bryde, author of *Modern Indian Psychology,* was a valuable teacher for my road. He contends that Native Americans trace back to 200,000 years.

When the Pilgrims first landed, they discovered a people living a distinct and different way of life. Since these newcomers were involved with a life or death situation, it behooved them to become friends with these people who would later be called Indians. The first observable act from the Indians' point of view was to watch these light-skinned Pilgrims steal one of their caches of corn. The Indians could have thought of these newcomers as thieves but being used to natural observation, they did not react to these takers as thieves. Remember, these east coast Indians did not have a value system that placed a high regard for possession or marked geographic boundaries denoting ownership of the land. It is possible that they thought that these Pilgrims were simply hungry or might be starving. The Pilgrims, on the other hand, had their point of view. They wrote down that the "Lord had provided for them." Different people have different reactions, different points of view, obviously. This historical comparison helps us to broaden our understanding. Viewpoint, judgement or value evaluation can have various interpretations.

The value system of different societies can come up with completely differing points of view. In this example, one could accuse the other of thievery, and throughout history, people went to war over such matters. Can you imagine Indians landing in England or up the Rhine River in Germany in those times? What would have been the reaction of the local populace viewing Indians appropriating a silo of oats or rye for food? In these two situations, one actual and one imagined, which value system would arrive at a closer verdict of the truth? "Those people must have been pretty hungry," might have been a fairly honest observation and maybe more accurate than, "those damned thieves are taking our grain." No war was the result. Harmonic friendship took place instead, albeit short lived.

The first Pilgrims remembered Indians saving their lives but when new settlers came to the eastern shores, they were taught how to survive by their own kind. The later arrivals might have heard stories about the friendship of the heathens who were camped close by, but when it came to expansion into new lands, appreciation of past deeds of honor were forgotten. The Pilgrim's European value system was too overpowering to learn differently, because in a short time they marked boundaries of ownership and began to annihilate these new found friends who initially saved European lives. Religion was used to ease their conscience. After all, these Heathens were not "chosen by God" to remain upon these lands.

Early indigenous society did not place a high value on materialistic acquisition, therefore, the foregoing historical event of true humanitarianism was made possible. Such a tragedy for humanity that early immigrants were not intelligent enough to recognize such charity. They were too steeped in their belief system that rigidly taught, "our way is the only right way." In light of this example, it is important to note that western material values should be introspected or lightened if one is considering the Natural Way as a spiritual path. If we are to consider the meaning of government then it must be recognized that values will determine our judgement as to what is government. We have learned how early native values allowed them a more humanistic perception and conduct towards others. How did Indigenous Spirituality affect their concept of government?

Let us look at some more history. In time, the colonists came to this land in a steady procession. Soon they were at odds with the British government, mainly the King's attempts to control their lives. When the Iroquois were still formidable as a military power, they were wooed by emissaries of both sides in the fight for early America between the British and the colonists. Fortunately for the entire world, perceptive men, the likes of Benjamin Franklin, Thomas Jefferson and Thomas Paine, became familiar with the early eastern coast tribes. Interestingly, these men were not bound up in zealous or eccentric religious beliefs. Maybe this characteristic of independence allowed them to be more observant than the average colonist of the times. As emissaries to the Iroquois Nation, Franklin and Paine were astounded to see Iroquoian Indians individually stand up in public assembly within their tribes. They saw that tribal members could speak freely to influence the social decision process. They also recognized that the native people had elected representatives and their equivalence of a king, their chiefs, were elected and not born into a position of governing power. Divine right to govern according to heredity had no place among nature-influenced people. No tribal member was considered lower or higher, nor were there levels of social or acquisition status. A landed gentry did not exist because the Indians considered the air and the waters as unowned, and the earth was equally immune to ownership. No priesthood existed, nor was there a nobility. Medicine or spiritual seers were not in league with any favored group and were readily accessible by all tribal members. Many other examples of democracy were also observed and well noted, except for suffrage. Iroquoian women voted and even had the additional power to recall leaders, but this finding, along with substantial evidence supporting matriarchy was omitted from the Bill of Rights and Constitution which would be drawn up later. The majority of these new observations, however, became the pattern for equality and justice within a free government which was about to evolve. Thomas Paine was so moved by his new knowledge that he went back to France to instill this new democracy into the French revolution.

Charles Van Doren's book, *A History of Knowledge*, has a serious omission concerning probably, the most important subject within his book—the history of democracy. An acclamation by the San Francisco Chronicle is also on the cover: "Fascinating... No less than the summation of the entire experience of the human race from the birds-eye view of a tremendous encyclopedic intelligence."[7] In my opinion, here we have the greatest gift to humankind and the givers are totally ignored because of Euro-centric supremacy that makes it so difficult for themselves to arrive at what is pure, factual truth. In the realm of spirituality, the errors are even more gross. I would like to allow Mr. Van Doren the benefit of the doubt however. He may have been misled by previous authors or had not yet had access to Jack Weatherford's historical findings. Hopefully, his (Van Doren's) later works will explore this new information.

Did the spirituality of the red people play the developing role in their own government before the colonists arrived? In my opinion, there is no question that Natural Way observation, together with respect and association with created nature, was the major influence. I highly doubt any degree of influence came somehow from ancient Rome or Greece.

How did this gift to humankind evolve? How was it discovered? What governmental form did the early colonists have? What was their concept of democracy? Did they have the freedom that the Indians had? These are important questions if we are going to realistically probe more deeply into a relationship with democratic government and resultant social structures.

This gift, democracy, which came from the North American Indian must have been derived from their closeness and observance of Nature. The idea that democracy came from the English Magna Carta is as foolish and erroneous as stating that you could walk only one direction across the Bering Strait land bridge that once existed. To say that it came from the slave states of Greece and Rome is equally erroneous. Yet our history books and encyclopedias are still teaching this Euro-centric propaganda. If that contention is true, then where was this Greco-Roman spawned democracy when the colonists first came to these shores? They had no concept of the democratic precepts which the original inhabitants were already practicing!

The North American Indians already had democracy and were thoroughly practicing and employing it. The colonists knew nothing about it and were not practicing it. The colonists viewed the Indians in their government and social structures. Suddenly the colonists were enlightened but, of course, not by the Indians. Somehow, by "divine inspiration," the colonists reinvented democracy. Years later we read from a proclaimed, widely published white man author and history scholar how it really did have its beginnings in Greece and Rome and absolutely no contribution of the Indians is mentioned.

Back in history, Natural Way spirituality was the basis for democratic government but European immigrants could not shed the virus of untruth which they brought over with them to believe this fact. The old values that caused them to migrate from their own lands have penetrated deeply to corrode and encrust natural truth. This <u>disguise, deception and untruth still prevails in government all the way from a Housing Commission to the highest office or judiciary seat in the land.</u> Elected officials have to run through a charade that keeps those who worship materialism in power. Their laws, decisions, appointments, exposures and scandals reflect that value system. In time, these precepts will either change or we will simply lose the planet.

What would be the function of government if Natural Way concepts and values were to be embraced? It would be to acknowledge that a truthful people did develop a workable government that did not tolerate any form of dishonesty. Iroquois women had the power to recall elected delegates, called *sachems*, for any such infraction. There existed definite sanctions and punishments severe enough to keep violations to a minimum. Wrongdoers became the victims, not the people as a whole. Wrongdoers were severely punished and not coddled in luxury confinement, as is the case with modern offenders who have held high political or corporate positions and a record of excessive material gain, regardless of how much damage they have done to the country. A moral government can evolve if the people can bring themselves to an exemplary state of awareness and have discipline as well, but it must be fairly administered with absolutely no favoritism as we see and experience now. Knowledge exists that can bring this country to a higher state. It happened before. It helps if the society believes that also, for violating a real truth, they will pay dearly as individuals in a spirit world that lies beyond.

Somewhere back in time this "right programming" was discovered and applied. In order to connect government with the point of view of early indigenous thought and influence, different values must be considered. These values must be centered on unbendable truth and be earth focussed. They would have to veer away abruptly from all forms of disguise or deception, which is so evident now in our government, law and judiciary. Some way, the sense of ownership by human will have to be confronted and reviewed. "This is communism and it (communism) didn't work," will be the first pessimistic statement of detraction. Communism was not associated with the spiritual or truthful focus and the absence of spirituality was a major reason this political idea was not successful.

"How could this possibly work out? It would be too drastic of a change. People won't stand for it!" I can hear the cry already. Those few in power will not want to stand for it, but if the situation merits needed change in light of drastic and severe suffering for the masses, it *will* change and possibly rather quickly. The dissatisfied masses will make it happen. Technology and its offspring, communication, will expedite its happening. The masses are becoming exposed to information on a daily basis. I strongly recommend that serious effort be applied now wherein a peaceful attempt can be employed rather than drastic measures taken before a riotous, frustrated public. In time, individuals who exist to appease the chosen few will no longer be allowed into political power. I am optimistic that beneficial change can happen, thanks to technology which is now establishing a new awareness among the people.

It has taken over two centuries for Americans to actually know their true democratic birthright and the majority still do not know these obvious facts. Who was responsible for the highest state of government that exists upon the planet? A freely elected government with inherent rights of individual freedom; such was the gift. Democracy, the greatest gift to humankind came from the North American Indian! Read *Indian Givers* by Jack Weatherford. In this country, I believe we can say that spirituality (religion) did affect government.

Is the religion politically active? Those who follow the Natural Way are concerned about politics but not to the extent that they are voting in blocks, nor devising methods to insure their way of thinking will control the legislative process. They vote, pay taxes, abide by laws and will even support political candidates of their choice. So far, from what I have observed, they will not scheme to pack a school board or support one-issue candidates. They generally suspect such candidates. The separateness of church and the state, so far, seems to be respected among the people of the Natural Way.

I am quite fearful of removing protections that uphold the separation of church and state. American Indians suffered serious effects from a government that conspired with a religion to destroy our culture and spirituality. To take children away from parents and cast them into cold institutions in the name of God gives me some strong reservations against such thought and practice. Along these lines, I cannot understand why churches do not pay taxes, especially since they now directly meddle and influence large voting blocks during election time. If they were honestly neutral then some argument could be made for less taxation. Now that they openly come out and promote their right wing candidates, it is time that they be treated like other non-religious institutions in regard to being taxed. Congress is attempting to cut back on expenditures by eliminating programs for the poor; by taxing the churches, this money can restore needed poverty programs.

Thomas Jefferson was strongly influenced when he observed the North American Indian tribes enjoying a sense of freedom nowhere to be found in the Old World. He was an intense scholar and knew the horrors of Old World abuses and devised safeguards against them. "He insisted on a "wall of separation" to prevent the church from using the state, or vice versa. He was proud of his authorship of Virginia's statue of religious freedom and had it cited on his tombstone. It begins: "No man shall be compelled to frequent or support any religious worship, place or ministry whatever...."[8]

Spirituality has proven that it can foster truthfulness, morals and ethics. Every politician who runs for office claims these standards. They soon forget these claims once elected, it seems. The American politician has a history of supporting those who put him in power. Ethics, morality, bravery, courage and truthfulness have virtually nothing to do with how the politician actually gets into office. He either accumulates an excessive amount of material gain or he allows himself to be controlled by powers of self perpetuation. It is basically that simple and clear. The appearance of morality, ethics, etc. is said to be a standard but in reality it is a smoke screen. Immediate gain has usually been the basis of political decisions. Focus for the future has too often taken a back seat.

The "American Dream" is now no longer realistic. The resources that allowed this philosophy have been depleted by the past generations who had absolutely no concept of "Living for the Generations Unborn." Other than agricultural resources, we are lying to ourselves if we deny that our natural resources are fairly well exhausted. Beyond this iron-clad fact is a related value, productivity. The Asian countries are far more productive and can out produce us any day in the week. They have little regard for fair wage standards and even employ child labor but it must be admitted that the average Asian worker is quite productive. Japan, especially, has treated sea life harshly and shown little regard for environmental standards when it comes to production. North America is becoming a service oriented society, rather than a mass producer for world consumption, which it used to be. This sobering fact is not an "un-American" finding. Balance of payments, competitive productivity and the thinning resources are proof enough.

Maybe it will not be a political system or maybe it will not be the system's leaders who will bring forth essential change in the future. Maybe it will be the entire focus of the tribe that can bring it forth. Maybe politics will become so corrupt that the people will no longer have faith in such a system. They themselves will tear down the "Wall of Untruth" in this land.

What are the moral standards of the religion? That which will bring back greater harmony to all related creations and of course, an ongoing determination to save the planet.

In the old indigenous system which existed before dominant culture exerted its influence, rigid tribal codes kept law and order. The moral standards of the people were also fortified by a belief system that included an afterlife. I believe that this statement would especially hold true for those tribes that had the power to conduct spirit-calling ceremonies. These ceremonies are quite convincing that a spirit world lies beyond.

It was not the influence of ceremony that preserved and fostered moral standards, however. Indigenous perception of created nature seems to be the basis of their primary influence. Their art, customs, song and even their languages are nature symbolized and reflected. Examples of their moral standards can be found in some of the writings of those who were connected with the old tribal ways. Ohiyesa, a Sioux, had the following to say;

"It is said that, in the very early days, lying was a capital offense among us. Believing that the deliberate liar is capable of committing any crime behind the scene of cowardly untruth and double-dealing, the destroyer of mutual confidence was put to death."[9]

On the other hand, Lakota people allowed the possibility of forgiveness, even for killing in retaliation, if the provocation was severe. To kill a harmful liar was an allowance which went a long way in keeping honest conduct among the people. You pushed a person only so far with untruth in Lakota society and they could retaliate.

"Murder within the tribe was a grave offense, to be atoned for as the council might decree, and it often happened that the slayer was called upon to pay the penalty with his own life. He made no attempt to escape or to avoid justice. ...He was thoroughly convinced that all is known to the "Great Mystery," and hence did not hesitate to give himself up, to stand his trial by the old and wise men of the victim's clan. His own family and clan might by no means attempt to excuse or to defend him, but his judges took all the known circumstances into consideration, and if it appeared that he slew in self-defense, or that the provocation was severe, he might be set free after a thirty days' period of mourning in solitude. Otherwise the murdered man's next of kin were authorized to take his life; and if they refrained from doing so, as often happened, he remained an outcast from the clan. A willful murder was a rare occurrence before the days of whiskey and drunken rows, for we were not a quarrelsome people."[10]

An effective check upon the actions and words of the old time Indians, was the belief that they would be accountable by their peers in the Spirit World for all that they said or did. In the old days, natural spirituality was part and parcel of the people.

Let us look at two countries to distinguish their evolution into their present status. We will explore two Asian countries that are very different in thought, religion and values. It will all come back to moral principles or sets of values conceived from spiritual and cultural thought. As a whole, did religion or indigenous choice affect the lives of the people within these two countries, including the present? Can we learn something from their example?

The Philippines and Japan are two countries that are modern examples of European influence versus indigenous practice, culture and the resultant mores. Japan threw out early European influence that had made inroads and divisions for a period of time in the era before the Pilgrims were landing upon North American shores. Japan retained its traditional identity while the Philippines converted significantly to the white man's belief system. The Philippines had numerous natural resources while Japan had few. Which country now is the most stable? Which is the least corrupt and which has the better standard of living? In which country would you feel safer to live, do business or walk the streets alone at night?

Antheaya Koppel, CNN, April 12, 1994, remarked in a news report; "It (Japan) is regarded as one of the safest countries on the earth." Which country has a closer tie to their indigenous or tribal influence?

Where can your country begin in order to have a better government in the sense of a truer realization of democratic government and moral standards? We can begin with new leaders and a new process of selecting a leadership that practices "hard-core" honesty. It is not an impossible task. We certainly have wide ranging technology on our side to inform, expose and educate. These are no longer medieval times so why should we allow destructive medieval values and methods to exist? A few still control just as in medieval days. Their method is still the same. Keep the masses in a stupor and repel any spiritual, religious or cultural thought that might enlighten and inspire the people. In time, maybe sooner than we think, this new ability to gather and share information will demonstrate its powerful effect because the present system is not addressing or even beginning to answer serious, social, national and environmental concerns.

What wars or conflicts has your religion been involved in? Tribes warred and fought in this hemisphere but even in this respect they were different. Their value system also reached into their warfare. Like wolves, they had flowing boundaries. They existed for thousands of years in that state and did not have a record of leaders who attempted or were successful in conquering massive areas of the continent. The Iroquois never had Iroquoian legions that invaded all of North America to establish themselves as rulers. The Sioux had no leaders equivalent to Caesar, Napoleon, Hitler or Alexander, who wept because he thought he had no more lands to conquer.

Tribes in North America did not fight over what would be regarded as a mystery. We only have to look at a portion of the Reformation in Europe to understand how futile it was to fight over dogma and religious domination. "The last great spasm of the Reformation was its worst. The Thirty Years' War, from 1618 to 1648, killed millions in Central Europe and left Germany a wasteland of misery...

"The Thirty Years' War was a human catastrophe. It settled nothing, and it killed uncountable multitudes. One estimate says Germany's population dropped from 18 million to 4 million. Hunger and deprivation followed. Too few people remained to plant fields, rebuild cities, or conduct education or commerce."[11]

Iroquoian, Siouan, Cherokee or Seminole influence did not reach out so far that cities, mountains and geographical reaches far beyond their tribal area reflected their language. Distant places did not bear their names or language except for the Siouan (Sioux). This tribe migrated and left their language across the continent. Missouri, Iowa, Minnesota, Dakota, Kansas and Arkansas were not names as a result of a tribe out to conquer and control. They were on the move because they were attempting to avoid being conquered and controlled.

Indigenous weaponry experienced little change down through the centuries. What indigenous people used for the hunt was sufficient for combat. In Europe, because of the endless wars for acquisition and gain, newer weapons evolved. The European mind became very inventive for better performing weapons to conquer other humans. It has evolved all the way to mass weapons of unimaginable destruction. When the Europeans came to North American shores, a diverse scattering of numerous tribes indicated that no one tribe, or even a few tribes, had dominated the continent through large scale warfare. Among the Indians, tribal warfare was on a much smaller scale and of much shorter durations. Military weaponry among the North American tribes did not evolve or change toward increased killing efficiency because mass destruction was not their main interest. They had no need to evolve beyond the bow or the spear. They evolved in a much different direction than the negativity of war. One of their customs was to ride into combat with little or no weapons and yet attempt to touch the enemy. No such custom existed in Europe.

I believe spirituality was the Native Americans' primary and highest focus. Usually a people's focus is evidence of their direction and interest. Maybe they were content that they had discovered the method, the government and the way of life to coexist within their environment which they related to their Creator. Maybe they no longer had to worry about evolving. They had reached their bliss, quite possibly and were close to being satisfied.

In this modern society, the turn of dominant culture people to Natural Way concepts has happened only recently. They have not yet established a firm enough track record to be judged. Since one of their guiding principles is that they believe in a universal relationship and they appear less covetous of other peoples lands or belongings, I believe that they will be less inclined to go to war. Woman is also well received among these people and her leadership and advice does not go unheeded. Most women exercise great restraint when it comes to making hasty decisions to go off to war. In time, I believe that history will acknowledge that those who espouse Natural Way thinking will be recorded as a peaceful people who sought to avoid war unless their freedom was seriously threatened.

What conflicts has my spirituality been involved in? The environmental issues are probably the major reasons why so many are starting to embrace the Natural Way. Many people are frustrated with the stance of major religious leaders who are avoiding confrontation over major environmental issues.

Paul and Anne Ehrlich, two leading world population scientists, warn us of world leadership indifference. "Yet the signs are also telling us that our society's leaders, with a few outstanding exceptions, do not get the message. For most presidents, prime ministers, and religious leaders, and those who advise them, "business as usual is the goal." They consider the environment just one more problem area kept on the political agenda by special interest groups. Environmental deterioration is viewed as a long-term problem, and foresight is not a prime characteristic of governments or most other social institutions. No agency in the United States is charged with overall assessment or planning for the next decade, let alone the next century."[12]

A half-century ago, Aldo Leopold wrote:

"One of the penalties of an ecological education is that one lives alone in a world of wounds....An ecologist must either harden his shell and make believe that the consequences of science are none of his business, or he must be the doctor who sees the marks of death in a community that believes itself well and does not want to be told otherwise."[13]

What stance does your religion take on recent social issues: abortion, euthanasia, the death penalty, pre-marital sex, unwed mothers, gay rights, feminism, birth control, etc.?

When you have questions on social issues, the more numerous the topics, the more diverse the answers will be from each person questioned. My response will no doubt differ from many people who share the Natural Way perspective. I have attempted to include historical indigenous perspectives, observations and relationship with Nature as my main forms of influence. I also refuse to answer from a "politically correct" perspective regardless of my degree of difference with the view or position of the dominant culture.

Abortion: World population alone justifies abortion in my opinion. Indigenous people had herbs that could prevent conceiving and also could cause abortion. They lived here for thousands of years, much longer than the European has been here and yet they kept their population in check.

Let us look at China. In China, an abortion can be obtained without any legal difficulties. China has had to keep its population in check and one important means has been the allowance of abortion. Japan is another country that readily allows abortions. In the Catholic countries of South America, thousands of orphans roam the streets of the large cities, unwanted and uncared for. This rarely happens in China and Japan.

Euthanasia: Wolves will go off by themselves to die when they become old and feeble. A herd in migration will not wait around for an older or wounded member that would otherwise hold back a necessary migration to better grazing or instinctive birthing or breeding grounds. In Sioux society, there are stories about injured or incapacitated tribal members who remained behind while the tribe or band embarked upon a movement. These members did not want to inconvenience or in some cases, endanger the tribe. Often, older members, who felt that they were a burden to their immediate families, would remove themselves voluntarily. How did they do this? They simply took a walk in a blinding blizzard or fell into a river or swift flowing stream. They removed themselves for the betterment of the tribe. In later years, once the dominant society took control of the native lifestyle by establishing tribal reservations, these old cultural practices were banned by the influence of the new religion that swept the reservations.

Many people fear growing old. Many people fear dying. I believe that once you begin to understand what Mitakuye Oyasin really means, and that you are related to all things which the Creator has created, you will have less fear of going on into the spirit world that lies beyond.

Actually, you come to believe that you do not die after all. Your spirit, simply goes on. There really isn't all that much to be afraid of. Has not the Creator shown so much of its vast creativity in innumerable miracles that are constantly placed before us? Even a mosquito or a lowly ant is a complex marvel if you were to study its inner workings and functions. What about the mysterious manner of electricity or energy transformation from the sun? This is all occasioned and designed by the very Mystery that designed us free, rationalizing, choice making humans. Do you really think that the Creator is going to let us merely die? I highly doubt such an end. We have placed too much knowledge and experiences in our Disks of Life to just fade away. If it were not for some younger children that I am still helping to raise, I would be looking forward to entering the spirit world. I also believe that this Creator, this Great Spirit, is a benevolent God and not an entity to be afraid of. Cheer up, if you are one of those who foolishly fears death.

I do not want to prolong my own death. It is so foolish to lie in a life support system especially if you have lived most of your life and your children are raised. I do not want to leave my earnings to the hospitals and rich doctors. I certainly do not want to be an expense or a burden to my children who are entitled to their own lives. I hope I have the courage and the dignity to be like the old time Indian.

Death penalty: I believe differently than most who follow the Natural Way. Most Natural Way people are against the death penalty. This is my presumption, and in a poll that I submitted, this was the general consensus. I favor the death penalty because the old time Indian had it (death penalty) but modern society is not fair with its use.

There are certain crimes that the death penalty can put an end to, especially if the criminal or perpetrator has a history of repeated offenses. I believe that the fewer the victims, the happier a society can be. Society has a duty to protect its members and an efficient method is to eliminate the source of much sorrow, anguish, despair, terror and fear. Unfortunately, the dominant society is unequal and unfair in meting out the death penalty or severe punishment to all of its citizens. If you are wealthy and have accumulated much, your chances of receiving a death penalty sentence or a life sentence without parole is extremely reduced. For this reason, I would not vote for a death penalty. My vote would be too unfair to the poor and the minorities.

Pre-marital sex: If one chooses a mate and discovers that they are incompatible in regards to their sexuality, it can be an unhappy partnership. I would not want to be in that situation. You are pretty foolish for not discovering your compatibility before you have expanded your relationship.

Unwed mothers: It is better be an unwed mother than to wed someone you are not in harmony with. Many of the animal world raise their young without mates. I am not condoning having children when you are least able to raise them in a proper manner, however. Young women as well as young men should develop a thirst for knowledge and spiritual contemplation before they decide to raise a family. Often, adventure and experiences will help them make decisions to postpone child bearing until later years. With so much worldview information now available, existing families can now inspire higher thoughts by providing an atmosphere that cultivates curiosity, individual philosophy and wonderment.

In Sioux society, there was no such thing as "going steady." Young men would have been laughed at and made fun of if they would choose to hang around a young girl all the time instead of preferring to becoming prepared in the art of hunting and becoming a protective warrior. There were no honoring dances for teen age pregnancies. You would be ridiculed for bearing children too early. Nature would make you pay a hard toll to provide for your offspring, especially if you had no one to hunt for you.

Gay rights: Homosexuality exists. I think that the Great Spirit creates all entities, including homosexuality. I also believe that most are born with this personal preference. It is not of their own choosing, no different than heterosexuality is of the majority's own choosing. It is the way one may come into this world.

Here again I can come back to the Natural Way for an answer. Does homosexuality exist? Who creates what exists? If the Great Spirit created it, how can it be bad? In light of the runaway population explosion occasioned by heterosexuals, homosexuality cannot be blamed for this approaching catastrophe.

In Sioux society, a person who displayed homosexual preference was called a winkte (pronounced wink-teay). Siouxs were quite practical, especially in matters of warfare. If a winkte did not express a profound desire to go forth on war parties or horse stealing expeditions, the winkte would not be forced to go. Why have someone along on a dangerous venture who did not have his heart in the endeavor? It would take considerable daring and risk because the enemy or the owners of coveted horses were also employing their skills and daring to protect themselves and their prized possessions.

If a winkte preferred to be among the women for social reasons and wanted to do the work of a woman, they were welcomed. Often, when a holy man needed an aide or assistant, the winkte was generally more available. Consequently a winkte would often become a medicine man's assistant and he, in turn, would often learn the ways of a medicine man. To make fun of or torment what the Great Spirit had created was considered highly disrespectful and could bring misfortune to the camp or the band. It would certainly bring eventual misfortune to the tormentor. According to my teachers, there was much less ridicule and more acceptance of homosexual people in Sioux society.

I disagree with the many organized churches who will not allow homosexuals to become spiritual leaders such as priests or ministers. What does leading ceremony have to do with whether one is a heterosexual or a homosexual? Eventually, a spiritual person will seek to lead ceremony or will be called on to do so. I cannot understand why humans should place a limitation upon a person, other than their sincerity and knowledge in the way of beseechment, appreciation and respectfulness of the spirit realm.

There will be many winktes in the spirit world. I caution all who do not treat them equally and fairly upon this planet; you probably will suffer some exposing ridicule and blame in the spirit world from innocent people whom you have tormented or harmed.

Feminism: I believe this movement is a needed means to restore balance into society. Nature definitely has balance and equality among the genders. Extreme patriarchy has caused feminism to finally stand up for basic human rights, fairness and respect.

Dominant culture has a history of patriarchy. When a society is materialistic, we should look at what motivates and promotes this lifestyle. What are the prime motivators, the primary influencers? What traits, goals or values are the forces behind patriarchy, wherein the male controls all major aspects of life? Commerce (trade), religion, politics, administration, war (decision to make war), judiciary (judgment of law), legislation (making of codes, rules, etc.), are all areas where patriarchal male controls. Lip service is given and some progress is made toward female representation, but there is a long journey ahead.

I look at feminism as feminine civil rights. Black people sought civil rights, Native Americans sought religious freedom and now the female citizen is seeking her equality. An important aspect of this equality is religion or spirituality. Woman, never be denied your right to conduct ceremony or to lead a beseechment to your concept of the higher power. Your wisdom and input is seriously needed here. If the spirits in the spirit world are former humans, then half of these spirits are former women!

Birth control: My view on the world population explosion favors birth control as a practical approach toward solving the population crisis. China has had to take effective birth control measures to stem their population problem. The following article, captioned, "Doomsday Coming?" appeared in the *Minneapolis Star Tribune*.

In 1960, Dr. Heinz von Foerster predicted that the human race would breed itself into infinity by November 13, 2026. We're halfway there and guess what? We're not on schedule, we're ahead of it!

The prediction was the conclusion of a scientific study on population growth and now, new evidence, according to a physicist for the Harvard-Smithsonian Center for Astrophysics, Owen Gingerich, states that we are 18 months ahead of schedule.

"Setting a specific date for "doomsday" is not part of my thinking, but we can certainly wreck the world systems and make them by present standards quite unlivable," says Nobel laureate Henry Kendall, MIT physicist and founder and chairman of the Union of Concerned Scientists (UCS). "We can do irreversible damage to the biosphere as well as to parts of the geophysical systems—the atmosphere, the oceans and the fresh water supply—which would stimulate enormous widespread and permanent misery everywhere in the world," says Kendall.

The proof of such contentions, in fact, is already starting to appear. "We have begun to see scientific evidence that our injury to the atmosphere, the ozone layer, is beginning to affect biological systems, " says Kendall.

Overpopulation and the issues of population pressure on food production will replace war as the greatest menace to survival on the planet.

The bulk of misery will be visited first upon the Third World, where it will occur "brutally," Kendall says, and then it will spread to the United States. "If we wait until we see the damage here, it will be too late. If we don't act now, Nature will curb the human population with mass starvation."

According to a study sponsored by the World Bank and United Nations, one in five people in the world today does not get enough to eat and one in ten suffers from serious malnutrition.

One of the earliest scientists in modern history to hypothesize about the threat of overpopulation was British political economist Thomas Robert Malthus (1766-1834), who theorized that global population tends to increase geometrically while food supply expands linearly. At some point, Malthus projected, population will outbreed the food supply. In scientific circles, that point is known as the "Malthusian limit."

In November 1992, the UCS published a "World Scientists Warning to Humanity," which Kendall called "the most authoritative document" that the world scientific community has published on the issues of global population, pressure on environmental systems and environmental damage.

Signed by more than 100 Nobel laureates and other senior scientists from around the world, the warning states, "No more than one or a few decades remain before the chance to avert the threats we now confront will be lost and the prospects for humanity immeasurably diminished."[14]

The following information is relative to this issue of Birth Control and population control.

WORLD POPULATION—THE BASIC FACTS

World population now exceeds 5.5 billion and is growing at the unprecedented rate of almost 100 million per year—over 10,000 every hour—and we are not increasing food, fuel and fiber to keep up with this huge gain.

1.2 billion people live in absolute poverty, more than the population of the entire planet only 150 years ago.

In recent years no other species of God's blessed creatures has increased like we have, while thousands of others have dramatically decreased or become extinct.

World population will grow by 3 billion people in the next 30 years, a number equal to the entire population in 1960.

Reducing birth rates to balance with deaths—population stabilization—will help preserve the planet's resources and environmental quality.

Reducing birth rates will reduce the number of people needing food, which means there will be more food for the thousands of children who now die each day because of poor nutrition—another good way of feeding the hungry.

If high U.S. growth rates continue for the next few decades, by the time your younger sister or brother becomes a grandparent there will be an additional 128 million people here, a gain of 50%—adding to pollution and resource depletion problems.

The United States population is growing by about 3 million people each year, with about 2 million from births and the other million from immigrants.

Because the average American consumes about 30 times more resources than the average person from a developing country, these additional 3 million people will have more impact upon the Earth than all of the millions added in China, India and Africa combined.

In terms of global resource depletion and pollution impact, the United States has the world's greatest population growth problem.[15]

What did Natural Way people do about Birth Control? The old time Sioux did not have the large families that the missionaries would come along later and urge them to have. The Sioux were nomads upon the Great Plains and it was a handicap to be burdened down with large groups of small children. The men married at a much later age in comparison to the dominant society. They wanted to prove themselves first, in hunting skills, adventure and upon the warrior road. Young men, the Dog Soldiers, lived together in separate, bachelor lodges to be the first line of defense. They looked down on anyone their age who would forsake the opportunity to seek honor and provide for the camp. Also, there was little preoccupation with premarital sex. In other words, no "Play Boy magazines" or related works would be found in their lodges or upon their war parties. Their stories and discussions focussed on a much higher plane.

Women nursed their children for a much later time period and therefore kept themselves from ovulating. This method imparted a closer relationship between mother and child. Grandparents, aunts and uncles helped raise the children. The lifestyle took its toll as well, in regard to the newborn. The strongest survived.

The proof is: Native Americans were on this continent for thousands of years and did not bring about overpopulation. The European has been here but a few centuries.

* * * *

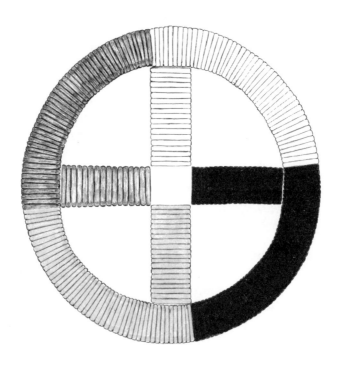

Following the Natural Way

I love a people who keep the commandments without ever having read them or heard them preached from the pulpit.

I love all people who do the best they can.

* * * *

How many followers of this religion are there?
Where are followers found around the world?
What are the obligations of the followers?
How do you relate your religion to your everyday life?
Can one convert to this religion?
Do members of your religion witness or try to convert others?
How does one go about learning more about this religion?
Do you feel you need to worship with a congregation?
Does your religion require a great time commitment?
How do you communicate the beliefs to children?
Do you or will you raise your children in this religion?
Do you feel your religion is superior over all others?
Why is this religion right for you?
What is the underlying theme of your religion?

* * * *

There are many who are influenced by the Natural Way and their numbers grow each day. The environmental dilemma is making people extremely concerned about their future and the future of the generations unborn. The inability of organized religion to address these serious environmental matters with their written words has been a decisive factor in pushing more people toward natural revelation. The apathetic attitude towards the world population explosion, the continual fighting between religious factions, and lack of leadership opportunities for women, are illustrative of many disappointments that are frustrating organized church members. People are seeking a closer connection to their Creator while they walk their life's journey. They want to feel and understand a relationship that is much deeper and broader than mere blood kinship. Many are taking a serious look at the Natural Way.

Environmental-minded people who never had strong religious ties are considering the Natural Way as a spiritual means. I think that the majority of those who are seeking to walk this path are finding satisfaction with what they are discovering. I do not know how many followers there are because it would be too difficult to count them. Every dawn the numbers increase significantly. Just go to your bookstores and see the many topics that are addressed in this area.

Followers are found around the world. Indigenous people who are still connected to their tribes are worldwide and those who see planet-saving values from indigenous wisdom and application are also worldwide. No membership list exists and I hope that such a record is never devised. For thousands of years, Natural Way people performed exemplary earth stewardship without one.

Obligations of Natural Way followers:

To bring back the natural harmony that humans once enjoyed.

To save the planet from present practices of destruction.

To find and reemploy real truth.

To promote true balance between both genders.

To share and be less materialistic.

To become rid of prejudice.

To learn to be related.

To be kind to animals and take no more than needed.

To play with one's children and love each equally and fairly.

To be brave and courageous, enough so, to take a stand or make a commitment.

To understand what *Generations Unborn* really means.

To accept mystery in order to end foolish argument over religion.

How does one relate this path to everyday life? My spirituality is easy to relate to. I can taste, touch and feel my spirituality every day. Each direction has an effect and I easily relate to what the Six Powers represent. It is easier to feel for your planet when you presume that the Earth and Sky are your Mother and Father. The whole universe is an expression of Wakan Tanka; the Great Spirit.

I have to hunt, make shelter, protect, give away and provide. While I am about such tasks my mind is immersed in a particular skill or calling and my spirituality is not in intense focus. What is at hand is my occupational and providing focus. Once, in time of war, I had a warrior focus. At times that focus had to be very intense. In the height of combat you must be extremely focused, otherwise you do not survive. Overall, I try to participate in life's functions with respect and acknowledgement because all of your life is a measurement. If I take a four legged or catch a finned, I tell it that I am taking it to provide and I thank it. Many finned I put back into the water and let them go. I can still laugh, play and make mistakes, many mistakes like all humans do. I hope that I never get so caught up with my occupation or travels that I lose the ability to admit that I still make mistakes, commit errors and do a "dumb thing" every so often. When there is time to focus on contemplation, however, then my spirituality comes into a stronger centralization.

Medicine Story tells about the Original Instructions that were handed down to his tribe. He remarked that most people who have an ancient oral tradition speak of such Original Instructions as having been issued from the Creator. Through these Original Instructions, the ancestral people related to their present life.

"It is this concept of Original Instructions that most profoundly distinguishes native spiritual belief from all man-made religions of the world. The Original Instructions are not ideas. They are reality. They are actually Natural Law, The Way Things Are—the operational manual for a working Creation. They cannot totally be explained in words. They must be experienced. Native People refer to the Original Instructions often in speech and prayer, but rarely attempt to say exactly what they are. They are not like the Ten Commandments carved in stone by a stern authority figure. We have no scriptures, no sacred books to be studied and argued over. The Original Instructions are not of the mind. They are of the spirit, the essence of Creation. Other creatures follow them instinctively. They are communicated to humankind through the heart, through feelings of beauty and love. We observe Nature, we tune in to the spirits and feel the creator's law all around us, silent, mysterious and immutable.

"The people of this continent at one time tried to live their lives according to these Original Instructions. They did not always succeed. They were human beings and were not perfect, but growing and learning like the rest of us. But their lives were structured around these Original Instructions: individual consciousness, family life, social organizations, educational and political and spiritual ways were all in harmony. Despite the frightening tales of the invaders, most of the over five hundred nations of this continent were among the most pacific people that ever inhabited the earth. Here in the Northeast our people created federations of peace that were in place when Alexander was trying to enslave Asia for the Greeks. The Houdinosonie to the west of us created the first United Nations in the world and a peace that has lasted among them for a thousand years. But the Great Law of Peace was not written down. It was kept in the hearts of the People of the Longhouse, so that the spirit, which was attuned to the spirit of Creation, would never be lost.

"The first people were in harmony with themselves and all Creation because their's was not written law. There were no Ten Commandments to be broken, no statutes for police to enforce and lawyers to find loopholes in. An ancient Chinese sage once said, "Where there is no law, there will be no criminals." Human laws create criminals, because they create opposition—they are based on fear and not love. The more laws, the lower the level of trust, and human community functions best on trust. Natural Law enforces itself, there are no loopholes in it. Four hundred years ago on this continent there was no need for a legal profession, and there was no such thing as a criminal profession.

"No one lived by hurting others. The Original Instructions are to be found in no book for the scholars to dispute. They are in our hearts, all the time. We all know what is right. You know what is right. You know when you are doing wrong. And when people point out to someone that he has made a mistake and hurt someone, if they are not condemning but helpful, that person will do anything he can to repay the hurt he has caused in order to feel good about himself again.

"There is no cruelty in the wilderness, in Nature, without human beings. Animals are never cruel. They do not act out of spite or revenge. They do not carry anger or fear beyond the appropriate moment. Only human beings think and understand with their minds that they must die. But with this understanding comes the knowledge of the Original Instructions. For we are the only beings on this earth that can feel and know Beauty in our hearts. When through our acts we create ugliness and imbalance and bad feelings we know this is not the Way of

Creation. When we create Beauty and Joy and Love we feel good. Our hearts tell us we are in harmony and in good balance."[1]

Medicine Story gives us more deep wisdom that is so appropriate to our journey which we travel on this planet. He tells us that people who live very close to the earth and the natural order of things are very simple and very real. I believe that they are the most happy on this earth. He tells us that the original people of this land embrace the essential spiritual and mysterious nature of the universe. Things are as they are. Whatever is, certainly is.

"Even though the Original Instructions are not written out in some book or scroll of the law, we can perceive them at work through the observation of Nature and by the experience of the people over the continuum of time, transmitted to each generation by tribal lore, ceremony, song and story. This is how we are one in a circle of time with our ancestors and with the unborn generations to come.

"Thus the Original Instructions suggest to us not only the reality, the "isness," of all experience and all things, but also their relatedness. All is one circle. We feel a kinship with everything. Animals, plants, stones, mountains, rainbows and stars are all to be addressed as relatives. Even those things which appear strange or frightening in lore or experience have some history, if we can discern it, which connects them in some unknown way to the circle. They have a necessary place.

"This is why we think and live in a realm of circles. We see circles in all of Nature. We gather together in a circle, we think of our communities as circles, of the races of humankind as a circle. The physical structure of the cosmos, from the smallest particle to the very walls of the universe, is a circle. And all these circles are part of one Great Circle of Existence."[2]

Can one convert to this religion, and do members of the Natural Way witness or try to convert others? There is absolutely no attempt to convert others to this spirituality. How would one bring about this conversion? Why would one want to attempt to erase another's accumulated knowledge upon their Disk of Life?

I think about my brothers and sisters all being taken to boarding school in the fall except for my sister Delores. We would not see them for a long time. A main emphasis at those schools was to convert and stamp out the Indian religion, our natural spirituality. How unnatural to separate little children at the age of five and six from their parents to foster assimilation and conversion. Tragic results happened. A high alcoholic rate was one result and there also was a high suicide rate. Self esteem is devastated when you are taught that your culture and your identity are inferior.

I think of the two little harmless dark specks sneaking into the back of that big cathedral because of the word—conversion. We were afraid and in fear that we would lose our souls as a result of what we were told. We were also in fear because we were meat eaters. We were so poor that often the only food in the house was deer meat which my brothers had provided. Breakfast, dinner and supper, we ate this deer meat. Besides, we preferred it over many of the white man's staples. We were taught to be in fear if we ate this meat on a Friday, and yet it was all that we had besides some potatoes or maybe corn. Would God actually put two little innocent Indian children in a burning hell simply because we did not attend a white man's ceremony or ate food according to our own customs? My Great Spirit does not indicate to me that It would do such a thing.

There must have been a bunch of sacrosanct, patriarchal old men, attempting to extend their personal power, who came up with these ideas; scaring little kids and actually the whole world with these goofy ideas that never considered the depth of Nature's revelations. Many intelligent people now laugh at and make fun of these bizarre pronouncements. Even their own flock makes fun of these "imprimatured" rulings. Strange written rulings and proclamations actually existed and were not mere suggestions of some fanatical zealot. They were carefully scrutinized, studied and forwarded on to higher authorities who were supposedly more learned. They even gave out compensation in purgatory, "100 days plenary indulgence from the suffering of purgatory." This promise was printed on pamphlets calling attention to certain events if you attended them. Purgatory is some human-devised place where your spirit is supposed to go and suffer for an untold amount of time. I do not believe that they were telling us the truth.

I am a dignified being, a creation of the Great Spirit. I want no part of a system that repels direct observation and daily knowledge. I have rejected this attempt at conversion. I hope that people will never spawn these kind of man-made fears in the Natural Way. Think all things over before you make proclamations. If you have a vision or a dream, keep it to yourself for awhile and think it over. Learn from Black Elk. He had a powerful vision yet kept it to himself for a period of time. How does it affect the tribe, Mother Earth and the Generations Unborn? Will it remove me away, or toward, direct knowledge from the Creator? This is a highly important question to ask yourself when you find yourself being fed religious information.

How does one proceed to learn more about the Natural Way? You are doing it now. You are reading and seeking knowledge. You can be in a wheelchair or you can be confined in a prison or an old folks home and have no one to take you to a ceremony, yet reading will take you there. Most people in this land have access to Nature, however. Go out and become a part of it.

In time, there will be those who will network and share their knowledge. It is starting to happen in the larger cities across the land. All of this takes time. Be patient, share your knowledge and be very concerned for the environment.

Do I feel that I need to worship with a congregation? I prefer to beseech by myself but I occasionally go to gatherings and group beseechments. It is enjoyable to be with nature appreciating people at times. Friendships begin and we come together for the essential tasks that lie ahead. During Earth Day and Earth Week, I find myself with many like-minded "congregations."

Does this religion require a great time commitment? This spirituality encompasses your entire life. It is not something that you put on when you walk into a ceremony and take off when you leave. Yet, I find that I have great independence and I rarely experience a boring ceremony. This spirituality is not centered on ceremony alone, however. It is mostly your everyday life, your commitment, concern and interest in what is happening to the planet and how you can be helpful, considerate and be a harmonic companion to all that exists. Dominant society has made it so easy to overlook the mystery that surrounds us in the natural world.

How do you communicate the beliefs to children? Children should be allowed to play, that is what the animal children do. Raise a pair of kittens in your home. You will understand what play is all about and will also find yourself laughing a lot at their antics. I love to see children play but gradually they are taught about life. I do not believe in pushing a religion or a spirituality onto children. Above all, I do not want to scare them about the Great Spirit and I certainly do not want to put an idea of evil spirits or a devil into their heads, especially when absolutely no proof of such human-contrived entities exist. In time, when they get older, they ask questions. I try to answer those questions from truthful experience.

Meanwhile, devote your time so that they can play and feel a sense of sincere interest and leadership from you who has many more life experiences than what they do.

One of the greatest gifts that you can give as a parent is to spend time with your offspring. Including other children is also honorable. This is more important than lacing down their minds with religion or spirituality, in my opinion. As they become older, they will choose what interests appeal to them. If they have had a stable relationship with their parents or a parent, they will most likely go forth into society with honorable ethics and contributing values. They will also be able to choose with confidence. My children have many pictures of our past adventures. I have an adult daughter who reads to me, occasionally, from her diary as a child. It is most satisfying to listen to your adult child tell fondly about adventures of the past, a past wherein both of you explored this life together.

Will I raise my children in this Natural Way and expect them to follow, or will I leave the decision up to them? If any of my children seek a different road, that is their choice and it will be honored. I have never attempted to force my children into the Natural Way, yet, when I conduct a sweat lodge and they are nearby, they often seek to take part in it and pray sincerely when it is their time to beseech or acknowledge. Often, some of them attend church services and that is fine with me.

Do you feel your religion is superior over all others and why is this religion right for you? It is dangerous to state that your religion is superior to all others. That is how many wars have started and are still being fought. Why antagonize another over what is Mystery?

To tell of happenings that you would not like to have repeated, may antagonize others but if you are doing this in the interest of truthful prevention, then you should be commended. The Jewish people do not want the Holocaust or the thinking behind it to return. They tell their story and have every right to if we believe that human decency should honor all beings.

What is right for a particular individual is another matter. We are all so very different from each other, especially those who have traveled far and often. New adventures and experiences give one many views, many imprints upon the Disk of Life. This increases our differences but that does not necessarily mean that we are not compatible or promoting disharmony. If Martin Luther King, Albert Einstein, Ghandi, Buddha, Fools Crow, Bill Eagle Feather, Black Elk or Jesus Christ were to give a lecture, most enlightened or high plane people would be there. They were very different and yet we would readily attend whatever event they would be associated with.

For those who cultivated this Natural Way Spirituality of which I speak, I believe the underlying theme was their ability to recognize a spiritual truth. They lived within that great truth to a much higher degree than what I have witnessed in this present day society. That alone is enough incentive for me to prefer my own path, my own spiritual road so influenced by the concepts of the indigenous people who were here before us.

Their proven ability to live in harmony as relatives to all surrounding creation gave me the clear mountain stream where I could swim as a child and the miles of room where I could walk and grow. Their traditions developed a kind mother and father who raised me in a happy home despite the prejudice and false stereotypes that we had to live with. I honor the millions of people who lived this nature-respecting lifestyle down through time, down through generation upon generation; each being contributing to the accumulating knowledge within those native people who were here when the first colonizing Europeans came to North American shores. The honor, the bravery, generosity and above all, the truthfulness of those Sioux warriors and women out on the Great Plains was shaped by their ancestors. The great gift to humanity— democracy from the Iroquois, was honed by those ancient and evolving ancestors who discovered that key of harmony within all of nature's knowledge. Nature is very democratic and equal. It is not difficult for me to understand why this gift could come from a natural system.

Atop the capitol of this nation there is a statue. Someday I hope that statue is taken down and replaced by a replica of the people who truly gave democracy to the entire world. Maybe a statue of a native woman reaching out to touch a flying butterfly or a winged one would be beautiful, truthful and inspiring. Maybe the other hand could hold out the power of the sacred hoop which embraces all races to the red dawn of knowledge. If there is a sculptor out there among you, this could be your challenge.

I must always strive to learn from the underlying theme of these Natural Way based people who actually existed and are not some mere, romantic myth or a fairy tale of magic wands. A pristine environment standing tall with stately trees amid clear flowing streams is solid proof that they were truly in harmony when the Pilgrims first landed. No detractor can deny this harmonious, environmental fact.

I thank the Great Spirit, Wakan Tanka, that the majority of these native peoples who once trod these lands; I thank you oh Mystery that they did live in the relative freedom of Nature. I am thankful that most of the natural people did experience a complete life out within the comforting yet challenging embrace of the Earth Mother in a time of clean streams and rivers, clear lakes, no endangered species and a land that needed no chemicals to bring forth bounty from planted seeds.

Yes, there were thousands, millions who lived upon this great continent for many, many centuries. These last few centuries of terrible change are but an eye wink of time in comparison. We are so caught up with our so-called modern lives that there is little realization that family upon family lived out their own lives back in time just as importantly as we consider ours. These families laughed, played, hunted, planted and provided. They took from the daily communion of Father Sky and the Earth Mother. They beseeched, acknowledged, honored and recognized the Higher Power. They knew how to truly share and when to be brave. I think that they laughed and played more than we in this modern era. Their bodies were healthier and they were also free from addictions. That in itself could lead one to laugh and play. Above all, in answer to our present dilemma, they give us the confidence to know that a workable way did exist for two legged habitation upon this planet.

I associate strongly with this past but I also realize that I am in a different time span. The whole landscape has even changed. This time span is fraught with serious environmental disaster. The present world situation that I confront has given me a mission, an essential purpose. I can even couple my concept of the beyond world into this mission. That is why I am comfortable with this spirituality or this religion, if you will. It certainly feels right for me.

What is the underlying theme of the Natural Way?

The underlying theme of my spirituality is:

1. To be thankful to a vast creative power that I live.
2. To gather as much knowledge as possible and imprint it upon my Disk of Life.
3. To believe that a spirit world beyond exists and that my reward will include being with others of the same level that I have endeavored to rise to. Also in that spirit world, I will be able to honor and tell good truths about all of those who were kind, considerate and fair to me. I will also condemn and chastise for an eternity, those who told untruths, deceived and lied as I will be challenged if I tell untruths or have harmed innocent others who have been upon my trail of life. The incoming Generations Unborn will challenge us all if we did not make a valiant effort to protect the Earth. Ina Makah Awanyanka (Mother Earth, we seek to protect you).
4. To kill the Blue Man of Black Elk's vision and help save the planet. This means that I must have the courage and bravery to share my knowledge and experiences. Others must realize that this is the greatest weapon which we have.

* * * *

In ending, I wish to restate that these <u>are not</u> necessarily the beliefs of indigenous people. These are simply my perceptions of the Natural Way and how I was strongly influenced by Nature's persuasion, my teachers, and the exemplary living standards upheld by certain indigenous societies.

Environmentally, how has this information affected you, the reader? We looked at a people who encompassed environmentalism within their spiritual beliefs. They had a spirituality that was very influential in their daily life style yet was not oppressive. It lasted for thousands of years. Hopefully, you now have an understanding that we are a part of the whole universe, especially this planet. Mitakuye Oyasin. We are related to all things.

* * * *

Oh Great Spirit

Who art everywhere
Mystery is thy name

I appreciate your allowance
that I live
And all mystery
which is put before me

Let me always seek knowledge
For you are the source of all knowledge
Help me to avoid ignorance
For it moves me away from thee

I seek to care for the home
This earth you have provided
Let my thoughts, actions and deeds
Lead me to you
And the Spirit World which waits beyond.

Humanities II Questions

* * * *

Ch 1 Who is God?
How does your religion define the Supreme Being?
Share your thoughts on God: Did He create us?
How does your religion explain the unknown, such as
creation?
Is this religion based on the existence of an immortal being?
How did the "higher power" become the "higher power"?
How does your God manifest itself to humans?
Is He always watching?
Does your God have a gender?
Is your religion defined by what one thinks and does?
What is the underlying theme of your religion?
Where do you believe your Supreme Being exists?

Ch 2 How did you become involved?
How did you become involved in this religion?
Does your God control all your actions?
Is there a book in your religion that is supposedly dictated
directly as the word of God?
What is the authority for your beliefs?
Where did the religion originate?
What is the history of your religion?
Has your religion changed over time? How?
How does your religion view other religions?

Does your religion have any God living on earth as a human?
Do you believe in a savior?
How does your religion view Jesus?
Does scientific evidence support your religion?
What are your fundamental beliefs?

Ch 3 Worldview Philosophy

Is the religion a "worldview" religion, or is it concentrated
more on itself and its members?
Who are your religion's prophets, if any?
Does your religion teach a view of the end of time?
Do you believe this world will end?
What is the purpose of humans on Earth?

Ch 4 Good, Evil and Afterlife

Is your God totally good? Does a totally bad God also exist?
Is your God all forgiving?
Do you believe in sin?
Does your religion have the concept of ultimate good and evil?
Is humankind inherently good or evil?
What does your religion teach about an afterlife?
Do people of other religious persuasions go to "heaven", or do
they all go to "hell"?
What does the religion believe about reincarnation?
What is your view of occultism and astrology?
How do the attributes of your Supreme Being relate to those
of humankind?

Ch 5 Beseechment

What ceremonies are carried out in this religion?
Describe a worship service.
How do you get in touch with your God?
Is prayer personal or relatively structured?
Where do you worship?
What do you worship?

Does this religion have an initiation procedure or
ceremony?
Does this religion have a language used in worship?
Does your religion have sacrifices?
Is there a holy place for the religion?
What religious holidays are recognized?
How has your religion shaped art, literature or music?

Ch 6 Miracles

Have miracles occurred in the religion?
Have you ever had a revelation, or intensely spiritual
experience occur?
What objects are sacred in your religion?

Ch 7 Rules, Restrictions and Conflict

Does the religion have a set of rules to live by?
What restrictions do members follow?
Are there restrictions on who may participate in the religion or
parts of it?
Do members have any special forms of dress?
Can a member marry outside the religion?
Can members practice more than one religion?
Is there conflict in this religion? Over what issues?
Have you encountered any prejudice because of your religion?

Ch 8 Hierarchy, Matriarchy and Patriarchy

Does any hierarchy in the religion oppress the common people
in any way?
Is there a human leader in this church?
Where is the leadership based?
Are there priests in this religion?
Is there room for independence of belief and action in your religion?
Is either sex seen as superior to the other in the eyes of the church?
What role do men and women play in this religion?
Are all people equal in this religion?
How is sex viewed in the religion?

Who supposedly wrote the books of authority in the religion?
Is doctrine in your church set in stone or is it changing?
How strongly and carefully is your spoken or written word
followed today?

Ch 9 Government and Social Issues

How does your religion affect government?
Is the religion politically active?
What are the moral standards of the religion?
What wars or conflicts has your religion been involved in?
What stance does your religion take on recent social issues: abortion,
    euthanasia, the death penalty, pre-marital sex, unwed mothers, gay
    rights, feminism, birth control, etc.?

Ch 10 Followers of the Natural Way

How many followers of this religion are there?
Where are followers found around the world?
What are the obligations of the followers?
How do you relate your religion to your everyday life?
Can one convert to this religion?
Do members of your religion witness or try to convert others?
How does one go about learning more about this religion?
Do you feel you need to worship with a congregation?
Does your religion require a great time commitment?
How do you communicate the beliefs to children?
Do you or will you raise your children in this religion?
Do you feel your religion is superior over all others?
Why is this religion right for you?
What is the underlying theme of your religion?

* * * *

List of Lakota Sioux Words

* * * *

This is a list of words, some of which may be heard in ceremony or associated with prayer. Spelling of most words is not consistent; the list below is usually spelled phonetically. Some variation in accent exists among the Sioux tribes. Chan and chun are examples; chanupa or chunupa for pipe. Definition of horse for example varies; <u>s</u>unka wakan or ta<u>s</u>unka wakan.

Often the n is barely heard at the end of a syllable. Wakan Tanka sounds like Wah kahhn Tahn kah. A smaller font n will be used for this expression since this is practical and a capability of the modern word processor.

<u>C</u>	ch as in chain	C	C as in cold
<u>H</u>	hk as in hahkk		
<u>K</u>	gutteral sound as in kh	K	K as in kite
<u>S</u>	sh as in Shell	S	S as in sit
<u>T</u>	gutteral sound as in tkh	T	T as in tie

* * * *

ahbleza	(ah blay zah) observer, literally perceives, look
ahitunwan	(a he toon wan) looking, watching
ah ho	exclamation of acknowledgement
ahpe	(ah pay) wait
ahte	(ah tay) father

ake   (ah khay)   again
akicita   (ah khee chee tah)   camp police, marshall;
                           a representative or messenger of a
                           supernatural being or power
akita mani yo   (ah kee tah mah nee yo)   observe
                           everything as you walk
alowanpi   (a lo wan pee)   singing in praise
anagoptan   (a nagho p' tan)   listen
anhe   (ahn hay)   exclamation of
                           acknowledgement or satisfaction
anpetu   (ahn pay too)   day, literally day-sun
anpetu wi   (ahn pay too wee)   the Sun
anpo   dawn light
anpo wicahpi   (ahn poh wee chak peh)   Morning Star
ate   (ah tay)   Father
awanyanka   (ah wahn yahn ka)   protect, to look over
awanyanke waste   (ah wahn yahn kay wah stay)   good
                           looking, handsome

bleaza   clear

canhanpi   (chan han pee)   sugar
cala   (cha lah)   baby
can   (chan) tree, wood; prefix for things made of
                           or related to wood
cancega   (chan chega)   drum
cangleska   (chan gleas kha) a hoop
cangleska wakan   (chan gleas kha wah kan)   sacred hoop
canku   (chan koo)   road, way, path
canli   (chan lee)   tobacco
canli wapahte   (chan lee wah pahk teh) tobacco offering
canhiya   (chan hin yan) love, of the heart
canpaza   (chan pah zah)   old term for tree
cansasa   (chan sha sha) red willow bark tobacco
cante   (chanh tay)   the heart
cantkiya   (chan teh kee ya) loving couple
canupa   (chan oon pah or chun oo pah)   peace pipe
canumpa   (chun oom pah)   peace pipe
canupa lutah   red pipe

Canupa Wakan	Sacred Pipe
canwi yuza	(chan wee yuza) small sharp stick for hanging meat
canwi yuza waopo	sharp piercing peg for a sun dancer
cekiya	(chay key ya) beseech, pray
cewakiya	(chay wa key ya I beseech, I pray
cicu	(chee choo) I give
cokato	(cho kah to) center
hakamya upo	(hah kahm yah you po) come, follow closely
hanbloglagia	(hahn blo glah gee ah) to tell dreams and visions
hanbloglaka	to tell of one's visions
hanblecheya	(han bleay chee ah) crying for a vision
hanblecheyapi	vision quest
hanhepi wi	(han heay pee wee) the moon
hanwi	(sacred term hanwikan) Moon
hau	(houw) exclamation, yes, agree, hello
hau!	interjection of affirmation
he	expression at end of sentence
Hehaka Sapa	Black Elk
hecitu	(hay chee too) it is so; amen
hecitu yelo, or welo	(yay lo, or way lo) It is very much so; it is so indeed
heyoka	(hee yoh kah) clown or a contrary, one who makes you laugh; those who do things backwards and wear shabby clothes; one who has dreamed of thunder and lightning and believes he should act in an unnatural or contrary manner
heyoka wachipi	clown at dances; funny dancer at dances
heyoka kaga	Ceremony of Clown Making
hina	(hee na) those
hinze	(hin zhee) blonde haired
hiya	no
ho!	interjection of affirmation, said at the end of an individual prayer

hocokan	(ho cho kan) circle, camp circle, sacred altar in a ritual
hoka	(hoke ah) I am not afraid)
hokahey	(hoke ah hey) war cry, let's go let's go, we are not afraid
hokh	expression of wonder by men
hokomi	beads
hoksi	(hoke shee) a child
hoksi cala	baby
hoksila	(hoke she la) boy
ho wana	(ho wah nah) now
hoye	(ho yay) send a voice, expression of assent
hoye wa yelo	(ho yay wa yelo) I'm sending a voice
hoyeya	(ho yay ya) to call or cry out
hunka	(hoon kah) ancestor, relative
Hunkapi	Making of Relatives Ceremony
hunkpapa	entrance to the camp circle Hunkpapa Tribe of the Sioux Nation
hununpa	two leggeds
hutopah	four leggeds
huya	(khoo yah) winged, bird
ikce wicasa	(eek chay we cha sha) a common man
icaga	(ee ca ga) to grow
ihanblapi	(ee han bla pee) they dream of
iktomi	(unk to mee or, ee kto mee) spider, the tricky spider fellow in Sioux stories, trickster or jokester
Ina	(ee nah) mother
Ina Maka	(ee nah mah kah) Mother Earth
inipi	(ee nee pee) sweat lodge ceremony, spiritual renewing ceremony
initi	(ee nee tee) sweat lodge, steam bath to become clean
inyan	(in yahn) rock, stone
inyansa	(in yahn shah) red stone
isna	(ee shnah) alone
ista	(ish tah) the eye
istima	(ee shtee mah) sleep

itancan	(ee tahn chan) chief, leader
itokaga	(ee toe ka gha) south
itokagata	in the direction of the south
Itokagata Ouye	South Power
itunwa	(ee toon wah) look
iya	(ee ya) say
iyaya	to speak
kigli	go
kihowaya	(ke ho wa ya) talk, speak
kile	(ke lay) with this
kin	(keen) expression at end of sentence
kinnic kinnick	(kin nic kinn nic) tobacco
kiwani	(kee wah nee) awakening
koda	(koe dah) friend in Dakota dialect
kola	(koe lah) friend in Lakota dialect
kta	(ktah) expression at end of sentence
kte	(ktay) expression at end of sentence
Kunshi, Unci	(koon she or oon she) Grandmother
Lakol wicohan	Indian way
Lakota	(lah koe tah) Allies, friends, Indian name for Western Sioux
le	(ley) this
Leksi	(lake she) uncle
lelah wah ste	(lee lah wah ste) very good
lena	(ley nah) these
lo	(low) expression at end of sentence
lutah	(loo tah) scarlet or red, color for east sa, (sha) is red but luta for red is used in naming, see Mahpiyah Lutah (Red Cloud)
Maka	(mah kha) Earth
Maka Sitomni	(mah kha see toe mnee) All things on earth
mahpiya	(mak pi yah) sky, clouds
Mahpiyah Ate	(Mak pi yah Ah tay) Father Sky
Mahpiyah Lutah Itancan	Chief Red Cloud, famous chief who won the Treaty of 1868

mini   (minn ee)   water
miniskuya   (minn ee sku ee ya)   salt
minksuyan   (mink sue yan)   remember
minne ahtah   much water, much rain, heavy rainfall
misun   (mee soon)   man's term for younger
                            brother
Mitakuye Oyasin   (me ta koo yea oh ya seen)   We are related
                            to all things; We are all related; We are all
                            relatives
miye   (me yeah)   me
mitawa   (mee ta wah)   my

nagi   (nah ghee)   spirit, ghosts

oglu wahste   good fortune, good luck
okiksapa   to have gained wisdom from experience.
olowan   (oh low wan)   song
omakiya   (oh mah key yah) help me
onsimala   (oon she mah lah)   have pity on me
onsiunlapi   (oon she un la pee)   pity us
ototola inyan   or skaya inyan   crystal stone
otuha   (o dtu ha) Give Away ceremony
omakiya   (o ma kee ya)   help me
omakiya po   all of you help me
owankinye   (oh wan keen yea)   flying
oyate   (oh yah tay)   nation, tribe

Paha Sapa   (pa ha sa pa)   Black Hills
pay sha   hair roach
peju ota   (pay zjhoo o tah) sage, sacred herb of the
                            north power
pejuta   (pay zjhoo tah)   medicine
pejuta wichasha   (pay zjhoo tah we cha sha)   medicine man
pejuta winan   (pay zjhoo tah we ahn)   medicine woman
pejuta makah wakan   the medicine world
peta   (pay tah)   fire
pilamaya, pilamiya   (pee lam ay ah, pee lam ee yah)   thank you
pilamaya aloh or yelo   thank you very much
pte   (ptay) buffalo cow

Ptecincala Ska Wakan Winan (ptay heen cha la ska wa kan we ahn) White Buffalo Calf Woman

sapa	(sah pah) black (color for the west, according to Black Elk)
s̲a	(sha) red (color for the east, according to Black Elk)
Shakopeh Ouye	Six powers of the Universe
sica	(she cha) bad, wrong, not good
sicun	(she chun) that aspect of the soul that lasts forever
sicun wotawe	(woe tah weh) special stone that has been invested with a spirit
ska	white (color for the north, according to Black Elk)
Tankashilah	(taunk ah she lah) Grandfather
tate	(tah teay) wind
tate topa	(tah teay toe pah) four directions, four winds
tiyospaye	(tee yo spi yeh) extended family
tokata	(toe ka tah) future
tokata wic̲ocage	future generations
Unci	Grandmother
unkinyan	(un keyn yan) flying
unsimala ye	(ounshee mah lah yey) have pity on me
waga chun	cottonwood tree
wakan	(wah kahn) holy, sacred
Wakan Tanka	(Wah kahhn Tahn kah) Great Spirit, Great Mystery
wakangli	lightning
wakanyeja makah	children of the earth
wakan wic̲ohan	ceremony
wakic̲aga	ceremony
wakinyan	lightning
wakinyan c̲etan	(wah keen yan che tan) thunder hawk
wakinyan hotonpi	thunder

wakinyan tanka	thunder beings
wamakaskan oyate	(wa ma ka skan o ya teh) the animals or animal nation
wanaca	(wah nah cha) flower
wanagi	(wah nah gee, wah nah ghee) soul, ghost, spirit
wana olowanpi	sing now
wanblee	(wanbli) eagle
Wanblee Wiyaka Itancan	Chief Eagle Feather
wanunyanpi	offerings
washichu	(wah she chu) white man, literally, he reaches for all things (wah she ee chu) he reaches for the fat
waste	(wash tay) good
wayaka	(wan yan ka) see
waziya	(wah zee yah) north
waziya ahtah	big storm, strong north wind
waziya ouye	power of the north, (prayer for the north)
wi (wee)	sun, moon
	anpetu wi sun
	hanhepi wi moon
	wiyosaya, wicahpi (wi chak pi) star
wichasha	(wee cha sha) man
wichasha pejuta	medicine man
wichasha wakan	holy man
wichasta	(wee cha stah) warrior
wichasta ohuze	(o hoo zhea) mystic warrior, also ohuze wichasta
wichoni mini	(wee cho nee minn ee) life giving rains
wichoni minne	life giving rains
wigmunke oyate	(wig muun key o yah teh) rainbow people
wignagnaye	(wi gna gna yeh) distract
wihaha	(win ha ha) jovial
wihahaya	(win ha ha yah) happy, pleasant
winan	(wee ahn) woman
winan wakan	(wee ahn wah kahn) holy woman
winkte	(weenk tay) broadly, one who is or has homosexual leanings

winyanktehca	(wee ahn khtay hey cha) basis of contracted winkte, wants to be a woman
wiwanyag wachipi	Sun Dance Ceremony
wiyaka	(we ya kah) feather
wiyakpa	shine, glisten
Wiyo Ate	(wee yo ah teh) Father Sun
wiyoheyapa	(wee yo he yah pa) east, rising dawn
wiyoheyapata ouye	east power; rising dawn of the east direction
wiyo ichoni	high sun, sun at its height is giving life
wiyopeyata	(wee yo peh yah ta) west, the sun is setting in the direction of west
wiyopeyata ouye	west power; power of the setting sun
woksapa	(woke sah pah) wisdom
woksapa kiwani	(woke sah pah kee wan nee) awakening to wisdom
wotai	(woe tie) personal stone that has appeared to you, you carry it at times, your personal gift from Wakan Tanka
wotawe	(woe tah weh) personal charm, broader term for personal stone
wowas ake iyuha	all powers
yupayo	close it, close the door
yusni yo	turn out the light
yuwipi	(yoo wee pee) spirit calling ceremony, they tie him up
zi zi	(zhee zhee) yellow (color for the south)
zintkala oyate	(zint kha la o yah teh) the winged people

* * * *

Animals:

	wamakaskan(wa ma kha skan)
antelope	heton cik'ala
badger	hoka
bat	hupakiglake
bear	mato (mah toe)

bear, grizzly	waonze
bear, black	mato sapa
bear, brown	mato hi
bear, polar	mato ska
beaver	capa (cha pah)
bobcat	igmu sinteksa
buffalo, (bull)	tatanka
buffalo, (cow)	pte
calf	ptehincala
cat	igmu
coyote	masleca, sunkmanitu
deer	tahca
deer, female	tahca winyela
deer, (fawn)	tingleska
dog	sunka
elk, (bull)	hehaka
elk, (cow)	unpan
ferret	itopta sapa, taunkasa
fox	sungila, tokala
frog	was'in, gnaska
gopher	itgnila, wahinheya
horse	sunkawakan, holy dog (horse), tasunkawakan, very large dog holy (horse) "A human can ride this large dog. It must be holy." Expression when Sioux first saw a horse.
jackal	mayasle
lizard	agleska
lion	igmu tanka
marten	wah'anksica
mule	sonsonla
mink	ikusan
mouse	(h)itunkala
muskrat	sinkpe
otter	ptan
porcupine	pahin
prairie dog	pispiza
rabbit	mastinca
raccoon	wica, wiciteglega

skunk	maka
squirrel	he<u>t</u>kala, zi<u>c</u>a (red)
wolf	<u>s</u>un<u>k</u>manitu tan<u>k</u>a

* * * *

Reptiles and Fish:

clam	tuki
fish	hogan
leech	tusla
minnow	hogan<u>s</u>anla
orca or porpoise	hogan wakan (It thinks like a human, is highly intelligent)
rattlesnake	sin<u>t</u>ehla
snail	mniwamnuh'a
snake	zuze<u>c</u>a
tadpole	hona it<u>k</u>ala
toad	mapih'a
turtle	<u>k</u>e or <u>k</u>eya
turtle, sand	pat<u>k</u>a sa
turtle, snapping	<u>k</u>eya samna
water snake	mni zuze<u>c</u>a
whale	hogan tanka

* * * *

Birds: Zintkala

blackbird	wablosa
bluebird	zintkato
buzzard	hecan
chickadee	skipipi
cowbird	pteyahpa
crane, white	pehanska
crow	kangi
dove, morning	wakinyela
duck	magaksica

eagle	wanbli
goose	maga
grouse	c̲ansiyo
gull	wic̲atankala
hawk	c̲etan
hawk, night	c̲etan, pisko
heron	hokagic̲a
hummingbird	tanagila
jay	zintkatogleglega
killdeer	pehincicila
kingbird	wasnasnaheca
lark	istanica tanka
loon	bleza
magpie	halhate, unkcekiha
meadowlark	winapinla, jialepa
mud hen (duck)	siyaka
oriole	skeluta
owl	hinhan
prairie chicken	siyoka
quail	siyo cik'ala
raven	kangi ta
robin	sisoka
sparrow	ihuhaotila
swallow	hupucansakala
swan	magaska
thrush	caguguyasa
turkey	wagleksun
woodcock	kankeca
wood duck	skiska
woodpecker	wagnuka
wren	c̲anheyala

* * * *

Lakota Spiritual Songs

* * * *

Beginner's Songs:

Beginner Song #1

Wakan Tanka	Great Spirit
Wakan Tanka	Great Mystery
Wakan Tanka	Great Spirit
Wakan Tanka	Great Mystery

Beginner Song #2

Wakan Tanka	Great Spirit
Pilamiya	I thank you
Wakan Tanka	Great Spirit
Wichoni hey	For my life

Beginner Song #3

Ina Makah	Mother Earth
Awanyanke	We seek to protect you
Ina Makah	Mother Earth
Awanyanke	We seek to protect you

Beginner Song #4

Shakopeh Ouye	Six Powers
Shakopeh Ouye	Six Powers
Tate Topa	Four Directions
Tate Topa	Four Directions

* * * *

Advanced Song

Wiyopeyata kiya etunwin na	Look to the west
Cekiya yo hey	Pray to them
Cekiya yo yo hena	Pray to them because
nitakuye yo hey	Those people are your relatives

Waziyata kiya etunwin na	Look to the north
Cekiya yo hey	Pray to them
Cekiya yo yo hena	Pray to them because
nitakuye yo hey	Those people are your relatives

Wiyoheyapa kiya etunwin na	Look to the east
Cekiya yo hey	Pray to them
Cekiya yo yo hena	Pray to them because
nitakuye yo hey	Those people are your relatives

Itokaga kiya etunwin na	Look to the south
Cekiya yo hey	Pray to them
Cekiya yo yo hena	Pray to them because
nitakuye yo hey	Those people are your relatives

* * * *

Wakan Tanka	Great Mystery
unsimala ye!	have pity on me!
Wakan Tanka	Great Mystery
wani kta ca hey ya hey ya	I shall live

* * * *

Notes

Foreword

1. George Catlin, *Episodes From Life Among the Indians* (Norman: University of Oklahoma Press, 1959), p. xxv.
2. Ed McGaa, *Mother Earth Spirituality* (San Francisco: Harper and Row, 1990), p. 29.

Chapter 1

1. Max Charlesworth, Howard Morphy, Diane Bell and Kenneth Maddock, *Religion in Aboriginal Australia* (St. Lucia: University of Queensland Press, 1984), p. 13.
2. Thomas Moore, *Care of the Soul: a Guide for Cultivating Depth and Sacredness in Everyday Life* (New York: Harper/Collins Publishers Inc.,1992), p. 204.
3. Ibid., p. 205.

Chapter 2

1. John Fire (Lame Deer) and Richard Erdoes, *Lame Deer Seeker of Visions* (New York: Simon & Schuster, 1972), pp. 155, 156.
2. Dennis W. Harcey and Brian R. Croone, *White-Man-Runs-Him (Crow Scout With Custer)* (Evanston, IL: Evanston Publishing, Inc., 1993), p.15.

3. William K. Powers, *Oglala Religion* (Lincoln: University of Nebraska Press, 1977), p. 16.
4. Dennis W. Harcey and Brian R. Croone,*White-Man-Runs-Him (Crow Scout With Custer)* (Evanston, IL: Evanston Publishing, Inc., 1993), p. 10.
5. William Unrau, *The Kansa Indians: A History of the Wind People, 1673 1873* (Norman: University of Oklahoma Press,1986), p. 16.
6. Bradford Keeney, *Shaking Out the Spirits* (Barrytown, NY: Station Hill Press, 1994), p. 161.
7. Ibid., p. 56.
8. Ibid., pp. 56, 57.

Chapter 3

1. Thomas Moore, *Care of the Soul: a Guide for Cultivating Depth and Sacredness in Everyday Life* (New York: Harper/Collins Publishers Inc., 1992), p. 208.
2. Ibid., p. 204.
3. Robert Redfield, *The Primitive World and its Transformations* (Ithaca, N.Y.: Cornell University Press, 1935), p. 85. Redfield was an anthropologist.
4. Dhyani Ywahoo, *Voices of Our Ancestors* (Boston: Shambhala, 1987), p. xiii.
5. Ake Hultkrantz, *Native Religions of North America* (San Francisco: Harper/Collins, 1987), p. 24. Hultkrantz is a professor at the Institute of Stockholm.
6. Ibid., pp. 24, 25.
7. John Neihardt, *Black Elk Speaks, Being the Life Story of a Holy Man of the Oglala Sioux* (Lincoln, NE: University of Nebraska Press, 1961), pp. 23—39.
8. Minneapolis Star Tribune, September11,1994, p. 21A.
9. David Paxson, *WORLD POPULATION BALANCE* Newsletter, (Richfield,MN: May,1994).
10. Minneapolis Star Tribune, February 22,1994, p. 1.
11. The Santa Fe Sun, May,1994, pp. 12, 13.
12. Melbourne Banksia News, January, 1995.

Chapter 4

1. Manitonquat (Medicine Story), *Return to Creation* (Spokane,WA: Bear Tribe Publishing, 1991), p. 28.
2. Ibid., p. 35.
3. Ibid., pp. 53, 54.

Chapter 5

1. John Fire (Lame Deer) and Richard Erdoes, *Lame Deer Seeker of Visions* (New York: Simon & Schuster, 1972), pp. 174—182.
2. Charles Van Doren, *A History of Knowledge. The Pivotal Events, People, and Achievements of World History* (New York: Ballantine Books, 1991), p. 13.
3. Ibid. p. 12.
4. Ibid. p. 15.
5. James A. Haught, *Holy Horrors. An Illustrated History of Religious Murder and Madness* (Buffalo, NY: Prometheus Books, 1990), pp. 61—64.
6. Ibid. p. 55.
7. Ibid. p. 57.
8. Ibid. p. 63.
9. Ibid. p. 65.
10. Ibid. p. 67.
11. Ibid. p. 75.
12. Ibid. p. 77.
13. Ibid. p. 64—68.
14. Ibid. pp. 73—76.
15. Ibid. p. 79.

Chapter 6

1. John Fire (Lame Deer) and Richard Erdoes, *Lame Deer Seeker of Visions* (New York: Simon & Schuster, 1972), pp. 183, 184.
2. Ibid. p. 184.
3. Ibid.

Chapter 7

1. Sandy Johnson, *The Wisdom of Native American Elders* (Willits, CA: Shaman's Drum, 1994/Spring Issue), p. 24.
2. Ibid.
3. Sandy Johnson and Dan Budnik, *The Book of The Elders* (San Francisco: Harper/Collins,1994).
4. Thomas Mails, *Fools Crow* (Tulsa, OK: Council Oaks Books,1991), p. 11.
5. Ibid. p. 18.
6. St. Paul Pioneer Press, September 29,1994, p. 2C.

Chapter 8

1. John Bryde, *Modern Indian Psychology* (Vermillion: University of South Dakota, 1971), p. 10.
2. Ed McGaa, *Rainbow Tribe* (San Francisco: Harper/Collins, 1992), p. 18.
3. Wm. K Powers, *Oglala Religion* (Lincoln: University of Nebraska Press, 1975), p. 64.

Chapter 9

1. Gary Presland, *Aboriginal Melbourne: The Lost Land of the Kulin People* (Ringwood, Victoria: McPhee Gribble, Penquin Books Australia Ltd., 1994), p. 50, 51.
2. Manitonquat (Medicine Story), *Return to Creation* (Spokane,WA: Bear Tribe Publishing, 1991), pp. 41, 42.
3. Jeffrey Goodman, *American Genesis* (New York: Berkley Books, 1982), p. 199.
4. Ibid.
5. Ibid.
6. Ed McGaa, *Rainbow Tribe* (San Francisco: Harper/ Collins, 1992), p. 46.
7. Charles Van Doren, *A History of Knowledge. The Pivotal Events, People, and Achievements of World History* (New York: Ballantine Books, 1991), Cover.

8. James A. Haught, *Holy Horrors. An Illustrated History of Religious Murder and Madness* (Buffalo, NY: Prometheus Books, 1990), p. 134.
9. Ohiyesa, *The Soul of the Indian* (Lincoln: University of Nebraska Press, 1980), p. 113.
10. Ibid.
11. James A. Haught, *Holy Horrors. An Illustrated History of Religious Murder and Madness* (Buffalo, NY: Prometheus Books, 1990), pp. 106, 107.
12. P. Ehrlich and A. Ehrlich, *Healing the Planet* (Reading, MA: Addison- Wesley Publishing Company, Inc.,1991), p. xiv.
13. A. Leoplod, *Round River* (New York: Oxford University Press, 1953), (Reading,MA: Addison-Wesley Publishing Company, Inc., 1991), p. xiv.
14. A.J.S. Rayl, Minneapolis Star Tribune, May 30,1994, p. 8A.
15. David Paxson,World Population Balance Newsletter, Richfield, MN.

Chapter 10

1. Manitonquat (Medicine Story), *Return to Creation* (Spokane, WA: Bear Tribe Publishing, 1991), pp. 45—48.
2. Ibid. p. 53.

* * * *

Suggested Readings

* * * *

Adams, Barbara Means. *Prayers of Smoke*. Berkeley, CA: Celestial Arts, 1990.

Arquelles, Jose. *The Mayan Factor*. Santa Fe, NM: Bear & Company, 1987.

Bend, Cynthia, and Tayja Wiger. *Birth of a Modern Shaman*. St. Paul, MN: Llewellyn, 1988.

Brown, Joseph Epes. *The Sacred Pipe: Black Elk's Account of the Seven Sacred Rites of the Oglala Sioux*. Norman: University of Oklahoma Press, 1953.

Brown, Tom. *The Vision*. New York: Berkley, 1991.

Brown, Vinson and William Willoya. *Warriors of the Rainbow*. Happy Camp, CA: Naturegraph, 1962.

Bryde, John F. *Modern Indian Psychology*. Vermillion, SD: Department of Indian Studies, University of South Dakota, 1971.

Campbell, Joseph. *The Power of Myth*. New York: Doubleday, 1988.

_____. *Transformation of Myth through Time*. New York: Harper & Row, 1990.

Carr-Gomm, Philip. *The Druid Tradition*. Shaftesbury, Dorset and Rockport, Massachusetts: Element, 1991.

Croone, Brian R. and Dennis W. Harcey. *White-Man-Runs-Him (Crow Scout With Custer)* Evanston, IL: Evanston Publishing, Inc., 1993.

DeLoria, Vine, Jr. *Custer Died For Your Sins*. New York, Avon Books, 1969.

Eastman, Charles A. (Ohiyesa). *From the Deep Woods to Civilization*. Lincoln: University of Nebraska Press, 1916.

_____. *The Soul of the Indian*. Lincoln: University of Nebraska Press, 1980.

Ehrlich, Paul R. & Anne H. *Healing the Planet*. Reading, MA: Addison-Wesley, 1991.

Fell, Barry. *America B.C.* New York: Simon & Schuster, Pocket Books,1976.

Fire, John(Lame Deer) and Richard Erdoes. *Lame Deer Seeker of Visions.* New York: Simon & Schuster, 1972.

Gallenkamp, Charles. Maya, *The Riddle and Rediscovery of a Lost Civilization*-3d rev. ed. New York: Penguin, 1987.

Goodman, Jeffrey. *American Genesis: The American Indian and the Origins of Modern Man.* New York: Summit Books, 1981.

Haught, James A. *Holy Horrors. An Illustrated History of Religious Murder and Madness.* Buffalo, NY: Prometheus Books,1990.

Hultkrantz, Ake. *Native Religions of North America.* San Francisco: Harper Collins, 1987.

Johnson, Sandy and Dan Budnik. *The Book of The Elders.* San Francisco: Harper Collins,1994.

Keeney, Bradford. *Shaking Out the Spirits.* Barrytown, NY: Station Hill Press, 1994.

Mails, Thomas. *Fools Crow.* Tulsa,OK: Council Oaks Books, 1991.

Manitonquat, (Medicine Story). *Return to Creation.* Spokane,WA: Bear Tribe Publishing, 1991.

McGaa, Ed, Eagle Man. *Mother Earth Spirituality.* San Francisco: Harper & Row, 1990.

_____. *Rainbow Tribe.* San Francisco: Harper Collins, 1992.

Medicine Eagle, Brooke. *Buffalo Woman Comes Singing.* New York: Ballantine, 1991.

Miller, David Humphreys. *Custer's Fall: The Indian Side of the Story.* Lincoln: University of Nebraska Press, 1957.

Morgan, Marlo. *Mutant Message.* Lees Summit, MO: MM Co., 1991.

Moore, Thomas. *Care of the Soul: a Guide for Cultivating Depth and Sacredness in Everyday Life.* New York: Harper Collins, 1992.

Neihardt, John G. *Black Elk Speaks.* New York: William Morrow, 1932. Reprint Lincoln: University of Nebraska Press, 1957.

Powers, William K. *Oglala Religion.* Lincoln: University of Nebraska Press, 1977.

_____. *Sacred Language.* Norman: University of Oklahoma Press, 1986.

_____. *Yuwipi.* Lincoln: University of Nebraska Press, 1982.

Ross, Allen Charles. *Mitakuye Oyasin.* Ft. Yates, ND: BEAR, 1989.

Sahtouris, Elisabet. *Gaia, The Human Journey From Chaos to Cosmos.* New York: Simon & Schuster, 1989.

Sams, Jamie. *Medicine Cards.* Santa Fe: Bear & Co., 1988.

_____. *Sacred Path Cards.* San Francisco: Harper Collins, 1990.

_____. *Other Council Fires Were Here Before Ours.* (San Francisco, Harper Collins,1991.

Sandoz, Mari. *Crazy Horse: The Strange Man of the Oglalas*. Lincoln: University of Nebraska Press, 1961.

Silverberg, Robert. *The Mound Builders*. Athens: Ohio University Press, 1970.

Standing Bear, Luther. *My Indian Boyhood*. Lincoln: University of Nebraska Press, 1988.

Stoltzman, William, S.J. *How to Take Part in Lakota Ceremonies*. Pine Ridge, SD: Heritage Center, Red Cloud Indian School, 1986.

Sun Bear. *Sun Bear: The Path of Power*. Spokane, WA: Bear Tribe Publishing, 1983.

Unrau, William. *The Kansa Indians. A History of the Wind People, 1673-1873*. Norman: University of Oklahoma Press,1986.

Vanderwerth, W.C. *Indian Oratory: Famous Speeches by Noted Chieftans*. Norman: University of Oklahoma Press, 1971.

Vestal, Stanley. *Warpath*. Lincoln: University of Nebraska Press, 1984.

_____. *Warpath: The True Story of the Fighting Sioux Told in a Biography of Chief White Bull*. Boston and New York: Houghton Mifflin, 1934.

Weatherford, Jack. *Indian Givers*. New York: Crown, 1988.

_____. *Native Roots*. New York: Crown, 1991.

Ywahoo, Dhyani. *Voices of Our Ancestors*. Boston: Shambhala, 1987.

* * * *

About the Author

The Author was born on the Oglala Sioux reservation and is a registered tribal member, OST 15287. Following the earning of an undergraduate degree he joined the Marine Corps to become a fighter pilot. Captain McGaa returned from 110 combat missions and danced in six annual Sioux Sun Dances. The Sun Dance led him to the seven Mother Earth ceremonies under the tutelage of Chief Eagle Feather and Chief Fools Crow, two Sioux holy men. Eagle Man holds a law degree from the University of South Dakota and is the author of *Red Cloud*, (Dillon Press, 1972), *Mother Earth Spirituality*, (Harper & Row, 1990), *Rainbow Tribe*, (Harper/Collins, 1992) and *Eagle Vision*, (Four Directions Publishing, 1998).

* * * *

Spirituality and philosophical books generate many letters. It would be most appreciated if you will please enclose a self addressed stamped envelope (SASE) and a return address upon your correspondence, should you consider writing to the Author. Please bear in mind, your letters are appreciated but it has become difficult to answer all correspondence especially while I still continue to journey upon the world to seek more knowledge.

Four Directions Publishing is dedicated to finding those special manuscripts that are spiritually fulfilling and which bring forth real-life experiences, rewarding culture, environmental preservation and/or traditional knowledge.

New Books from Four Directions Publishing

Kayhut - A Warrior's Odyssey by John Metcalf (deceased).

A powerful Northwest Coast legend. Pre-European setting and rich in traditional culture. Like Neihardt of **Black Elk Speaks**, the author lived when old timers spoke real knowledge of the past. Written with a gifted, descriptive style devoid of the customary paternalism and Euro-centrism of that era: The old Indian story-tellers obviously sensed Metcalf's perception to pass on this fascinating legend of a warrior who lived a life of harrowing travels and spellbinding adventures. Unedited by the publisher to avoid modern "political correctness" and dilution of the pre-20th century story tellers. Cover by Daryl No Heart. $15*

Fallen Feather - A Spiritual Odyssey by Deborah Chavez, M.A., a psychotherapist, begins her intership at a woman's shelter in the Black and Native American community. A Sioux family residing at the shelter introduce her into a world of intrigue with spiritual trials and tribulation. She meets a teenager and a Sioux teacher who guide her towards her spiritual path. Deborah embarks on a mystical journey beyond the boundaries of ordinary human encounters and discovers the powers of Natural Intuition. $11*

The Last Mission by Cliff Santa. (Edited by Eagle Man).

Unable to find employment, two part Indian pilots enlist in the British Air Force in 1939. Exciting aviation combat in a time when air battles raged daily. The author writes with historical accuracy. Rich Siouian culture is entwined in the thoughts, attitudes and dreams of the two warriors. A love story ensues for one of the pilots. $15*

Journey Song - A Spiritual Legacy of the American Indian by Celinda Kaelin, daughter of pioneers, a poet, philosopher and historian, finds her unque spiritual view which is strongly reflective of the powers she learns within Black Elk's vision. She is gifted with unfolding experiences beginning as a child. Celinda takes us out of the spiritual desert and puts us on a path of nature blessed wisdom that will make the desert bloom with soul refreshing knowledge and understanding. Cover by Daryl No Heart. $15*

Eagle Vision - A Sioux historical novel by Ed McGaa/Eagle Man. Chief Fools Crow and Chief Eagle Feather, two Sioux holy men rebirth the Sun Dance ceremony which has been wrongfully banned by the Federal government. Kyle Charging Shield, a modern warrior, receives a mission to thwart the reservation missionary who seeks to prevent the return of Native Spirituality. A love story, combat in Vietnam and the eerie mystery of the Blue Man of Black Elk's vision are entwined. Sioux culture, ceremony and history from the Indian's point of view are portrayed. 35 illustrations by Sioux artists, Daryl No Heart and Harrisson Lone Hill. $15*

*Add $2.00 per book for shipping.

Audio Tapes and Video Tape

Audio tapes are $15 each, plus $2 mailing charge.

☐ Audio Tape - **Finding Wakan Takan** by Eagle Man with Catherine Freidrich. Beseechment Song in Lakota to Four Directions and Six Powers. Haunting drumbeat. Reverse side narrates Black Elk's Vision.

☐ Audio Tape - **Black Elk's Prayer on the Mountain** by Eagle Man. A moving remembrance of a great visionary's last lament.

☐ Video Tape - **Native Wisdom** by Eagle Man and moderator Pete Carlson. Filmed outdoors. A hour and half discussion and demonstration relating to the Four Directions and the Six Powers of the Universe. Excellent educational projection of Siouian cultural concepts and spirituality. $25 plus $2 mailing.

Check or Money Order only.
Please remit in U.S. funds.

Four Directions Publishing
Box 24671
Minneapolis, MN 55424
Phone: (952) 922-9322
Fax: (952) 922-7163
E-mail: eagleman4@aol.com
Website: http://members.aol.com/eagleman4

Book stores please order **Native Wisdom** from the following distributors. Tapes and posters can be ordered directly from Four Directions Publishing.

Distributors:

The Bookmen; Minneapolis, MN; (612) 341-3333, FAX (612) 341-3065 (800) 328-8411, Fax ordering (800) 266-5636

Ingrams; La Vergne, TN; (615) 793-3845, FAX (800) 876-0186

Dakota West; Rapid City, SD; (605) 348-1075, FAX (605) 348-0165

New Leaf; Lithia Springs, GA; (770) 948-7845, FAX (800) 326-1066

Baker & Taylor; Momence, IL; (815) 472-2444, FAX (800) 775-1300

Maverick Dist.; Bend, OR; (800) 333-8046

The Bookhouse; Jonesville, MI; (517) 849-2117, FAX (517) 849-9716

Living Drums, Rockford, IL; (815) 397-9042

Four Winds Trading Company; (800) 456-5444, FAX (303) 499-6640

Grey Owl Crafts; Jamaica, NY; FAX (718) 527-6000

Gemcraft Ltd.; Melbourne, Australia

New distributors will be listed in subsequent reprintings.

Eagle Vision Native Wisdom, Mother Earth Spirituality, Rainbow Tribe and Kayhut Order Form

Enclosed is $15.00 plus $2 postage for:

☐ **Eagle Vision - A Sioux Novel**

☐ **Native Wisdom**

☐ **Mother Earth Spirituality**

☐ **Rainbow Tribe**

☐ **Kayhut**

☐ **Finding Wakan Tanka**
(Audio Tape) Eagle Man narration and song.

☐ **Black Elk's Prayer & Vision** (Audio Tape)

Upon Request; Books will be Autographed by Author

Add $1 postage for each additional book or tape.

Check or Money Order only.

Please remit in U.S. funds.

33% off for any book or audio tape delivered to a state or federal prison.

Four Directions Publishing
Box 24671
Minneapolis, MN 55424
Phone: (952) 922-9322
Fax: (952) 922-7163
E-mail: eagleman4@aol.com
Website: http://members.aol.com/eagleman4

Plains - style Necklaces
by Eagle Man

These attractive necklaces utilize carnelian, jasper, hematite, turquoise, bone, buffalo horn, shell, abalone etc., along with animal fetishes — bear, wolf, turtle, dolphin etc. as the principle make-up materials. Pony beads (size 5^0 & 6^0) blend the color arrangement. Expect many compliments when you wear your necklace.

$35, $40 and $50 are average prices. (necklaces bearing turquoise are usually $50.) Please E-mail or call for special requests.

View these necklaces in color on the website listed below.

Four Directions Publishing
Box 24671
Minneapolis, MN 55424
Phone: (952) 922-9322
Fax: (952) 922-7163
E-mail: eagleman4@aol.com
Website: http://members.aol.com/eagleman4